LOSER NO MORE!®

NEGOTIATE BETTER AND WIN MORE OFTEN - AT HOME, ON THE JOB, AND IN BUSINESS

Igor S. Popovich

Career Professionals
Australia

Disclaimer

The information contained in this book is to be taken in the context of general overview, not specific advice. You should not act on the information contained herein without seeking professional, financial or legal advice.

Neither the author nor the publisher nor any person involved in the publication, distribution or sale of this book accepts any responsibility for the consequences that may arise from readers acting in accordance with the material given in the book.

Published by Career Professionals
P.O. Box 5668, Canning Vale South, WA 6155 Australia

First edition, 2012

Bulk purchases

This book may be purchased in larger quantities for educational, business or promotional use. Please e-mail us at
sales@careerprofessionals.com.au

National Library of Australia Cataloguing-in-Publication Data:

Popovich, Igor S., 1962 -
   Loser No More! Negotiate better and win more often - at home, on the job, and in business

   ISBN: 978-0-9806223-0-0

   1. Business 2. Negotiation 3. Personal improvement
   I Igor S. Popovich II Title

658.4

To Isabella

Loser No More! Training

Loser No More! negotiation training course was designed to meet the needs of managers, professionals and anyone who has to negotiate as part of their working life. It will improve negotiating performance both within your organisation and in business negotiations with other organisations - clients, vendors, contractors, consultants, government agencies.

Loser No More! can be run as a 1-day executive overview, a 2-day comprehensive seminar or a 5-day advanced negotiating workshop. It can also be customised to suit your specific needs and to target particular personal and organisational goals and outcomes.

By presenting *Loser No More!* or any of our management training courses in-house for your employees, your organisation will benefit in six significant ways:

- ✓ <u>Cost-effective solution</u> that represents maximum value for a minimal investment - save on travel, accommodation costs and multiple registration fees
- ✓ <u>Quality training</u> - Igor S. Popovich, the expert who designed this course will personally deliver your course in-house.
- ✓ <u>Confidentiality</u> - participants can openly share their experiences, without a danger of disclosing sensitive information to participants from other companies
- ✓ <u>Flexibility</u> - course content, duration, venue and timing can be selected and adjusted to suit your needs
- ✓ <u>Convenience</u> - participants don't have to travel far or be away from their jobs for too long
- ✓ <u>Teamwork</u> - participants will share the same ideas and support each other in implementing them in the workplace

E-MAIL	
	To work with us on improving the negotiating and deal-making performance of your team, contact us today on:
	training@careerprofessionals.com.au

About the Author: Igor S. Popovich

Igor is one of Australia's most prominent and acclaimed thinkers, writers and presenters in the business and self-improvement fields.

He is the author of *You Can Have It My Way!*, *Winning at Job Interviews*, *Kaizen and You*, *Managing Consultants*, and other management and personal improvement books.

A professional engineer by education, he is currently the Principal Consultant of Career Professionals, an international management training, coaching and consulting business based in Perth, Western Australia.

Since 1996, Igor has trained thousands of managers, engineers and other professionals in the art and science of negotiation, persuasion and conflict resolution. His public and in-house seminars have been enthusiastically received in more than a dozen countries.

Igor's extensive experience and expertise in project management and consulting skills development provides his clients with additional value on their projects and change management initiatives. As a consultant, he can help you with various aspects of individual, team and organisational learning and improvement.

E-MAIL	
	Should you have a negotiating, consulting or training project, Igor is here to help you make it a success. For a confidential discussion of your needs and goals, contact Igor today on: **igor@careerprofessionals.com.au**

Management Training Courses

These practical, effective and life-changing training courses from Career Professionals will have an immediate and long-lasting positive effect on your team, department and organisation:

- ✓ Internal Consulting Skills @ Work
- ✓ Knowledge Management @ Work
- ✓ Powerful Business Presentations @ Work
- ✓ Time, Stress and Priorities Management @ Work
- ✓ Cross-Cultural Skills @ Work
- ✓ Managing Projects, Consultants and Contractors
- ✓ People Management Skills @ Work

These workshops can be run anywhere in the world, at the time that suits you. No matter how many employees you have that would benefit from such training, from five to five thousand, we have a training solution for you!

All you have to do is send us a brief e-mail outlining your business situation, project or training needs, and we will do the rest: **training@careerprofessionals.com.au**

WEB LINK	TRAINING COURSES AND CONSULTING SERVICES
	For more information on these courses and our services, please visit Career Professionals web-site: **www.careerprofessionals.com.au**

Contents

Why You Need This Book

"Our Age of Anxiety is, in great part,
the result of trying to do today's jobs with yesterday's tools."

Marshall McLuhan, philosopher and scholar

Getting married. Having children. Changing professions. Facing a job interview. Conflict at work. Asking your boss for a raise or promotion. Buying property or investing your hard-earned money. Starting your own business.

These are all significant, life-changing situations, and they all involve negotiation in some form. Positive or negative outcomes of these defining moments will have a marked impact on your life. Yet, strangely, nobody teaches you how to deal with these pivotal events and situations.

Schools don't teach such skills to any meaningful extent, employers even less so. Our parents may try to help us, but their knowledge and experience is limited. Plus, they don't have either the time or the skills required to pass on that wisdom. Even if they did, we wouldn't listen. Pride, impatience, or the adolescent feeling of invincibility and infallibility would get in the way. So, you end up unprepared and on your own. Worst of all, you are guided by myths and misconceptions.

Life is one long-winded negotiation game. The game is relentless, the stakes are high and the opportunities for losing abound. The price you could pay may be financial, emotional, physical or psychological. Yet, life is too short to make too many mistakes.

A great deal of this anguish is preventable. The skills required to effectively and confidently negotiate through or around most life situations can be learned, and major mistakes can be avoided.

Negotiation is a journey. Travel light and enjoy yourself along the way.

HOW *LOSER NO MORE!* CAME ABOUT

To understand what this book is and isn't about, let me tell you how it was conceived and created. It is not just an ordinary introduction to the book, but an illustrative story with some important lessons for would-be negotiators.

Most of the material for this book originates from my "Successful Negotiating Strategies & Tactics" seminars, but that title didn't seem exciting or inspiring enough for a book. The alternatives - *Power Negotiation, Negotiate and Win!, Become a Master Negotiator* - either didn't sound right or had already been used. I wanted something bolder, more provocative.

9

After a long contemplation, I finally settled on *Guerrilla Negotiating*. I liked the idea of little guys winning over the more powerful opponents, using an unconventional approach to battle, winning the guerrilla way. My search was finally over! I sat on this idea for another two years, while busily presenting my negotiating seminars.

Tragedy Strikes - My Title Gets "Stolen"

> "Experience is the name everyone gives to his mistakes."
>
> Oscar Wilde, writer and poet

One murky and generally unhappy day, I got a rude shock while browsing through business books in my local bookshop. There it was, a new book, just published, called *Guerrilla Negotiating*. Somebody beat me to the title! I was really pissed off, with the authors and the publishers, the bookshop that was selling a book with a clearly "stolen" title, and their greedy, opportunistic attitude. Then I realised I only had myself to blame.

I learned a lot that day. If you have an idea, act on it while it's hot. The world will not wait for you to decide if your timing is right, if you are ready or not, or if there is a better way of doing whatever you are planning to do. Somebody else will have the same idea sooner or later. There is nothing worse than the feeling "Why didn't I try? Who knows how my life would have improved had I tried?"

It is easy to recognise a loser. Procrastination is a dead give-away. Interestingly, procrastination is caused not only by the fear of failure, but also by the fear of success. You know if you did "it", things would improve. You would be better, richer or happier. Becoming a better person *is* scary. Paradoxically, you may not like your "new self". "I am comfortable with my old mediocre self, thank you!" we comfort ourselves.

So, instead of regretting your inaction for the rest of your days, get the ball rolling.

The Procrastination Conundrum

Losers wait and hesitate, until it's too late. Winners get on the ball.

Why I Named This Book *Loser No More!*

> "Nomen est omen." ("Name is a sign.")
>
> Latin proverb

I picked myself up and continued my title search for my still nameless new baby - yes, it's true, authors do treat their books like children. I forced myself into designing the title for this book using key words like "winning", "negotiating", "power", "achieve", and tried all possible combinations. It proved futile. The rational way, which the engineer in me advocates, does not always work. The creative process is like pregnancy - it has to take its course. You need inspiration, time, even a little providence or serendipity.

The Pregnancy Rule

Some things take a certain time, and no amount of money, effort, planning or praying can make them happen faster or sooner.

Why do I call it a Pregnancy Rule? Because you cannot get a baby in a month by impregnating nine women. Likewise, most things in life you simply cannot rush through; they have to run their own course. Ideas need time to ferment in your subconscious mind. Eventually, triggered by a thought, a word, a sight, a smell or a taste, they will pop out, to your genuine amazement.

Serendipity finally happened one afternoon in Malaysia, where I was presenting my negotiating seminar. I was reading a book on cross-cultural management, when this sentence caught my attention: "The Americans like to win and hate to lose". The statement intrigued me. I don't think Americans are that different from any other nationality - who, after all, prefers losing to winning? Who doesn't want to be a winner in life? The "Aha!" happened. I had finally found my title!

WHY IS THIS BOOK BETTER THAN THE REST?

"That is a good book which is opened with expectation
and closed with profit."

A. Bronson Alcott, writer and philosopher

A decade ago I wouldn't have even dreamed about making a cocky statement like the subtitle above. I used to be very modest, even shy. Then I realised that false modesty is a recipe for a lifetime of sorrows and regrets. Now I tout my own horn whenever I can. Try it - highly recommended!

What kind of book is *Loser No More!*? I'm not really sure, you'll be the ultimate judge of that. I've tried to make it provocative (in a positive, motivating sense), sometimes tongue-in-cheek, other times cynical, but I hope, never boring.

Every now and then you will find exercises, short stories, negotiating hypotheticals and quick quizzes. Some are business examples, while others are situations we find ourselves in when shopping, travelling, or interacting with our friends and family.

I strongly urge you to go through those exercises and examples without skipping forward to the answers and explanations that follow. To make it easier for you to remember certain principles and concepts, I've highlighted them and called them laws, rules, myths and paradoxes. I'm sure you understand they are not laws in a legal or scientific sense, but simply a naming convention I've used.

In this era of sound-bites, I too have used one-liners in this book, not because I necessarily believe in them, but because the readers expect it. Plus, I must admit, they are convenient. Don't you just love titles like, *Get Rich, Get Richer*, or *Get Stinky Rich*? I've come up with my own version. If this book sells well[1], I could quickly botch-up another one, *Loser Never More - How to Lose Even Less and Win Even More!*

Why I Wrote This Book

> "Writing is like prostitution. First you do it for love,
> and then for a few close friends, and then for money."
>
> Molière, French playwright and actor

We are still far from the level of negotiation competence needed to cope with these complex times. I've found that even experienced professionals and managers, who negotiate on a daily basis, aren't really that good at it.

Most of the participants in my training courses told me they have read a few books on negotiation, but either failed to learn much from them or forgot to practice what they've learned. I became curious as to why or why not? After probing further, I've complied a list of the "suspects", i.e. the likely causes. Here is the composite profile of a typical book on negotiation:

- Strong, assuring title (*Power Negotiating, You Can Negotiate Anything*). Some are condescending (*The Only Negotiating Guide You Will Ever Need*), some offending (*The Complete Idiot's Guide to Negotiation*), others plain misleading (*Instant Negotiation*).
- Written by a lawyer or an agent of some sort (sports agent, real estate agent, secret agent). Can ordinary people relate to those hot shots pulling off grandiose contracts and head-spinning sums of money?
- Full of self-aggrandizing stories and billion dollar deals the author clinched, against all odds and nasty regulatory agencies.
- Liberal use of sports analogies, bursting full of hardball tactics.
- Based on a personal opinion without any grounding in research. Opinions are authors' best friends. They cannot be disputed, as facts can.
- Examples are idiosyncratic. You are unlikely to find yourself in such situations. Try applying such atypical lessons in your life.
- Examples were carefully chosen to support the author's point-of-view, while those that contradict it were conveniently ignored.

---

[1] Please ask all your friends, neighbours, relatives and their pets to buy a few copies each.

- Once all the fishing, hunting and baseball stories are excised, it can all be distilled down to a list of a dozen simple tips.
- Simplistic. Way too simplistic.

There are some exceptions to these examples, but apparently those books aren't selling too well. A creepy thought entered my mind. Am I shooting myself in the foot?

So, since most of the existing material on negotiation is either boring or self-aggrandizing, too generic or too nit-picking, I decided the world was ready for a negotiation book of a different kind.

This is Your Handbook For Success

"Miss a meal if you have to, but don't miss a book!"

James E. (Jim) Rohn, self-help philosopher

I am so glad you didn't miss this book. Among all the business and self-improvement books, and all those authors spreading their "mantra" and competing for your attention, time and money, you honoured me amongst such a fierce competition.

Instead of saying thank you, which is nice and thoughtful, but does not instil confidence in this choice you've just made or are about to make, I will say only this: After reading this book you'll be a better, smarter and more competent person than you are now!

Some Description, Less Prescription, Mostly Provocation

"The philosophers have only interpreted the world in various ways;
the point, however, is to change it."

Karl Marx, revolutionary

Personally, I dislike generalisations. I also abhor simplistic advice and silly stories about chained elephants, slowly boiling frogs, ships and lighthouses, to name just a few overused examples from contemporary management literature.

If you haven't read these old-and-tired "stories" in management books, don't worry, you haven't missed much. They are not only daft, but grossly misleading.

I find the majority of management books too prescriptive, too "black & white", "do this" or "don't do that" type of affairs. Most look at negotiation from a certain (usually narrow) perspective and fail to integrate negotiation with other related life concepts such as problem solving, decision making, or relationship building.

My aim in creating this book is to do just that, so you, as a negotiator, not only understand the building blocks of negotiation but also be able to integrate them into a coherent whole.

13

The haphazard, ad-hoc way of negotiating does not work. Only an integrated approach leads to consistent, predictable results.

My other goal is to stir you up and provoke you into thinking and making your own conclusions. If you agree with what I'm saying, great; if you don't, even better - you have an additional learning opportunity.

Stop and think. Ask yourself, "Why do I disagree with Igor here? Why do I see this issue differently?" Such inner reflection or self-talk is the best way to learn about yourself.

Yes, I am biased, just as you are in your own way, and these biases and prejudices will come out in these pages. All you have to do is read carefully and pay attention to clues, and you'll form a pretty accurate intellectual profile of yours truly or any other author.

Likewise, interpersonal dealings in general and negotiation in particular are full of clues; you've got to be a detective and find them.

There is No Advice Like Practical Advice

"There is nothing more practical than a good theory."

James C. Maxwell, theoretical physicist

The principles outlined here are not theoretical, untested concepts. They've been used in various industries and cultures, on all continents and spheres of life. They work in large companies, small firms and for individuals. Some are from people I know, others from my own experience.

As an engineer and project manager I negotiated with consultants, contractors, suppliers, stakeholders, and upper management. Just as they've worked for me and for the others, these lessons learned will work for you too.

There isn't much difference between negotiating in business, on the job and at home. While the relationship dynamics may be different, the underlying principles are the same.

Welcome to the Eagle School!

In his book *Seven Strategies for Wealth and Happiness,* Jim Rohn proposes that the first rule of successful management training is "Don't send your ducks to eagle school."

Then he elaborates: "Because it won't work. All you'll get are unhappy ducks. They won't soar like eagles. They'll just quack, quack, quack. And then they'll 'poop' on you."

I hope you are in the right school here. This is a school for eagles, not for ducks.

IF I COULD DO IT, SO CAN YOU!

Understanding Losing is the First Step Towards Winning

"While winning is the best feeling in the world, losing need not necessarily hurt either. Losing should be a lesson in how to win more often. I learned a lot from my failures. Losses fed my fervor to win."

Al Neuhart, *Confessions of a S.O.B.*

Have you noticed how most sport coaches are not the former star players? You know why? Star players are naturals. They play instinctively, almost effortlessly and that makes it hard for them to teach those skills to others. It is hard for them to understand the struggles of those who have to overcome their less-than-stellar natural ability by hard work and practice.

By the same token, people who never failed or lost in business or personal life can never fully understand winning and cannot be great teachers or coaches.

The question about credibility to teach is best answered with another question: "Why should we learn only from winners? Can't we learn a great deal more from losers?" Yes we can. It's a pity losers don't write books and give seminars more often.

There is only a limited number of winning strategies, but the repertoire of losing moves seems endless. That is actually and opportunity in disguise, an opportunity for learning. Losing is the first, almost necessary step towards winning.

A Matter of Personality - Yours and Mine

"Try not to have a good time ... This is supposed to be educational."

Charles Schultz, cartoonist

Inevitably, every book reflects the personality of its author, especially a self-help book such as *Loser No More!* You will learn a lot about me here, but, more importantly, I hope you will learn even more about yourself.

You may find some of my attitudes intriguing or some of the advice dubious. That is perfectly normal; nobody expects you to agree with everything I say here.

Just as it is impossible to separate the chef from his dish or the author from his book, the way you negotiate is uniquely yours. It reflects your background and personality, your feelings and attitudes.

Not all of the strategies and tactics outlined here will be appropriate for your gender, age or occupation. Some will suit your circumstances and your personality, others won't. If you haven't done so already, try everything a few times and see what works for you and what doesn't.

15

Pick & Choose
Adopt the methods and strategies that suit your circumstances and your personality - make them part of your negotiating toolbox.

I've had lots of fun writing this book and can only hope you'll be able to say the same about reading it. Having fun is extremely important. Without fun, what are we doing here?

Who Am I to Tell You What to Do?

> "My Daddy doesn't have a job. He talks the whole day to people in companies and gets paid a lot for that."
>
> Isabella Popovich, age 5, when asked in pre-school what my job was

I'm not some hot-shot lawyer, a psychologist , not even an MBA, and I'm quite proud of that fact. MBAs are a dime-a-dozen, psychologists are so confused they often disagree with their own ("professional") opinions, and lawyers, well, we all know what that bunch is like.

You may think that to teach negotiation, one should be a lawyer or have a PhD in conflict resolution or mediation. This is like saying one needs a degree in child psychology or a doctorate in marriage counselling in order to get married and have children. Nothing is further from the truth. In my view, many lawyers are not good negotiators just as many academics are not good teachers.

I was an engineer in my previous career. Now I train professionals and managers in the art and science of negotiation and other so called "soft skills". "Soft skills" is an obvious oxymoron. These skills are anything but soft. They are hard to learn and even harder to apply. Above all, I'm a practitioner - I practice what I "preach".

Although I do like abstract ideas, I am also firmly grounded in reality. You should be too, if you want to get what you want out of life. Pragmatism works fine for me. It will work for you, too.

You Have Always Been a Negotiator ...

People often ask me how I made the transition from an engineer to a negotiator and management trainer[2]. Actually, it was surprisingly easy.

Negotiation is the discipline of engineering a deal and designing your desired outcome. It requires most of the skills engineering does: investigation, preparation, critical thinking, creativity, problem solving and decision making, communication, persuasion and persistence.

Just as you have, I've always been a negotiator - without realising it. I simply did not think of myself as one. The only thing that did

---

[2] I prefer to be labelled "educator" or even "provocateur", rather than "trainer". Dogs and horses are trained, people should be educated.

change was my focus. Instead of technical issues and projects, I now "engineer" deals. Negotiating your way around a technical problem is surprisingly similar to striking a business deal or creating a change in your personal life.

The good news for you is that no matter what your "profession" or background is, you can use those skills and knowledge in your negotiations, as a foundation to build upon.

... Although Probably Not a "Born Negotiator" ...

"A happy childhood is poor preparation for human contacts."

Sidonie Gabrielle Colette, novelist

My childhood was a happy one. As a result, I had no knowledge of negotiating concepts and principles. I lacked assertiveness and didn't know how to get what I wanted. My toughest period of life was late twenties and early thirties, during which I'd had a rich and varied experience as a loser. I had to learn it all the hard way - by making lots of mistakes.

You can do it too!

If I could master negotiation skills, starting from zero, so can you, no matter what level of negotiating proficiency you are starting from.

Then I started reading self-improvement books. What I read came as a revelation to me; it was a real eye-opener. I recognised myself in those books, I'd made most of the mistakes they talked about.

My feelings of exhilaration ("I can do that?!?") were mixed with regrets ("How come I didn't think of that at the time?"). In such moments of catharsis, most people blame others and look for excuses. I blamed my parents, friends and teachers for not teaching me how to negotiate better. Then I realised they didn't teach me not because they didn't want to, but because they couldn't - they themselves didn't know how.

Such a lack of real-life role models was a huge impediment for me; you may have been luckier.

... Because There is No Such Person as a "Born Negotiator"!

"The way to avoid mistakes in negotiating is to gain experience. The way to gain negotiating experience is to make mistakes."

Negotiators' Catch 22

I'm not a natural-born negotiator and I suspect, if you are reading this book, neither are you. I believe negotiators are made, not born. Most of us stumble from one episode to the next, trying to make some sense out if it all. Sometimes we succeed, other times we fail, dust ourselves off and carry on regardless. I've made my fair share of mistakes. I am not some sort of a guru or a role-model, but a struggling human being, just like you.

I have studied negotiation for almost three decades. In my corporate roles I negotiated with bosses, colleagues, subordinates, consultants, contractors, suppliers and government authorities.

Now, in my management training and consulting business, I deal with clients, partners, agents and suppliers. I can tell you what works and what doesn't, why or why not.

When people hear that I present negotiation training courses in Asia and the Middle East, they think I'm very bold, even brazen. It is like selling ice to Eskimos, they say.

Sure, the Chinese and the Arabs are known for their bargaining skills, but that doesn't mean they are (on average) better negotiators than their Western counterparts. As we are about to see, bargaining is only one aspect of negotiation.

I suspect the main difference between you and me is that I have devoted more time and effort to the study and practice of negotiation. That is about to change. You and me are about to embark on a discovery mission together.

In order for us to succeed, three things have to happen. Firstly, I have to provoke you (in a positive and constructive sense, of course) into thinking for yourself, about yourself and about the way you go about your daily business.

Then, you need to take in all the knowledge and the ideas put forward in this book, and internalise it.

Finally, you have to put your valuable new knowledge into practice by applying it in your daily life, at work and at home.

The First Law of Punditry

When the student is ready, the teacher will appear.

Well, I am here, and you are ready!

Helpless No More!

HOW THIS BOOK WILL HELP YOU WIN

Now that you know a bit about me and my other reasons for writing this book, apart from making tons of money, let's look at the issues of winning and losing, not just in negotiation, but in life in general. Then I will show you how this book will help you negotiate better and win more often.

After reading *Loser No More!* you'll be able to:

- Understand constructive, win-win deals;
- Analyse situations and prepare for negotiations;
- Manage and control the negotiation process;
- Protect yourself from negotiating games, tactics & tricks;
- Enhance your power in the negotiation process;
- Get what you want, when you want it, on your terms.

LOSERS AND WINNERS - A WORKING DEFINITION

People feel like losers for various reasons. You may be a person to whom things don't come easily, so you have to work harder and longer than others to achieve them. It may be your unhappy emotional state or the low level of success you have attained so far in your personal or professional life. You may be falling short of your potential, with a large gap between your reality and your aspirations.

Or, it could simply be a perception others have of you - as a pushover, also-run, has been or "going nowhere fast" type of person. If one or more of those describe your present state of affairs, don't worry. Together, we'll prove them wrong!

For the purpose of this book we will define a loser as a person who does not get what he needs and wants, either in business (at work) or in their personal life. We should add a qualifier "as much or as often as they would like to." Nobody gets everything they want, all the time.

LOSERS	WINNERS
■ Don't get what they deserve.	■ Get what they want.
■ Reactive. Blame others.	■ Proactive. Search for solutions.
■ Victims of circumstances.	■ Make their own circumstances.
■ Rigid, set in their ways.	■ Flexible and adaptable.
■ Want short-term success, end up long-term failures.	■ Accept short-term "failure" to achieve long-term success.

The "Grass is Always Greener" Syndrome

"The grass is always greener over the septic tank."

Erma Bombeck, humorist

One reason we may feel like losers is our "grass is greener on the other side of the fence" perception. We don't deal with others as they are and with the world as it is, but as we see them. We base our judgements, evaluations and comparisons on our perceptions of reality, not on the realty itself. And perceptions are often deceiving.

Hyping and hiding - the facade of success

To look better, people, organisations and governments all hype their winnings and hide or deny their losses.

You may feel jealous of somebody or think they are better, stronger, smarter, happier, or richer than you. You could be wrong. Your perception could be flawed.

Comparing yourself to others does bring certain benefits, if you look at things realistically and critically. Benchmarking is a fine practice in business, but it may be discouraging and counterproductive in your personal life. Accepting appearances at face value is the surest way to misery.

The Watermelon Story: The First Time I Felt Like a Loser

"Win as if you were used to it, lose as if you enjoyed it for a change"
Ralph Waldo Emerson, philosopher and essayist

It was a hot summer day. I was about nine or ten, playing outside with the neighbourhood kids. The mother of one of the guys brought out a plate with half-a-dozen watermelon slices. She gave a slice to each kid, all except one. Guess who missed out?

I don't know why it happened that way; she may have miscalculated or simply did not have more. Or perhaps she didn't think it was a big deal. But it was to me. They were all busy slurping the juicy fruit, while I just stood there looking dejected. This was the earliest instance when I truly felt like a loser.

The story did not end there. Seeing what happened from her window, another lady came out and brought, just for me, a large slice of watermelon. That was the sweetest tasting watermelon I've ever had.

People never forget such gestures. When you restore their self-esteem or help them save face, they will be grateful to you forever.

Start Your Negotiation Journal

"Journal writing is a voyage to the interior."
Christina Baldwin, writer and seminar presenter

We are about to do our first exercise. But, before you start, get yourself a notebook. We'll do a few more exercises as we continue our journey, so keeping them all in one place makes sense. Make it small enough to carry it with you in a bag or your briefcase, and large enough so it can last you for a year or two.

The power of the journal

Keep a "Lessons Learned" diary.

Use this notebook to prepare for your negotiations and as a "Lessons Learned" diary. Jot down your experiences and any ideas, tools and tactics you come across. Be honest. Don't sugar-coat your comments or rationalise your actions. The journal is for your eyes only!

✐ EXERCISE: Things I Didn't Get

Our first exercise consists of three steps. In Step 1, recall a few cases when you wanted something but didn't get it: a promotion, a contract, somebody's love, or anything of significance to you *at the time*. In

Step 2, try to identify the reasons that caused this problem or failure. Perhaps it was your lack of knowledge or experience (you didn't know what to do or how to get what you wanted). Maybe you said or did something wrong or somebody prevented you from achieving your goal. Don't worry if it sounds like you are bitching or blaming others. Again, this exercise is for your eyes only.

✎ EXERCISE: Things I didn't get

1. I didn't get ...
- _____
- _____
- _____

2. Because ...
- _____
- _____
- _____

3. What I SHOULD HAVE done is ...
- _____
- _____
- _____

In Step 3, ask yourself "What could I have done to achieve a better outcome?" or "What would I do today in the same situation?" Answer as much as you can, based on your current knowledge. As you read the book, keep adding new ideas and alternative solutions.

CHECKLIST	WHY DO WE LOSE IN THE NEGOTIATING GAME?
	■ We don't negotiate at all or do it the wrong way.
	■ We deal with the wrong people at the wrong time.
	■ We don't know what we want.
	■ We allow others to decide what we should do or have.
	■ We make assumptions or jump to (wrong) conclusions.
	■ We cut corners and expect something for nothing.
	■ We don't know when to persist and when to move on.
	■ We assume fixed, inflexible positions.
	■ We are too trusting (gullible) or too suspicious.
	■ We overuse logic while not trusting our intuition.
	■ We don't learn from our or others' mistakes.
	■ We repeat our dysfunctional patterns of behaviour.

THE GOOD NEWS: HOW THIS BOOK WILL HELP YOU

You Will Play With New Cards in a New Kind of Game

"I don't think of myself as a poor deprived ghetto girl who made good. I think
of myself as somebody who from an early age knew
I was responsible for myself, and I had to make good."

Oprah Winfrey, talk-show host, entrepreneur

Some say we cannot change the cards we were dealt at birth, that the only thing we can change is how we played that hand. Such a fatalist outlook is not only unhelpful, it is also untrue.

Sure, you cannot choose your biological parents, or where and when you were born, but you can change pretty much everything else. I migrated to another country, learnt another language and completely changed my profession - all in a few short years.

Many individuals, organisations and governments suffer from the same debilitating belief. If something doesn't work, just try harder, they say. Redouble your efforts and it has to work sooner or later. Instead of changing their cards, or redefining the game by changing the rules, they keep playing the same hand over and over again, adhering to the same old, arbitrary rules.

It's like riding a dead horse. No matter how good your riding skills are, you won't get very far. Plus, what is the use of riding fast if you are heading in the wrong direction?

Insanity defined

Hoping for or expecting better results but using the same old ineffective techniques.

If you keep doing what you've been doing, you will keep getting what you've been getting. If you are not happy with what you are currently getting, you must change what you are currently doing.

THE OLD PARADIGM

YOU

THE *LOSER NO MORE!* PARADIGM

YOU

You Will Get Things Done Even When Not in Charge

In my previous career as an engineer, I had goals to meet and tasks to accomplish, just like you have in your profession. Formal authority gives you control over people using the leverage of force or fear. Yet, I had no such authority over anybody, only managers did.

Responsibility without authority is a very frustrating predicament. I had to quickly find another way to enlist people's co-operation and get the job done. The way out of that predicament was in developing my influencing and negotiating skills.

Paradoxically, my lack of formal authority turned out to be a blessing in disguise. I learned how to approach people, how to discover their pet peeves, their interests and "pain points".

The Authority - Responsibility Conundrum
The less authority you have, the more important your negotiation skills become.

A pain point is a pressing problem hanging over someone's head, negatively affecting their financial, emotional or psychological well-being. The pain points I helped others with were of job-related nature, things that were bothering them on a daily basis, yet were not that hard to fix once correctly identified and analysed.

Then I would show them how working with me or helping me would also help them by making their lives easier. Without exceptions, I got co-operation and respect.

Self-interest is the most powerful persuasion tool.

I strongly suggest you adopt the same approach. Don't boss people around even if you do have the authority. Approach them as a friend and helper. I assure you, more often than not, they will help you achieve your aims. Your performance, image and status will improve, along with your chances of promotion.

You Will Get Better Control Over Your Life And Relationships

"If everything seems under control, you're not going fast enough."

Mario Andretti, racing car driver

Your improved negotiation skills will put you in the driver's seat. You will depend less on others and more on your own actions.

The bottom line is simple: If you don't take control of your life and your future, somebody else will. The problem is that you may not like what they've got planned for you. Those who are not in control end up being controlled. I've tried both in my life so far; being in control is infinitely better.

The Control or Be Controlled Axiom

If you don't take control of your life, somebody else will.

You Will Break Out of the Perpetual Losing Cycle

"Failure is not a single, cataclysmic event. You don't fail overnight.
Instead, failure is a few errors in judgement, repeated every day."

Jim Rohn

Your current knowledge, attitudes and actions have taken you to where you are today. It should not be difficult to see where you will end up if you don't change one or more of them. You will be in exactly the same situation you are in today. And the bad news? The more you lose, the harder it is to start winning. The Perpetual Losing Cycle is hard to break out of.

The Losing Streak Rule

The more you lose, the less likely it is you will win again.

Your success is directly linked to your self-image and self-confidence. The better you feel about yourself, the easier it is to become successful. By negotiating well and getting what you want as a result, you will see your confidence rise dramatically. This will, in turn, make it easier for you to get what you want next time around and to further improve your negotiating skills. I call it "The Compounding Success Loop" or "The Winning Streak Rule".

The Winning Streak Rule

The more you win, the easier it becomes to win more.

You Will Achieve Better and Faster Results

"A competitive world has two possibilities. You can lose.
Or if you want to win, you can change."

Lester C. Thurow, economist

Most negotiators settle for compromises, consolation prizes, and lowest-common-denominator outcomes. *Loser No More!* will show you how to be a player and go for the jackpot.

The Shaft-or-Be-Shafted Rule

Conventional "wisdom": Don't get mad, get even.
Igor's wisdom: Don't get mad or get even, just get what you want.

Negotiating skills will give you the power to create the outcomes and the rewards you want. You will achieve better outcomes in all sorts of situations. When buying, you won't be taken for a ride again. You won't pay too much, agree to unfavourable terms, or be tricked into buying something you don't need. When selling, you will not be intimidated by buyers into accepting a pittance for the value you are providing. I have yet to meet a loser with good negotiation skills or a winner with poor negotiation skills.

You May or May Not Become a Happier Person ...

> "What do you take me for, an idiot?"
> French president Charles de Gaulle, when asked if he was happy

More than thirty years ago my father prophetically told me that the more I knew, the more miserable I would be. While negotiation can make you a more successful person, it does not automatically follow that you will also become happier. You may or you may not achieve happiness by getting more and achieving more.

The Happiness Curse
The more you know, the less happy you will become.

Indeed, no truly intelligent and self-conscious person can ever be completely happy, only ignorant fools can. After reading this book you may not become any happier, but you'll definitely be less ignorant.

... But You Will Certainly Become a Different Person!

> "If I don't practice one day, I know it; two days, the critics know it; three days, the public knows it."
> Jascha Heifetz, violin virtuoso

Your transformation from loser to winner in life will not be obvious from the start. Most human transformations are initially gradual and subtle but eventually become noticeable. Others may notice it before you do. Sometimes you will be complimented by others who will be impressed by your markedly improved performance - be it on the job, in your interpersonal relationships or in achieving your financial and other goals.

The Self-Improvement Law
To improve your outcomes, you have to first improve yourself.

Your Relationships Will Change

I believe that the fear of change is the mother of all fears. Fear of failure is understandable, but that people may be afraid of success is far less intuitive. No change happens in isolation - when you change, others will change too, or, at least, your relationships with them will change. Consider it the ultimate of all relationship tests!

Most people who truly care about you will love the new, more successful you. Significant improvements will happen in your dealings with bosses, colleagues, prospective employers, the opposite sex, your children (if you happen to have them), neighbours (almost everyone has them) and relatives (some people regret having them).

Not everybody appreciates winners, though! Some of these people will not like the new, better you. Relationships based on dependency or power imbalance will undergo a significant transformation.

You will not allow others to ignore you, use you or cheat you. They will not be able to pretend any more, to promise without delivering, to coerce or demand. You will stand your ground, draw the boundaries and tell them in no uncertain terms how you want to be treated - what is acceptable and what is not. In short, you will negotiate to protect your interests, your dignity and your sanity.

People who have been exploiting and mistreating the old, unsuccessful you, will like you less, but will respect you more. Now you have to decide up-front what is more important to you, to be liked or to be successful!

Once others start to envy you, take notice. Jealousy is a good sign, meaning that whatever you are doing is working.

Jealousy as a success indicator

Nobody envies a loser. When others start being jealous of you, you know you are on the right track. Keep going!

Your Financial Situation Will Improve

"Formal education will get you a job; self-education will make you a fortune!"

Jim Rohn

How would you like to earn $15,000 per hour? That is the equivalent hourly rate I got "paid" for my negotiating effort. Let me tell you how I saved $125 in thirty seconds.

Upon completing my tax return, my accountant - a nice Indian lady - presented their bill for $375. It did seem quite high for the amount of work involved, one or two hours maximum. I flinched. I also said I expected the figure to be about $180, since that was the figure my previous accountant charged me. Nothing works better than the good old precedent plot.

I admit, my approach was a bit flawed. Last year was last year, this year is this year. The complexity of one's tax returns does vary. Secondly, each firm has its own rates. The other accountant was a one-man-show and worked from his kitchen table. This was a large firm with higher overheads. Plus, some professionals are more efficient than others.

Noticing my disappointment, she said she could reduce the fee "a little". So, I braced myself for a figure of around $350 or thereabouts.

When she asked me how $250 sounded, I went against my own advice and accepted her first offer, hoping she wouldn't change her mind. She didn't.

The significance of this discount was even more pronounced in the long run. The first amount charged set a precedent, it anchored the expected charge for years to come.

For simplicity sake, let's assume the same price for all subsequent tax returns. With $375 annually for ten years, the total charge would be $3,750. With the reduced amount of $250 over the same period, the total is $2,500, a long term saving of $1,250, all as a result of one little flinch.

The sum wasn't important. Saving $125 on a dishwasher or a sofa purchase wouldn't bring me much satisfaction. You would expect such results from the guy who teaches negotiation for a living.

Wrestling any amount of money out of your consultant's, accountant's, financial advisor's or lawyer's hands, however, is far from easy. Perhaps that is why we miss opportunities to save significant amounts of money while dealing with these professional money snatchers!

Negotiation is the highest paid activity you will ever undertake.

Negotiation will save you lots of money as a buyer, just as it will make you lots of money if you are selling goods or services. In the chapters to come I will show you exactly how.

Your Life Will Get Easier

> "Life wasn't meant to be easy."
>
> Malcolm Fraser, former Australian Prime Minister

I want my life to be easy and I suspect you want the same. Easy means enjoyable, pleasant, not hard or stressful. However, it shouldn't mean too easy. When things are too easy, we lose interest, motivation and passion. We don't feel challenged. A certain degree of struggle is desirable. Think for a second or two: what would making life easier mean to you and how would you go about it?

When I ask people such questions in my negotiating workshops, married men (half jokingly) mention a disappearance of certain persons, most often mothers-in-law.

To single men, making life easier is about meeting women. Sellers mumble about difficult and demanding customers, while buyers wish for sellers who tell the truth and don't use any tricks. Managers would like to see more co-operative employees while employees mention dealing with difficult bosses (not in such polite words, though!). That, they say, would make their jobs and their lives easier.

Negotiation is not a solution to all life's problems, but it gets pretty darn close. I cannot help you get rid of your boss or your mother-in-law, or with getting laid, but I can help you in your struggle on other fronts.

More gain with less pain!
Negotiation is the ability to minimise pain and maximise gain.

✓ CHECKLIST: The Big Wins Negotiation Will Bring You

- You will understand yourself better and respect yourself more. You will demand and get such respect from others.
- Rather than allowing others to use and control you, you will be in control of yourself, situations and outcomes.
- Instead of being a victim of circumstances, you will create your own circumstances, conducive to your own success.
- Instead of relying on others to give you what they think you should have, you will get what you want.
- Instead of being swamped by problems and discouraged by difficulties, you will effectively, efficiently and confidently overcome those setbacks and progress towards your goals.
- You will be able to anticipate developments and people's actions, prepare for them and deal with them in the best possible way.
- Instead of using a few old and tired approaches that don't work well, you will have a range of strategies and tools to choose from.
- You'll be able to look back at your life with pride, without sorrows or regrets, knowing you always did your personal best.

THE BAD NEWS: WHAT NO BOOK CAN DO FOR YOU

It's Simple, But It Ain't Easy

> "All good is hard. All evil is easy.
> Dying, losing, cheating, and mediocrity is easy. Stay away from easy."
>
> Scott Alexander, British millionaire, media personality

Now that you are ecstatic about the good news I just gave you, I have to give you the bad news too. Just because negotiating concepts are relatively simple and easy to understand, this does not automatically mean they are actually easy to implement (put into practice).

The Implementation Paradox
Simple does not mean easy.

Success depends on various situational factors. This doesn't just apply to negotiation, but to every worthwhile human activity.

After reading about something, we enthusiastically embark on the life-changing path, thinking, "How hard can this be? It is all so simple!", only to get discouraged when the gap between theory and reality becomes obvious. We'll talk about bridging this knowing-doing gap in the last chapter.

Negotiation is a far too complex subject to be categorised into "21 Greatest Negotiating Tools & Tactics". There are very few universal recipes. We are all unique individuals, so what works for me, may not work for you or vice versa.

Most books on negotiation tell you to forget your own circumstances and to follow the rules: "Do the things I tell you, and you'll succeed." I wish it was that simple.

The Theory - Practice Gap

A good cookbook does not guarantee a perfect meal.

Slim, Sexy & Successful: It's All Cinderella's Fault!

"Fairy Godmother, where were you when I needed you?"

Cinderella, fictional character

Cinderella is a fairy tale, but its appeal is real. We all wish we could instantly be transformed into slim, sexy and successful achievers who will fulfil their dreams and aspirations and live happily ever after. In the negotiating arena, we expect an overnight transformation from a timid pushover into a charismatic deal-maker.

Becoming a winner is also a transformation. However, it won't be easy and instantaneous, like Cinderella's magical transformation in a fairy tale. Transformations in real life aren't easy because they require a significant investment of money, time and effort.

Fairy tales are dangerous. They encourage unrealistic expectations and instant solutions. What message do little girls get from such Prince Charming type fairy tales? How does Cinderella escape poverty and oppression, through her own efforts and slow-but-steady progress? No, by marrying a prince. By hoping someone else ends her predicament and makes her rich and happy.

The Cinderella Delusion

Expecting others to improve your situation or get you what you want.

Life is often Cinderella's story told backwards. Instead of a humble pumpkin turning into a golden chariot, or an ugly frog into a handsome prince, your expensive "luxury" car may turn out to be a lemon and your dream job may prove a boring dead-end.

If you are a woman waiting for a handsome prince on a white horse to make your dreams come true, you have an additional work in front of you. Your Prince Charming may turn out a total loser who will run away with his bimbo secretary and leave you with two young kids and an oppressive mortgage. You'd better get prepared!

Life is no fairy tale; it requires hard work and even harder negotiation.

I also blame cartoons for this unfortunate human tendency. For instance, Popeye becomes strong in a couple of seconds after he gulps down a can of spinach. At least Popeye is for children. It seems adults can be fooled just as easily.

To Go Forward, You May Have to Backtrack a Bit

"It is only because of problems that we grow mentally and spiritually.
It is through the pain of confronting and resolving problems
that we learn."

M. Scott Peck, psychiatrist turned best-selling author

To advance in negotiation, as in life in general, you may have to go backwards first. Don't expect smooth and constant progress. Two-steps-forward situations are quite rare in life. Most are one-step-back and then two-steps- forward.

Say you want to change careers. Negotiating a career change is one of the most difficult human undertakings and the price we usually have to pay is substantial. Getting an additional qualification requires an investment of time, money and effort. Then, starting at the bottom again and working your way up tests your self-esteem and represents a lost financial opportunity. Too much certain pain for not enough uncertain gain. No wonder many of us stick to boring or demeaning jobs while our real talents and aspirations lie elsewhere.

All change comes at a price. Whoever tells you that change is free, or that it comes easy, is misleading you. It took me five years to reach the income level I had before changing careers. But it can be done, and if you feel stuck in The Vicious Losing Cycle, you should do it, too. At least you will not keep regretting your inaction for the rest of your life. "If only I tried ..." is the most tragic of all regrets!

Transformational Miracles in 21 Days? Oh, Please ...

"If self-help is so effective at what it's supposed to do,
then why is there so much evidence that Americans,
and the society they inhabit, are so screwed up?"

Steve Salerno, *SHAM (Self-Help & Actualization Movement)*

Lots of "self-help"[3] literature promises miracles in seven or twenty one days. Nicely sounding numbers, reminding you of your 21st birthday

---

[3]A total misnomer. If it was *self*-help, why would you need to read books and go to courses? You'd be able to improve all by yourself.

and the coming of age scenario. I won't insult your intelligence and make a similar claim.

There is instant coffee and two-minute noodles, and we all know how bad they taste compared to "the real thing." Likewise, the instant improvement promise, peddled by false gurus of flamboyant style but feeble substance, fills you up quickly with hope and hype, but doesn't provide any long-term benefits.

Your transformation will take more than three weeks, that's for sure. It may take months or years, but it will happen. Just don't get discouraged. Gradual improvements can be disheartening, and that is why they aren't very appealing.

You cannot avoid the "pain-in-the-arse factor". That is the highly scientific name I use for those difficult and discouraging aspects of any worthwhile human activity.

WINNING TIPS: What I Wish I Knew Twenty Years Ago

- Life is no fairy tale; it requires hard work and even harder negotiation.
- If you don't take control of your future, somebody else will.
- To improve your outcomes, you have to first improve yourself.
- The more you win, the easier it becomes to win more.
- Negotiation is the highest paid activity you will ever undertake.
- The less authority you have, the more important your negotiation skills.
- Envy is a good indicator of success. When others start being jealous of you, you are on the right track.
- Conventional thinking: "Don't get mad, get even". *Loser No More!* mantra: "Don't get mad or even, get what you want."

Confused No More!

WHAT NEGOTIATION IS AND WHAT IT ISN'T

In this chapter we will define negotiation and dispel some common negotiating myths. These fallacies and delusions may hamper you on your way towards winning, so we'd better put things straight from the start.

Coming up:

- If negotiation is so important, why are we so bad at it?
- Why do we like "pre-negotiated" deals?
- Negotiation defined
- "Hit & Run" and "Nice & Easy" negotiations - which approach to use and when?
- Debunking common negotiating myths

THE MANY FACES AND MEANINGS OF NEGOTIATION

The Image of Negotiation

"Almost anything that can be praised or advocated
has been put to some disgusting use. There is no principle, however
immaculate, that has not had its compromising manipulator."

Wyndham Lewis, painter and author

What comes to your mind when the word negotiation is mentioned? A meeting of people in suits discussing a business deal? A family considering the upcoming holiday? Perhaps it invokes images of political talk, diplomats and international conferences? A bargaining scene from a Sunday market or Arabian souk? None of these are far off the mark. Negotiation means various things to different people.

I still dislike negotiation. If you are anything like me, I suspect you associate negotiation with tense, unpleasant situations and conflict. Very few people seem to enjoy it. If you are one of them, consider yourself fortunate. Things we enjoy doing we usually do better, with more enthusiasm and dedication.

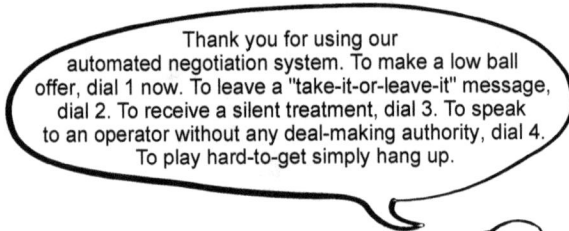

> Thank you for using our automated negotiation system. To make a low ball offer, dial 1 now. To leave a "take-it-or-leave-it" message, dial 2. To receive a silent treatment, dial 3. To speak to an operator without any deal-making authority, dial 4. To play hard-to-get simply hang up.

One reason for the prevalent distaste of negotiation may be the confusion between negotiation and haggling or bargaining. Negotiation is a much more complex and diverse process than bargaining, which is only one stage of the negotiating process - talking about money.

Negotiation is often erroneously associated with intimidation and coercion, which is the use of fear to force others into compliance. Negotiation doesn't have to be that way. Constructive and principled negotiation is a process based on dialogue and co-operative problem solving.

DEFINITION	NEGOTIATION
	■ Discussing common and conflicting interests in order to reach a mutually satisfactory agreement. ■ Achieving goals through collaborative problem solving. ■ Enlisting the support of others, in order to get what you want, while helping them get what they want. ■ Resolving conflicts and clarifying misunderstandings. ■ Bridging differences in opinions, values or preferences.

The word negotiation comes from Latin *negotium,* which, literally translated, means "not leisure". And we know what the opposite of leisure is - it is business. In its broadest definition, negotiation is the art of conducting business.

Instead of Losing, You'll Be Choosing!

"It is our choices that show what we truly are,
far more than our abilities."

Joanne Kathleen (JK) Rowling, author

We'd all like to think we make our own choices in life, while (in many cases) the truth is that others make those choices for us. They decide what rewards we may get if we outrun numerous competitors for the same job, promotion, contract or business deal.

Unless you make your own choices, sooner or later somebody else will make those choices for you. If that happens, you may not agree with what they have in mind for you or not like what little they've decided you may have.

This is the rat-race to get out of the pits. Millions rely on the lottery, on a one-in-ten-million chance of winning, or hope for an inheritance or a similar windfall, forgetting there are others waiting to spoil their gains - the insatiable tax man, jealous relatives, shameless marketers, greedy bankers and other vultures.

Who is deciding for you?

You either make your own choices or allow others to choose for you.

I see negotiation as the power or the ability to make your own choices. You will not leave it to others to decide for you. You will be in a position to choose jobs, clients, bosses and, generally, your own circumstances.

The choices you make and the steps you take in life all leave their imprint on you. They shape your personality and determine your destiny. By mastering the art of negotiation, instead of losing, you will be choosing.

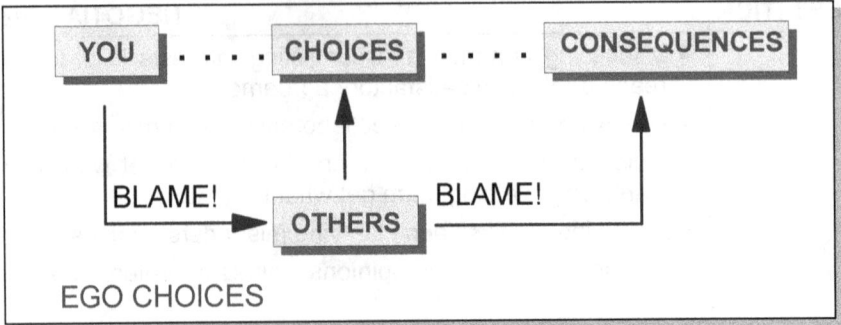

```
  YOU  . . . . CHOICES  . . . .  CONSEQUENCES

                          ↑                      ↑
  BLAME!                       BLAME!
        ──────▶  OTHERS  ──────────────────┘

  EGO CHOICES
```

Choosing is closely related to and dependent on confidence. Many times you will have the answer on your mind. You will intuitively feel what the right course of action is. Don't ask others what to do when you already know it yourself. Why would you respect or value the opinion of others more than your own?

The CCC framework: Challenges - Choices - Consequences

The challenges we brave and the choices we make determine the consequences we face.

Study the two diagrams on this page. Notice the difference between "responsible" choices and "ego-choices". With ego-choices, you blame others for presenting you with unappealing options or forcing you to make a choice you wouldn't make otherwise. Then you blame them for the consequences of those choices, although it was you who made those choices.

Most poor negotiators don't negotiate, they egotiate! The main criterion they use for making decisions and choices is to protect and preserve their egos.

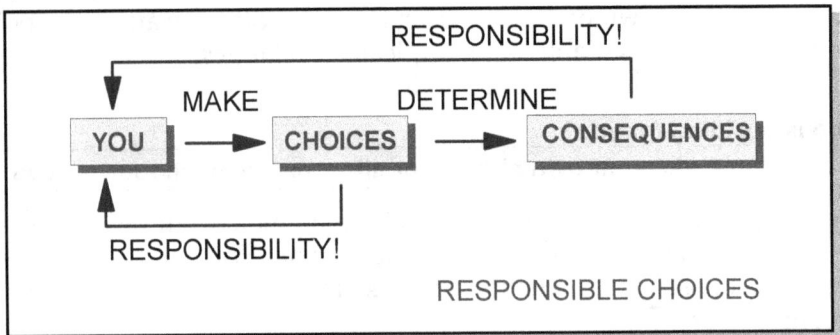

```
                     RESPONSIBILITY!
        ┌──────────────────────────────────────┐
        ▼        MAKE          DETERMINE
      YOU  ──▶ CHOICES  ──▶  CONSEQUENCES
        ▲           │
        └───────────┘
      RESPONSIBILITY!
                                 RESPONSIBLE CHOICES
```

Responsible choices are those you assume responsibility for. By making your own choices you determine appropriate consequences, and you admit full responsibility for both. You don't blame others for the consequences of your own choices.

Is Negotiation a Science or an Art?

"Deals are my art form. Other people paint beautifully on canvas or write wonderful poetry. I like making deals, preferably big deals.
That's how I get my kicks."

Donald Trump in *Trump: The Art of the Deal*

Negotiation is not a science. Just because some negotiating decisions and outcomes can be evaluated from a statistical perspective, that does not make it a science. The main aspects of negotiation are communication and persuasion, which are personal skills, and, if done masterfully, can be considered an art form.

Science is (or should be) impartial and impersonal. Its rules are valid everywhere and for everybody. Breaking them would render the invention unusable or the experiment invalid.

Art is situational and perceptual. There are rules, but breaking them makes for an even more interesting and challenging art.

Pablo Picasso drew women with both eyes on the same side of the face. Negotiation allows for the same type of artistic freedom. Providing both sides are happy with the process and the outcome, you are welcome to experiment by bending and breaking the rules as much as you please. In fact, calling them rules could be misleading; guidelines is a more appropriate term.

Negotiation as a Fruit-Tree

One hot day under the Arabian sun, a course participant brought in a selection of dates from her father's date farm. Palms grow in a harsh, unforgiving climate and dates appear without any human intervention. As such, palm trees do not provide the best analogy to negotiation. Fruit trees need continuous tending and care, a situation that resembles the negotiation process much more closely.

The foundation of any negotiation is the relationship between the parties involved. This is the soil into which we plant the seeds.

The success or failure of our planting efforts also depends on the climate. The fruit tree needs sun, air and water to grow and flourish. Negotiating does not happen in a vacuum, either. Political, organisational, interpersonal and other contextual factors are critical.

Just like strong trees grow from healthy roots, strong agreements have their roots in the proper preparation.

The trunk determines the strengths and the direction of the tree. It carries all the branches, leaves, flowers and, ultimately, the fruits. Its equivalent in negotiation is the strategy, our master plan, the journey between where we are now and where we want to be.

Branches of a tree are negotiating tactics, the manoeuvres we use to bring the negotiation back on track or to make it go faster, smoother or more favourable for us. Strategy is about effectiveness, being on the right track. Tactics are concerned with efficiency, achieving more with less.

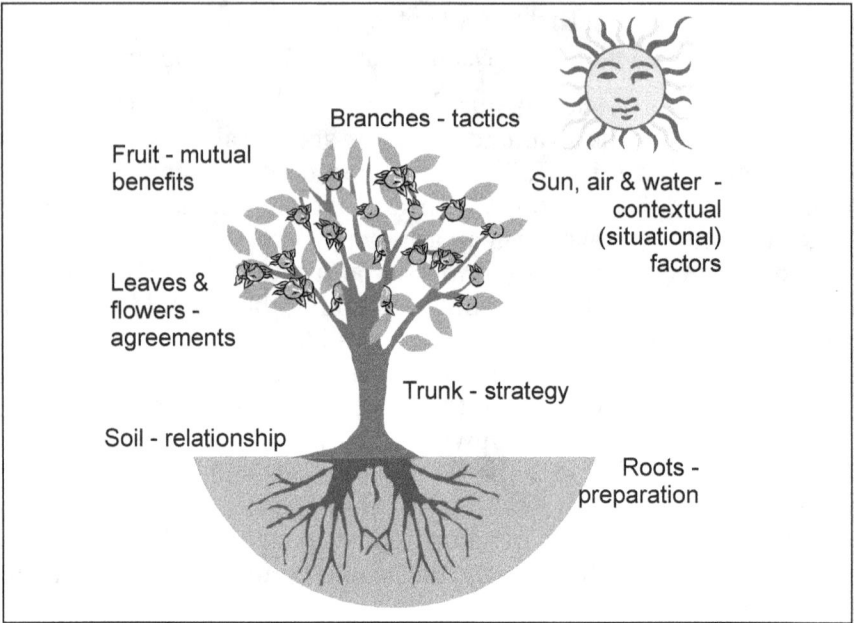

The leaves and flowers are like the agreements we reach. No matter how important these agreements are, they are not the end in themselves. The fruit of a negotiation is in the ultimate benefits to the negotiating parties. The ultimate goal is to eat and enjoy the fruit of the negotiating tree.

WHY ARE MOST OF US SO BAD AT NEGOTIATING?

Negotiation is not some esoteric concept or some manipulative skill only lawyers, real estate agents and used car dealers possess. Negotiation is not just a professional or business skill, but a life skill. It's an activity all of us engage in.

We negotiate dozens of times every day, from sales and contract negotiations at work, to numerous small negotiations at home: To go out for dinner or not? Who should wash the dishes? Who will do the shopping? Who should we invite for dinner or to spend the holidays with us?

At work, restructuring and outsourcing trends have made negotiation skills more important than ever. Flattened organisational structures, collaborative arrangements and partnerships require new approaches in dealing with suppliers, consultants, clients, and other stakeholders.

Most people have a vague and mostly superficial knowledge of this important subject. They not only lack education and experience in negotiation and conflict resolution, but are also confused and misguided by myths and erroneous beliefs.

Negotiations are about some interest, in most cases self-interest. We are not dealing with fences, cutlery or engines here. Negotiation involves people's feelings, aspirations and emotions. Nothing dealing with emotions, perceptions and self-interest is ever easy. We bring our emotions, expectations, biases, idiosyncrasies and previous experiences with us.

Negotiations are frustrating, confusing and emotionally charged encounters. It is next to impossible to tell facts from fiction. The line between what is honest and what is misleading is often very fine. The truth and the intent of one or both parties is open to interpretation.

Why Don't We Negotiate Better, or More Often?

> "What a fine comedy this world would be
> if one did not play a part in it."
>
> Denis Diderot, writer and philosopher

There are many reasons people fail to negotiate. The first pitfall is emotional attachment. People fall in love with an item, an idea or a person and would do anything or pay any price to get it. Most human disasters happen when emotions overpower reason.

We make conclusions about ourselves and others based on our previous experiences. Those who have been on the losing side for most of their lives, simply give up. "What is the point of negotiating when I will lose anyway?", they claim. People with such defeatist attitude don't make good negotiators.

We may be afraid that we will hurt others' feelings and appear pushy, greedy, difficult or demanding. So we just give them what they want (all they want!) and keep our relationship cosy and untroubled. More on this debilitating delusion later on.

A poor return on the investment required in negotiation is another common reason we choose not to negotiate. We look at the likely savings or other benefits gained by a specific negotiation and conclude that we shouldn't bother. It simply isn't worth our time or effort. Perhaps. It all comes down to a simple choice: Do you have more time or more money?

The fifth cause is the nature of the system, or our perception of it. The system, for example, can be the use of price lists and price tags. So, we think, how can we negotiate when the price is fixed? It's all in black and white and everybody is paying the same price ...

Some people don't negotiate due to snobbery. They consider

39

negotiation (which they equate with haggling) an unsavoury activity below their status. "Only small minds argue over small matters," they claim, "we would never lower ourselves to such a level."

Some of these explanations do make sense and may even be valid in certain situations. Most, however, are just excuses for not making an effort.

Why Do We Like "Pre-Negotiated" Deals?

Most buyers dislike haggling and will do anything to avoid it. These irrational fears of negotiation have been noticed by shrewd sellers. You may have seen car dealers' advertisement or commercials, where the message is "All the haggling has been done for you!", "The same price for everyone!" or "No negotiation required!"

Buyers get attracted to those dealerships based on the premise of "lowest prices" without haggling. "The same price for all" message appeals to egalitarians and is perceived as fair and equitable.

However, the claimed savings are off the list prices, which are nothing but dealers' wildest dreams. Nobody in their right mind should pay those amounts.

This perceptual tactic is called anchoring. Just as an anchor positions a ship and prevents it from drifting off, the initial figure positions buyers' expectations.

Anchoring

Positioning buyers' perceptions and modifying their expectations of the final price by mentioning the inflated price or value first.

No matter how arbitrary anchors may be, and most are, research shows they do influence negotiators' perceptions of the value of the deal. That is one of the reasons it is better to start very high if you are selling (to anchor buyers' perception to the high value of your wares) and to make your initial offer a low one if you are buying (to deflate sellers' expectations from the start).

TWO TYPES OF NEGOTIATIONS

Hit & Run

> "SELFISH, adj. Devoid of consideration
> for the selfishness of others."
>
> Ambrose Bierce, *The Devil's Dictionary*

"Hit & Run" is a negotiating approach where there is no long-term relationship. You don't care about your negotiating counterpart. You hit them on the head[4] and take as much as you can from them.

---

[4]Not literally, of course!

Parties compete for the same rewards or resources. The goals of the two parties are mutually exclusive or even opposite.

If you are looking to buy a house, the less you pay for the house, the less the seller gets. Some call it a "fixed pie" situation. The bigger the piece of the pie you get, the smaller slice the other person gets.

STRATEGY	HIT & RUN
	■ One-off deal. You will never see the other person again, so your relationship is not of any concern. ■ The deal is simple and money is usually the main issue. ■ Minimum investment of time and effort, quick gains wanted. ■ Parties are competing against each other, emotions may be running high, possible deterioration into a conflict.

You could also call it "Tough & Dirty". One-off purchases fall into this category, such as buying a computer, a TV set or a car. Both parties resort to tricks and exaggerations, while overstating their cases and making dubious claims. Buyers instantly turn poor, afraid of their spouses and reluctant to commit to the deal: "This is way over my budget ... I can get it much cheaper elsewhere ... My wife will kill me if I pay that much ..."

Supposedly inundated with offers, sellers suddenly play "hard to get" and cannot possibly supply all that demand: "This is our last one! You better make an offer right now, I have three more buyers waiting! Even my brother paid more than what you are offering!"

Nice & Easy

> "There is a sufficiency in the world for man's need
> but not for man's greed."
>
> Mohandas (Mahatma) Gandhi, Indian leader, statesman

Many negotiations of the "Nice & Easy" type are actually quite the opposite, ugly and difficult, but that doesn't mean they have to be that way. "Nice" means both parties should be nice to each other, because it is in their mutual interest to behave in such a manner. In this context, "easy" means going slowly and systematically, rather than "without difficulty".

The "Nice & Easy" approach is used when parties have a valuable working relationship and are likely to do more deals in the future. Preserving and even developing the relationship is of paramount importance. "Nice & Easy" is not based on appeasement but on a set of mutually-agreed-upon collaborative principles, such as ethics, fairness, mutual respect and joint problem solving.

41

STRATEGY	NICE & EASY
	■ The deal is more complex, price is not the only issue. ■ Relationship has to be preserved or developed. ■ Collaboration prevails over competition. ■ Tricks and tactics are not used. ■ Long-term solutions are sought.

When negotiating the "Nice & Easy" way, you have to understand and satisfy not just your own needs, but also those of your negotiating counterpart.

**If "Hit & Run" was a one-night stand,
"Nice & Easy" would be a marriage.**

DEBUNKING DEBILITATING NEGOTIATION MYTHS

"The reason people believe weird things is because they want to.
It feels good. It is comforting. It is consoling. "

Michael Shermer, *Why People Believe Weird Things*

Myths are misconceptions, erroneous views or misguided beliefs, usually spread around by well-meaning but poorly informed lay people. Even some experts contribute to this confusion, either through their incompetence or, more often, because they directly benefit from their clients' or buyers' belief in these myths. As such, myths are a powerful selling and persuasion tool.

It is often next to impossible to draw a line between fact and fiction, myth and reality, persuasion and manipulation.

The following list of delusions is not in any particular order of importance. All can affect your performance as a negotiator and have a debilitating impact on your results. Pushing the boundaries of our own ignorance is a crucial task, one you have to tackle if you want to achieve better and faster results. Let's do it now!

The Everything is Negotiable Myth

Negotiation is *not* the best thing since sliced bread. It doesn't always work; nothing does.

Negotiation assumes some sort of a working, functional relationship. If the relationship is so damaged that the sides cannot stand each other and refuse to even sit and talk, an intervention by a third party is needed. This could be a mediator, a marriage counsellor, an expert, an arbitrator or a judge.

The "Everything is Negotiable" Myth

Negotiation always works and everything is negotiable.

Just because an issue can be negotiated, it does not mean the other side will actually negotiate with you. There is no such thing as the sound of one hand clapping. The "take it or leave it" attitude is alive and well, both in business and in personal relationships.

The Invincibility Myth

EXERCISE: Rate yourself as a negotiator

How would you rate your current negotiating skills on a scale of 1 (non-existent) to 10 (outstanding)? Circle one number:

1 2 3 4 5 6 7 8 9 10

Negotiation is one task most people think they are good at. It is so easy to overrate one's negotiating ability. When I ask the participants on my negotiation seminars to rate their negotiation skills, most give themselves a rating of around seven. In my opinion, that is far too optimistic. When I present simple negotiation situations to those same participants, most of them fail to move beyond the obvious or trivial solutions.

The Invincibility Myth

I know how to negotiate. I don't need anyone to tell me how to do it!

The Real-life Experience Myth

"Experience is a dear teacher, yet fools will learn in no other school."

Benjamin Franklin, American scientist turned statesman

Most people believe the best way to learn anything, including negotiation, is through personal experience. Is experience really the best teacher? Experience *by itself* will not make you a great negotiator.

The Real-Life Experience Myth

The best way to improve my skills is through my own experience.

Most aspects of negotiation cannot be mastered by reading books or attending negotiating courses. They have to be experienced. Plus, the retention factor is there. You will definitely remember real-life lessons.

On the other hand, learning from experience is a slow, frustrating and expensive ordeal, and somebody has to pay for it. Business owners have to pay for their own real-life education. Perhaps this is one of the reasons so many small businesses fail so soon.

If you work for an organisation, you have the luxury of having them to pay for your bad decisions. Just make sure you don't make too many of them. The lower down the pecking order you are, the less your expensive mistakes will be tolerated.

Experience = expensive

Experience is an expensive way to learn and somebody has to pay for it. Make sure it is not you. Learn at somebody else's expense.

Time is not an accurate indicator of someone's experience, either. Most of us don't really have ten or twenty years of experience, but one or two years of real experience repeated ten or twenty times. We do the same things again and again and rarely venture into something different or more challenging. If we always use the same negotiating tactics (and we all have our "favourites" we swear always work!), how can we hope for any improvement?

It pays to look at negotiating experience as a two-dimensional matrix. We can make it broader (wider or more diverse), or deeper (more intense and reflective). Ideally, one should strive for both.

Most of us intuitively understand the difference between these two dimensions. In reality, we are more likely to work on broadening our experience by negotiating in a variety of situations and with a wider spectrum of people, while neglecting the depth aspect of those experiences.

Quiet reflection, soul-searching and lessons learned sessions haven't been in vogue for a while. Deep thinkers are in short supply.

We seldom analyse what is happening to us or reflect on these developments, so we don't capitalise on the lessons learned. We fail to see the alternatives, the cause-effect links and similarities. We miss patterns and trends, and ultimately, repeat the same mistakes.

The Complexity Hurdle

Life is not a neatly designed and carefully rehearsed management seminar. It's messy, confusing and often irrational. Luck often wins over logic, style over substance.

Analysing our performance and the quality of our decisions isn't without problems, either. We have no way of knowing what the alternative outcome would have been if a different decision was made or if different actions were taken, either by ourselves or by the other party. In negotiating workshops we can look at various scenarios, analyse them and draw conclusions, but life is not a management seminar!

Many important negotiating situations are unique and provide little scope for generalisation, and therefore, do not result in extensive learning. Change just one or two factors, and the entire dynamics of a negotiation change beyond recognition.

Perspective is always better than retrospective

**Experience is the worst teacher.
It gives the test before presenting the lesson.**

Both in corporate and personal life, most outcomes of our actions (or inaction!) are delayed and cannot be easily causally-linked with a particular deed or decision. Not only we don't know what was the cause and what its effect, we may not even realise that the two events or outcomes were linked. If results aren't immediately obvious, determining with certainty that some things were right while others were wrong is impossible, and without such conclusions there can be no learning.

The Win - Win Myth

"Win-win" is a typical example of how a valuable concept degenerated into an overused cliché. It belongs to the same unfortunate group of clichés as "collateral damage", "diplomatic solution" or "positive discrimination".

I still notice a great deal of confusion about the win-win concept among the participants in my negotiating seminars. Although most claim they fully understand the concept of win-win, once I ask a few poignant questions, it becomes obvious they don't really understand what win-win means.

The Win-Win Myth

Win-win is always possible.

The main reason win-win is not always possible is scarcity. If the amount of goodies is limited, no matter how much we brainstorm, we cannot make two pieces out of one.

Remember the "Hit & Run" negotiations, those revolving primarily around one issue? The possibility for a win-win outcome in those fixed-pie situations is slim. The less money you pay as a buyer, the less money the seller gets. It is impossible for you to get a bargain and for a seller to make a huge profit.

The Cookie Mentality

I better get my cookies before somebody else gets them!

Win-win does not automatically mean that parties[5] got everything they wanted. A more realistic term would be "I win some - You win some". Win-win does not mean the benefits were shared *equally,* either. One side usually gets a larger slice of the pie, but that doesn't mean that the other negotiator will go home hungry!

As for the satisfaction with the deal, win-win does usually mean that both parties are happy with the deal, although it doesn't guarantee that *an optimal deal* has been reached or that benefits were maximised for both parties.

---

[5]There is no precise word in English language for the person you negotiate with. Opponent, counterpart or even partner don't cut it for me.

In short, when negotiators declare a win-win outcome, it has more to do with their perceptions of the deal and how they feel about it, than with the quality or fairness of the achieved outcome!

Finally, and perhaps most importantly, the win-win philosophy does not work with selfish negotiators. Win-win negotiators believe (or want to believe!) in abundance. People whose world-view is based on scarcity are more likely to be win-lose negotiators. They simply don't care if you win or lose; all they care about is themselves.

If you are a win-win type negotiator and meet a win-lose intimidator, beware! He will interpret your win-win frame of mind as a weakness to be exploited for all its worth!

SCARCITY	ABUNDANCE
■ There isn't enough for both of us so I better get my share first. ■ You want the same things I do. ■ The more you get, the less is left for me.	■ There is enough for both of us. ■ Our needs may be complementary. ■ The more you get, the more you will want to deal with me again.

The Appeasement Myth

> "Do not be so sweet that people will eat you up,
> nor so bitter that they will spit you out."
>
> Pashto saying

You may remember an important lesson from your history class, a prelude to the second World War, when then British Prime Minister Neville Chamberlain "negotiated" with German Chancellor Adolph Hitler.

The first test of the British and international community's firmness came in 1932 when Germany declared it would no longer abide by the 1919 Treaty of Versailles. They claimed the surrender and subsequent reparations terms from the first World War were harsh and unfair. No response from the British.

In 1936, Germany reoccupied the Rhineland demilitarised zone. Emboldened by the British weakness, Hitler claimed that Austria should not be a separate country. It was populated by Germans, not Austrians, he asserted, and all Germans should live in one country. To appease him, the British promptly agreed again. Austria was annexed in March 1938.

Things started moving quickly from there. The world was sliding toward another disaster and Germans were again the main culprits.

Encouraged, under the pretext of supposed protection of their population in the Sudetten region of Czechoslovakia, Germans demanded an unprecedented change of the borders. European "powers" acquiesced and in September 1938 the Third Reich annexed half of another sovereign country.

After all, what did Chamberlain care, he wasn't giving away British soil. Emboldened by his own guile and his opponents' vacillation, in March 1939, Hitler occupied the rest of Czechoslovakia.

By then, British voters finally got the message and booted Chamberlain and his inept government out. The British government finally woke up and warned Hitler he should not push his luck any further.

By then, it was too late. The mad corporal from Berchtesgarten had already armed himself to the teeth (another violation of the Treaty of Versailles) and set his shifty eyes on his next prey, neighbouring Poland. When Hitler called the British bluff and invaded Poland on September 1st, 1939, even the duplicitous British could not renege on their publicly made promise to protect Poland and had to declare war on the German Reich. The rest is history.

Chamberlain's government believed in the Appeasement Myth and made a mistake that inexperienced or "would-be negotiators" often make. Their fallacy is in thinking that quickly accepting all the terms and conditions demanded by the other side will make them respected, loved or valued. They are afraid of asking for what they want. Ultimately, they are afraid of damaging the relationship with the other side.

The Appeasement Myth

If I negotiate, I will lose their respect, be seen as difficult and jeopardise the whole relationship.

Appeasement doesn't work, neither in politics nor in business. If others "love", respect and value you *only if* you say "yes" to everything they ask for, yours is not a healthy relationship.

Real relationships in business (as in marriage) are based on respect, commitment and mutual satisfaction (happiness). Notice that I didn't mention lack of conflict. A certain degree of conflict and disagreement is natural. Being liked and being respected are two very different things.

QUICK QUIZ: Negotiating at a job interview

You've been looking for another job with more responsibility and higher pay. The interviewer seem impressed by you. She offers you the job and tells you the salary on offer. What would you do?

a) Accept. The figure is higher than your present salary anyway and you really hate your current job. Plus, if you negotiate, they may think you are being difficult or greedy so they may even withdraw the offer.

b) Tell her you'll think about it. Let them "simmer" for a while.

c) Summarise your past achievements and remind them of the higher salaries in the same industry for the equivalent positions. Then, ask for 10 percent more.

d) Ask for 20 percent more and see how much they really like you. Ask her to put her money where her mouth is!

STOP & THINK! What would you do?

a) LOSER THINKING: If I try to negotiate, they will lose interest in me. I will appear difficult, demanding, opportunistic, even greedy. I better be nice and reasonable, so I won't rock the boat! Winners' thinking: If I start low, it will take me much longer to get to my desired income level.

b) RISKY MOVE! You may come across as indecisive or unsure if you even wanted the job. Better negotiate now, face-to-face, while they are still crash hot on you.

c) GOOD MOVE! If you just accept the first offer the employer may think: "Since he accepted our first offer, he will be equally meek and timid in dealing with suppliers, contractors and consultants. He will not fight to get the best deal for us!" This way you display ambition and send a message to prospective employers that you know your own value.

d) WINNING MOVE! Now you are really testing their commitment. Even if you don't get 20% more, you should get 10% or possibly even 15%. You are learning fast.

WINNING TIPS: WHAT I WISH I KNEW TWENTY YEARS AGO

- While your professional skills are a given, your people skills will make the difference between success and failure.
- Negotiation embodies a wide range of skills such as influence, persuasion, communication, critical thinking, conflict resolution and problem solving.
- Negotiation is not only a business tool, but a life-skill.
- Some people have a talent for negotiation, others have to learn it the hard way. Either way, negotiation skills can be improved.
- Negotiation is full of myths that can hurt your interests and your sanity. The sooner your debunk those, the better.

Erratic No More!

NEGOTIATE SMOOTHLY AND SYSTEMATICALLY

Amateurs negotiate in a haphazard, hit-and-miss manner, relying on tricks or luck. Master negotiators approach negotiation as a process that is predictable and, therefore, controllable. They advocate a planned, rational and systematic approach to deal making.

Coming up:

- The 4P's of negotiation: People, Problem, Process & Power
- The seven stages of negotiation
- Meta-negotiation: agree on how you are to negotiate
- Team negotiations
- Packaging and implementing the deal

STAGES OR PHASES OF NEGOTIATION

The 4P's of Negotiation: People, Problem, Process & Power

Even if you forget everything you read in this book, except these four P's, you will still benefit immensely. These four P's also apply to other situations, such as investigating, problem solving and consulting. To remember it better, look at this way:

Problem is about "what", *process* is about "how", *people* is about "who" and the concept of *power* ties the other three P's together.

Problem is about asking "what?": What happened? What is this about? What are the issues here? What are the risks? What are the benefits?

Process is about "how?": How should we negotiate? How should we approach the problem and get the people involved? How should the negotiation proceed and unfold?

People is about "who?": Who was involved? Who contributed to the problem? Who are we negotiating or dealing with? Who can help us with a solution? Who are the stakeholders? Who are the blockers and who are our supporters? Whose approval do we need?

Power is about "When?" and "How?": How can I leverage my strengths and minimise my weaknesses? When should I do certain things for maximum impact and benefit?

PEOPLE	PROBLEM
■ POSITIONS AND INTERESTS	■ CRUCIAL ASPECTS (FACTORS)
■ PERCEPTIONS	■ RISKS & REWARDS
■ EMOTIONS	■ OPTIMAL SOLUTION(S)
■ RELATIONSHIPS	■ CREATING & SHARING VALUE

POWER	PROCESS
■ STRENGTHS & WEAKNESSES	■ STAGES OR PHASES
■ OPTIONS & ALTERNATIVES	■ NORMS & RULES
■ TRICKS & TACTICS	■ DYNAMICS & MOMENTUM

Negotiation as a Process

Negotiation is primarily seen as an event. However, the process aspect to negotiation is even more important. Brushing your teeth or driving a car now come so naturally to you. These processes are permanently programmed into your subconscious mind. Most processes we go through in life are run on auto-pilot, except those we are currently learning. Those we have to think about every step of the way. Likewise, in the beginning, you'll have to consciously and deliberately follow your negotiating plan step-by-step. With time and experience, negotiating will become as natural to you as getting dressed or going shopping. As with most things in life, the beginning is the most difficult step.

Every process is a sequence of stages or phases. There is the ultimate outcome, called an aim or a goal. The process steps happen faster or slower, depending on the timing and the momentum, which may also be called the speed of the process or its dynamics. Finally, every process is governed by a set of norms and rules; what is allowed and what isn't, how the process is carried out.

Negotiation is obviously a communication process; without communication negotiation is impossible. Listening, questioning and clarifying are the communicational components of negotiation.

Nothing happens until somebody sells something to somebody else - an idea, a proposal or a deal. Negotiation is a sales process.

To achieve desired outcomes, negotiators have to make numerous decisions, some mundane, others critical. Negotiation is the process of making decisions and taking actions.

Negotiations are about disputes and disagreements that need to be resolved if an agreement is to be reached. Negotiation is a problem solving process. In seeking alternative solutions to these problems, negotiators use innovation and creativity. So, negotiation is also a creative process.

No deal is *only* about money. An exchange of value is always involved. Negotiation is thus a value-creating process.

Negotiation involves a potentially explosive mix of perceptions, expectations, feelings and emotions. Various conflicts may develop, from simple misunderstandings and personality clashes to cultural conflicts or conflicts of values. Negotiation thus becomes a conflict resolution process.

All this happens between people, whose relationships affect the outcomes. Ultimately, negotiation is a relationship-building process.

Negotiations Are Predictable, Therefore Controllable

Every process (beer making, oil refining, car driving) has a structure; so does negotiation. This is excellent news. The fact that most negotiations are structured in a similar way, along the same principles, makes them predictable - and anything that can be predicted, can be controlled.

Predictability = controllability
Negotiations are predictable and, therefore, controllable.

The Seven Stages of Negotiation

Let's have a look at the flow or progression of a typical negotiation. After preparation, we go face-to-face and ask questions. The aim of the probing stage is to determine if the assumptions our preparation was based on were correct or if major changes to our strategy are needed. We probe for our negotiating counterpart's interests and check their responses to our tentative or preliminary proposals.

Then, one of the parties puts a proposal on the table. This could be anything, from a tentative "trial balloon" ("What would you say if we took the training out of the main contract and added it to the ongoing technical support agreement? That way you can reduce your capital expenditure and pay for it from you operations budget!") to a tangible, multi-page written proposal and full costing.

The first three stages usually happen in the preparing - probing - proposing order. The advanced stages, on the other hand, may happen simultaneously or in a different order, they don't necessarily follow in the manner presented in the table below. That is the first aspect of the negotiation structure that complicates its planning and understanding.

PRELIMINARY STAGES	ADVANCED STAGES
■ PREPARING (planning) ■ PROBING (asking open-ended questions) ■ PROPOSING (solutions)	■ PERSUADING ■ PROBLEM SOLVING ■ PRICING (bargaining) ■ PACKAGING (integrating)

The second difficulty with the negotiation process is that one or more steps may have to be repeated at least once. Don't expect these seven steps to happen only once during a particular negotiation.

For instance, no matter how thorough your preparation is, there are facts and issues you cannot anticipate - they manifest themselves only during the face-to-face stages of probing and proposing. Such new developments warrant going back to prepare some more and then submitting a revised proposal.

Persuading usually goes hand-in-hand with proposing. The side making the proposal usually tries to persuade the other side that their proposal is fair, reasonable and mutually beneficial. The other party may or may not agree. If they disagree, we get into a problem solving situation.

MISTAKE: Jumping to solutions

Don't start negotiating a specific solution or an outcome before 1. the "problem" is correctly identified, 2. both sides agree on the problem definition, and 3. all possible solutions are explored!

To bridge the gap between the two parties during problem solving and pricing, it may be necessary to go back and do some more probing and proposing.

Pricing or bargaining is about money. It isn't always a separate stage, in many cases pricing is part of problem solving, since money is often the biggest gap that separates the two negotiators.

Finally, the aim of the packaging or integrating stage is to add various smaller or peripheral issues under the umbrella of the main deal and to build a bridge towards future deals.

Due to exhaustion after a tough and prolonged negotiation or a whole series of meetings, or due to the excitement of the moment when the agreement is reached, negotiators generally pay very little attention to packaging. A failure to properly package the deal usually results in disputes and disagreements at later stages, during the implementation of the deal! More on packaging later on.

📖 *You Can Have It My Way!* by Igor S. Popovich

The issue of persuasion (as we have just seen, one of the seven stages of negotiation) hasn't been extensively covered in this book, especially not in its wider context. My material on influence and persuasion, if included, would blow out this book's size to over 500 pages.

No matter how important the subject may be, I'm not a sadist (to expect you to read it all), so I've devoted my next book, a sequel to Loser No More!, exclusively to this crucial skill. Keep pestering me about the books availability, constant nagging from readers can drive authors to success (or to despair)!

META-NEGOTIATION: SETTING THE NEGOTIATING TABLE

Meta is a Greek word meaning "above" or "beyond". Meta-negotiation is a negotiation about the negotiation.

The goal of meta-negotiation is to agree on who will negotiate, where, when and how. If the negotiation itself was a dinner (cooking, serving and consuming a meal), meta-negotiation would involve fixing the date and time, choosing a dining room, deciding who will be invited, planning what meals will be served, and deciding how the table will be set.

Before the negotiation proper begins, it pays to think about, discuss with the other party and agree on the following issues: Who is going to negotiate and how? Where is the negotiation to be held? When are you going to schedule your negotiation meetings? How to negotiate, issue-by-issue or the whole package at once? What issues will and what issues won't be a part of the deal?

How Would You Like Your Deal Done?

> "We think in generalities, but we live in detail."
>
> Alfred North Whitehead, mathematician turned philosopher

I like the steak analogy of deal-making. Detailed agreements are like overdone steaks, while "in-principle" deals are like rare steaks. Neither is without problems.

An overdone steak is tough - all the juices have been sucked out during grilling. Similarly, an overdone deal is too prescriptive and too restrictive. It limits the freedom required to keep the deal flexible and to implement it creatively. While rare steaks are still bloody inside, under-done deals usually get bloody later, when disputes arise about important aspects of the deal that had not even been considered, let alone specified.

Details (specifics) or framework (principles)?

Decide up-front what would suit your purpose better - a detailed or a broad, "in principle" agreement, and negotiate accordingly.

Your personality impacts your preference for a certain type of an agreement. *Planners & Organisers* usually prefer detailed agreements, spelled out to the last letter, while *Improvisers* tend to aim for broad, "in principle" deals.

No matter which camp you belong to, decide early on what kind of agreement you want and discuss your preference with your negotiating partner. You may prefer a broad, in-principle understanding, while they may have been burned in similar cases in the past or they don't fully trust you, so they want a detailed, water-tight agreement.

What to Negotiate First - Details or Framework?

> "A process cannot be understood by stopping it. Understanding must move with the flow of the process, must join it and flow with it."
>
> Frank Herbert, *Dune*

There are two options when it comes to negotiating complex deals. We can start discussing various issues, agreeing on some easy ones while leaving the more contentious ones for later. Then, we'll move towards larger and more significant issues. We may call that an inductive approach (from specific towards generic) or inside-out way of negotiating.

The alternative is to first agree on how and what to negotiate. Discuss the basic framework of the deal first, what rules are to be adhered to, what is acceptable and what isn't. I call this a deductive approach (from generic towards specific) or an outside-in deal.

When it comes to minimising risk, a simple prescription I suggest is based on the size of the deal, its complexity and criticality. For SS negotiations (Small or Simple deals), do the deal first, and the relationship can develop later. With CC deals (Complex or Critical), develop the relationship first, and do the significant deal once the trust has been established.

Draw Boundaries, Clarify Expectations

"It's a funny thing about life, if you refuse to accept anything but the very best you very often get it."

William Somerset Maugham, playwright and novelist

Trying to play a game without understanding its rules is absurd. One of the aims of meta-negotiation is to clarify expectations and agree on what type of deal may serve the best interests of both parties. You are telling the other side who you are, what you have to offer (benefits you are bringing to the negotiating table), what you want from them (in broad terms) and how you expect to be treated. You are also emphasising where the boundaries are - what is acceptable and what is not. Just as good fences make good neighbours, so clear limits make good negotiating partners.

Many negotiators feel that these preliminary discussions are a waste of time. They are keen to get into the negotiation itself, assuming the other person somehow discovered their needs and understood their preferences. Big mistake. People can do many things, but mind reading is not one of them.

Choose the Location Carefully

"I like to drink to suit my location."

Tom Jones, entertainer

Most negotiators prefer negotiating on their home turf; in their office or home. There are no travel expenses, no time invested in travel, no jet-lag or tiredness, no culture shock or dodgy food. All the information is available at hand, it is easier to consult with the boss or stakeholders, and you can play the hospitality tactics.

There are some disadvantages, too. A friend of mine recently commented, "I don't like negotiating on my home ground. How can I walk away or threaten to, if the other guy is sitting in my office?"

There are even more important reasons why you should consider negotiating away from home. First and foremost, for intelligence gathering purposes: You will see more, talk to more people and get a better picture about their situation, how urgent or important your deal is to them.

Negotiating at home may also give you a false sense of security. The comfort factor may be working for you or against you. We are usually more alert when away, in an unfamiliar environment.

Negotiating on a neutral ground, such as a hotel or resort, is a third option. After all, don't forget to look after number one, enjoy your trip and have fun. Business expenses are fully tax-deductible. Just don't overdo the cocktails; these aren't so easy to justify to your accountant or the tax man.

TEAM NEGOTIATIONS

Should You Negotiate on Your Own or as Part of a Team?

> Dirty Harry: "We are not just going to let you walk out of here."
> Crook: "Who the hell is 'we' sucker?"
> Dirty Harry, pointing his .44 Magnum at the crook: "Smith, and Wesson, and me ..."
>
> Inspector Harry Callahan in movie "Sudden Impact"

Most negotiations don't leave us any choice. We either negotiate on our own, or, mostly on large business deals, as part of a team. Most of us believe negotiating as a team will be easier for us and better for the deal itself.

The most important advantage of negotiating as a team is a division of tasks amongst two or more negotiators. Each team member assumes one or more roles. When you negotiate on your own, you have to perform all those tasks yourself. It is extremely difficult, if not impossible, to observe, listen, ask questions, evaluate proposals, devise options, and take notes at the same time.

The personality factor should not be underestimated. Your personality makes you suitable for some roles and unsuitable for others. For example, if you are a conceptual person, it will be difficult for you to pay attention to details, and we all know that small issues can have big consequences. If your strength is in your analytical skills and the analysis of the deal, are your creative skills at the same level of proficiency? Remember, when you negotiate alone, you have to do *everything* yourself, and nobody is equally good at everything.

During the preparation stage negotiators can act as each other's sounding boards. They can bounce suggestions off each other, constructively criticise and contribute to each other's ideas. The synergy effect should not be underestimated. More heads, more ideas.

Let's not forget the proverbial "run over by a bus" problem. When something happens to a lone negotiator (urgent commitments of business or personal nature, illness or worse), what happens to the negotiation? It grinds to a halt. Very few business negotiators have a replacement ready to step in. A lengthy familiarisation process of catching up is usually required, and such a setback may be advantageous to the other party.

When negotiating as a team, there is usually someone who can step in and take over some or all of your responsibilities.

Finally, we come to the perception of power. Have you ever arrived for what you thought would be a one-on-one talk, only to be ushered into a room with six stone-faced negotiators seated at an enormous table, facing a solitary chair - yours? Even if you haven't, I'm sure you've been to a job interview where you were seated opposite a panel of three or four interviewers. How did you feel? Intimidated? Outnumbered? Lonely?

TEAM ADVANTAGES	TEAM DRAWBACKS
■ roles and responsibilities can be divided ■ show of strength (intimidation) ■ stakeholders are part of the team, so buy-in is ensured ■ specialist knowledge available within the team	■ high expenses (travel, time) ■ disagreement, role confusion or conflict within the team ■ more communication, longer discussions ■ longer planning and more co-ordination is needed

Pitfalls to Watch for In Team Negotiations

There are many obvious dangers in team negotiations. If responsibilities are not clear, some tasks will not be done, while other efforts may be duplicated. There is always the "I thought you were doing that ..." danger.

Conflicts of interest or opinion happen often. These internal disagreements between operations, projects, purchasing, maintenance, finance, contracts and other stakeholders have to be resolved promptly and properly, otherwise a sub-optimal deal may be reached. Any disagreement within the team will eventually become obvious to the other side, who will exploit such differences for all they are worth.

There is a fine line between leading and dominating a team, especially when stakes are high, when the team is under pressure from stakeholders or when imminent deadlines are looming. Team negotiations often degenerate into a one-on-one duels between team leaders, while the other team members become spectators. The opposite may also happen. In some negotiating teams, it is not clear who has the final authority.

Another obvious disadvantage of sending your team instead of a lone negotiator is the required investment in terms of cost (travel and accommodation), as well as expenditure of time and effort. Protracted negotiations will prevent team members from performing other tasks or managing or participating in other projects or deals.

Apart from these universal pitfalls, Westerners are also

disadvantaged by their cultural predispositions. Books on teamwork are rare in Japan; Japanese are instinctively good team players (and negotiators, too)! Not so with the strongly individualistic Americans, Britons or Australians.

In the west, there seems to be a certain fascination among both writers and publishers with the subject of teamwork and team building. Supply is usually a good indicator of demand. The more books there are on a particular topic, the higher the need for those skills amongst the prospective buyers.

✓ CHECKLIST: Three Critical Conditions For Team Success

- *Roles and responsibilities* should be clear and appropriate. Assign roles based on personalities, individual strengths and preferences.
- *Unison performance:* The team should speak with one voice. Team members should not contradict each other or openly disagree with each other in front of the other side.
- *Efficiency:* There should be no tourists or loafers on your team.

PACKAGING AND IMPLEMENTING THE DEAL

Super-sizing the Deal

Win-win is often confused with compromise. The only thing you can achieve on single-issue deals is compromise. You don't pay the asking price, but you don't get it for the bargain price you were hoping for either. I call these "SO-SO" or "not bad" deals. Just like people who, when asked, "How are you today?", reply "Oh, not bad." But that usually means they are not very good, either. Just so-so.

Moving away from a one-issue-deal to a multiple-issues-deal is the first step towards a win-win outcome. How many times have you heard "Would you like fries with that?" in a fast-food joint?

How do we upsize or even SUPER-SIZE a deal? How do we convert a single-issue deal into a larger deal? Well, that depends on the deal itself. Simple deals, where price is the main or the only issue, cannot be upsized.

If there are follow-up deals, you may choose to let the other side "win" on the first deal (or the first few deals), and then change the dynamics into a win-win later on. You may call it short-term-pain for a long-term-gain. It pays to look at the whole series of deals as one bigger upsized-deal.

Another upsizing option is a trial deal. The buyer gets a lower price or better terms now in return for future orders. This arrangement is disliked by sellers because many unscrupulous buyers use it is a trick, promising future deals that usually don't happen.

Wrapping Things Up

> "Life is too short to live with a bad deal."
>
> David Geffen, record executive, film producer

The aim of the integrating phase is two-fold. The immediate aim is to tie-up all the loose ends. The outstanding issues should be agreed upon, and, as much as possible, grey areas as possible should be identified and addressed. That often implies that further smaller negotiations will be required along the way. Very few agreements are complete or immutable; most are living, changing, and ultimately, imperfect - just as the people who produced them.

Imperfect (real) people cannot produce perfect (ideal) agreements.

The longer-term aim of the packaging stage is to make the current negotiation (deal) a bridge or a link with future ones. Just as every deal sets a precedent for the future dealings between the same parties, it should also develop the relationship so the deals that follow are even more beneficial and profitable for both parties.

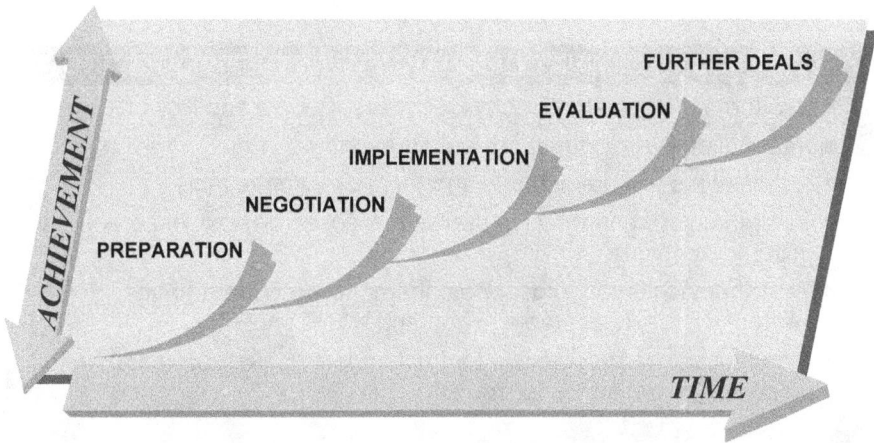

The integrating phase provides a feeling of continuity. Its aim is not the agreement itself, but its implementation and easier, more productive future negotiations. Instead of a series of one-off deals where everything starts all over each time, the parties realise it is in their best long-term interest to bridge the deals and slowly-but-steadily grow and strengthen their relationship. The integrating phase thus sets the scene for additional, mutually beneficial deals.

The Perpetual Journey Theory

Every destination is a starting point for another journey.

A Deal is Not Done Until the Fat Lady Sings

Less experienced negotiators erroneously define the reaching of the agreement as the last step of negotiation. I consider a deal done deal when the agreement is implemented, not when the handshake happens, not even when the contract is signed.

The aim of negotiation is not only to agree on the deal, but to implement that agreement and to realise or distribute the benefits to all involved.

Implementors make the most motivated negotiators

Whoever has to carry out the agreement in practice or live with the results of a deal, is the best person to negotiate it.

Even if negotiators pay attention to details and are on guard during the actual negotiations, once the deal is agreed upon, they relax, move to the next deal and forget about implementation. One team or department negotiates a deal while another has to implement it in practice. This creates all sorts of problems. It's easy to agree on something you don't have to do yourself.

WINNING TIPS: WHAT I WISH I KNEW TWENTY YEARS AGO

- Use the 4 P's system: Problem, Process, People and Power.
- Negotiation is a process, not just an event.
- Negotiations are predictable, and therefore, controllable.
- Before you start negotiating the issues, agree on how you are going to negotiate.
- Tell others what you expect from them, how you want to be treated, what is acceptable to you and what is not.
- Whoever will be responsible for implementing the deal should be the one to negotiate its terms.

Perplexed No More!

PROBLEM SOLVING IN NEGOTIATION

If you know how to investigate, define and solve problems, you are ready to become a competent negotiator. Negotiators are deal-detectives.

Coming up:

- How to define and analyse problems
- Crucial or pivotal aspects of a deal
- Obvious versus optimal solutions
- How to complain and get satisfaction

HOW TO DEFINE AND ANALYSE PROBLEMS

Which should we concentrate on first, the people or the problem side of negotiation? Since they are usually entwined, you have to work on both simultaneously. Important issues shouldn't be tackled in a piece-meal fashion.

In business, many management initiatives fail for that particular reason. We either focus solely on the technical or business side of a problem and ignore the people aspect, or we put pressure on people to perform better and faster, while the real problem lies elsewhere - on the technical or system side.

You cannot solve people problems by technical means.

What if people are the problem? To most negotiators, the main problem about negotiation is "the other person". To achieve a successful outcome, you have to work on two fronts: Understanding and improving yourself, and understanding and helping the other person. Notice I didn't say you have to change or improve the other person; that is not your responsibility.

Don't try to fix the system or the other person (unless you are a psychotherapist or a sado-masochist). Fix the problem.

You Cannot Negotiate Things You Don't Understand

"Where the broom does not reach, the dust will not vanish of itself."

Mao Tse-Tung, Chinese revolutionary leader

I often get asked if there is such a thing as a "universal negotiator", someone who could negotiate any type of deal, in any situation, with anybody. When a bank in Hong Kong asked me to run an in-house seminar on negotiating bad loans, I declined. I know that bad loans are situations when borrowers stop paying interest back to the banks, but that is hardly enough to talk to bank's senior management about for two days!

While the framework of all negotiations is universal, the details and specifics are not. A professional hostage negotiator would not be very successful in negotiating oil tanker leasing deals in Dubai, or an oil exploration deal between a mining company, local, state and federal governments, and traditional Aboriginal landowners in the Australian outback. The devil, as they say, is in the details.

The Lemon Problem

Although problem solving is a crucial and fascinating subject, we cannot cover it comprehensively in a book on negotiation. I will use the simplest possible case, a negotiation between two people and involving only one issue. Most real life negotiations are much more complex.

NEGOTIATING CASE: The Lemon Problem

A teenage daughter comes into the kitchen and asks her mother: "Mum, have we got any lemons? I need one ..."

"Sorry, honey, we only have one left, and I need it for the cake I'm baking," replies the mother.

"But Mum, it always has to be your way! I never get what I want!" She storms out and slams the kitchen door behind her.

✋ STOP & THINK! What's the problem? How would you fix it?

No matter how knowledgeable you may be about the negotiating principles, you will not be a successful negotiator until you master the details of the subject you are negotiating. Negotiating franchise deals is quite different from negotiating divorce settlements.

The key to the solution of our case is not the mother, or the daughter, or their relationship. Sure, all these factors are important and will impact the outcome, but the key here is in the lemon. To become a great negotiator you have to know the lemon - you cannot negotiate something you don't understand.

Problem Definition is Half of the Solution

"The obvious is that which is never seen
until someone expresses it simply."

Khalil Gibran, Lebanese American poet

Possibly the biggest mistake that inexperienced negotiators make is discussing possible solutions before the problem itself is fully understood and properly defined.

Every problem is a black box - open it and investigate it inside out. Take it apart. Break it down into factors or components. These factors should be as independent of each other as possible and they should be exhaustive - no significant factors should be left out. Apply the 80/20 rule: 20 percent of the factors determine eighty percent of the deal. Focus on these "significant few" and avoid getting confused by the "trivial many".

Next, see how these issues or factors relate to each other and how they fit together into the overall picture. Some factors will be in a parent-child relationship with others; they will be causally linked. That will help you to prioritise them properly. Parent problems should be dealt with first, and most of the children (flow-on problems) will automatically be solved.

Before you start preparing for any negotiation, ask yourself a simple question: "What is this situation (negotiation / conflict / problem) all about?" Remember this question well. The answer will take you a long way towards finding the optimal solution.

The ultimate question

What is this *(situation - negotiation - meeting - problem - conflict)* fundamentally about?

The most obvious issue may not be the most critical. When one aspect of the deal stands out, we may fail to discover other issues at play.

For example, while money is always a significant aspect of a business deal, it isn't always the most important one. People just make it seem that way. There may be something hidden behind sellers' demands for more money or buyers' demands for a cheaper price.

The Crucial or Pivotal Aspects of a Deal

"Negotiations are about
whatever the parties involved think they are about."

Howard Raiffa, academic, negotiation theorist

The Lemon Problem involves an *imbalance of power*. The mother has the authority to make decisions. If say, a sister was baking a cake, there would be no power imbalance. The daughter could just take the lemon without asking and a cat fight could have ensued.

Another important aspect is *the daughter's attitude*. She was impatient and behaved immaturely, approaching her mother from the position of a rebellious child. She failed to motivate her mother to even consider giving her what she wanted. There was nothing for the mother to gain.

The last sentence ("But Mum, I never get what I want ....") indicates another critical factor - *past or previous dealings* between the two of them. This is not the first time the daughter lost. It is almost as if she expected to go away with nothing. Perhaps that is why she gave up so easily.

Timing could also be an issue here. One or both parties may face a deadline, or one person chooses the wrong time to approach the other. The mother may have a real deadline (dinner party at seven) and is running late. That could explain her firm attitude toward her daughter's request.

The relationship between the parties could be of competitive nature. In our vignette, the mother and daughter may see each other as rivals. Or, it may be a loving and nurturing relationship, where parties involved would be likely to adopt a self-sacrificing stance, putting the other person's needs before their own.

✓ **CHECKLIST: Common Crucial Aspects of Various Deals**

- *Relationship:* Is this a "one-off" or repeat (regular) negotiation? What sort of relationship is it? Do parties trust each other? What is the influence of stakeholders (on both sides)?

- *Previous Dealings (History):* What happened in previous negotiations? What precedents were set?

- *Time & Timing:* Is there an element of urgency? Is one or both sides are in a hurry? Is there a real deadline looming? Is anybody stalling, playing a delay tactic?

- *Power:* Is one party dependent on the other (parent, boss, client)? Are there are differences in options or alternatives? Does one side have more options than the other?

- *Money:* How can the price be reduced? Clearance or superseded models, large quantities or as introductory discount for a new client)? Are there are any trade-offs or substitutes?

- *Culture:* Are there substantive differences in customs, mentalities, expectations, norms, ethics or values? Any taboos, sensitivities, religious differences, language barriers?

- *Efficiency and Effectiveness:* If something is proposed, should it be done? If yes, what is the best way to do it? When is the optimal time? Who is the best person to do it and why?

The Perception Paradox

> "The words of truth are always paradoxical."
>
> Lao Tzu, ancient Chinese Taoist philosopher, sage

Perception is of such significance in negotiation and problem solving, that I was tempted to include it as the fifth P in my Four Ps model of negotiation. Instead of asking, "What is the problem here?" we should be asking, "How does the other side see this problem?"

We see the same event but often interpret it differently. Police face such a problem on a daily basis when they interview eye-witnesses of traffic accidents or crimes. Some people see more, some less. Often, eyewitnesses tell completely opposite stories, especially if some time has passed after the event. Human memory and perception are both unreliable and volatile. The line between our imagination and our memory is often blurred. So, before we start search for possible solutions, we have to agree on what the problem actually is.

The Perception Paradox

We don't see things as they are, we see them as we are.

YOUR	PROBLEM FOR	THEIR
PERCEPTION	MUTUAL	PERCEPTION
	SOLUTION	

As if conflicting perceptions weren't enough, our search for meaning complicates things even further. When we cannot explain something, we assign, without adequate justification or proof, causes to those unexplainable events.

For instance, just because the cancer rate is higher in one suburb, does not automatically mean the local factory is the cause of the illness. Random events do cluster, but we feel more comfortable and look much smarter when we pinpoint the cause, no matter how erroneous such a conclusion is.

The Closure Principle

When the cause of a problem isn't found, we invent it.

So, when you and your negotiating counterpart don't see eye-to-eye, don't push for the solution. Step back and compare your views of the situation with theirs. You cannot explore potential solutions, before you fully understand how they perceive the situation or the deal you are negotiating.

MOVING TOWARDS SOLUTIONS

Obvious Solutions Are Seldom Optimal

"Thinking is the most unhealthy thing in the world, and people die of it just as they die of any other disease."

Oscar Wilde, Irish writer and poet

When I pose the Lemon Problem to participants in my negotiating seminars and ask for suggestions on how to solve it, the first solution is inevitably "Maybe they can cut the lemon in half!"

Compromise is an obvious option, an easy way out. Unfortunately, an obvious solution is seldom the best one. The mother would not get enough rind (assuming she only needs the zest) and the daughter would get only half of the lemonade she may be after.

The Obvious Solution Trap

An obvious solution is seldom the optimal one.

"The daughter should do what her mother tells her to!" is another common response. Authoritarian negotiators solve problems by resorting to force, authority and exercise of power. Mothers may have power over their daughters, as long as the daughters are economically dependent, but such autocratic attitude won't get you very far in the long run. Remember, always be nice to your kids, because one day they will choose your retirement home!

"It's all the mother's fault because she did not buy enough lemons." This is the least constructive of all suggestions. Blaming others for their past omissions or lack of foresight doesn't bring us any closer to a satisfactory resolution of this situation.

"The mother should choose a recipe without a lemon." True, the mother *could* bake a different cake. But why would she? Has the daughter motivated her to do so? Has she explained why she needs the last lemon? No, she hasn't. You cannot expect others to change their plans without offering them something in return!

Optimal solution

In negotiation, an agreement that allocates the maximum possible benefits (both short- and long-term) to both sides.

Should We Justify Ourselves to Others?

"Never explain - your friends do not need it
and your enemies will not believe you anyway."

Elbert Hubbard, writer and philosopher

"Being a mature adult, the mother should justify her decision to the daughter." There is some truth in this suggestion, but there are also wider implications here. Should parents justify their actions and attitudes to their children? Should bosses justify their requests to their employees? I think not, at least not always.

Justifications invite arguments and arguments may lead to conflict. Justifications are defensive and may perceptually weaken your position.

The Justification Trap

The party that feels the need to justify themselves to the other side is perceptually in a weaker position.

"The mother should buy a cake and give the lemon to her daughter. That way, she would save the time and effort of baking a cake, and the daughter would be happy!"

This is a typical "money can buy you anything" approach. What if she doesn't have the money to buy a ready-made cake? What if her cakes are much better than commercially-made ones? If the mother goes out to buy a cake, she may as well buy more lemons.

67

Complementary Versus Conflicting Needs

Our Lemon Problem lacks contextual information. We don't know why the daughter needs the lemon. Just because the daughter said she needed the lemon does not necessarily make it so. She just got bored, snooped around the kitchen, and decided she wanted a lemon.

We have been conditioned to minimise the use of "I want ..." and substitute it with a more socially acceptable "I need ..." Wanting sounds selfish and arbitrary, but is closer to reality.

Life is selfish and most rules and conventions are arbitrary. By replacing "I want" with "I need", the terminology starts shaping our thinking. We rationalise and convince ourselves that we really do need it.

We don't know much about the mother's needs, either. Neither of the characters tried to understand or clarify the needs of the other person or explained her own needs. The daughter's behaviour was impatient and immature. The mother immediately assumed her own needs were more important.

Finally, we come to the ultimate question: Is win-win possible here?

Let's assume the daughter wants to make herself a glass of lemonade. She may be thirsty, or she may have a sore throat and feels vitamin C would do her good. Assuming the daughter wants a lemonade, now it all depends on the mother's needs. There are two possibilities:

1. *Complementary needs:* The mother needs the rind to bake a cake. She will grate the lemon skin first, then the daughter will make herself a lemonade. All they have to do is to explain their requirements to each other and they will quickly find an optimal solution. Their needs are not mutually exclusive, but complementary. This is a typical win - win situation.
2. *Conflicting needs:* The daughter needs the lemon juice for a lemonade. The mother also needs all of the juice. The rind is irrelevant. It is *not* possible to satisfy both requirements with only one piece of lemon. A typical win-lose situation ensues.

🛠 The Ideal Solution Method

"The greatest challenge to any thinker
is stating the problem in a way that will allow a solution."

Bertrand Russell, philosopher, mathematician, Nobel prize winner

Before you start negotiating any issue or resolving any conflict, ask the other person to outline their ideal outcome or preferred solution. Say something like, "Please understand this is just an exploration of views and ideas. I cannot guarantee we will be able to satisfy your needs or comply with your demands, but if we could, what would you like to see happen? What could we do to bridge the gap between our positions? What outcome would make you happy?"

Only when you fully understand the other negotiator's preferred solution, their ideal outcome, will you be able to move to the next stage, designing a realistic solution that comes closest to both yours and their ideal solutions. Of course, success is not guaranteed. If the two ideal solutions have little in common and if the parties stick too rigidly to their own ideal outcomes, a compromise will not happen.

Let's go back to the Lemon Problem and assume we are facing conflicting needs - a more difficult scenario where win-win is not possible. If you were in the daughter's shoes, how would you persuade the mother to give you the lemon?

Pushing Mother's Hot Buttons

"The principle of give and take is the principle of diplomacy -
give one and take ten."

Mark Twain, novelist

To persuade the mother to give her the lemon, the daughter first has to understand why the mother is baking the lemon cake. Perhaps the father likes lemon slices, or has invited his boss and his wife home for dinner, and knows it's his boss' favourite. Or, she just saw it in *Women's Weekly* and wants to try it for no particular reason.

Once the mother's motivation is explored (and it is a simple matter of asking her a question or two), the daughter can identify her mother's "hot buttons". These are pivotal motivational factors that cause a person to do what we want them to.

She could say something like, "Mom, why are you baking a cake on such a hot day? Why don't you have a rest and I will call Dad and ask him to stop at the cake shop on his way home from work?"

Or, if the mother still insists on baking the cake, the daughter could try to make her change the recipe: "Mum, the strawberry flan is everyone's favourite, and I've noticed we have some strawberries in the fridge. If we don't use them very soon they will go off ..."

Hot buttons

Pivotal motivational factors that help us persuade others to do what we want them to.

The Lemon Problem is a simple example. On a complexity scale of one to ten, it would be around two. It is far from trivial, though. It illustrates important issues also present in the more complex deals and situations.

HOW TO COMPLAIN AND GET SOME SATISFACTION

The Room Service Rule

I tend to spend lots of time in hotels. I like hotels. Somebody cleans up your mess daily, you don't have to cook, make your bed or wash your clothes. And best of all, there is room service.

Unfortunately, life is not as neat and predictable as dialling 9 for service and getting what you want twenty minutes later. It is a rather messy and unpredictable affair, where nice things usually don't happen by themselves. You have to make them happen.

Sitting in your room and twiddling your thumbs will not make room service take place. Sure, it is available, but you have to get on the phone and ask for it. I call this mental delusion "The Room Service Rule" or "The Silver Tray Trap".

The Room Service Rule (The Silver Tray Trap)

To get something, you have to ask for it.
If you expect others to read your mind and bring you the things you want on a silver tray, you are in for a very long wait.

How often do you expect others to give you what you want, only to realise you hadn't actually asked them to do so? Have you ever assumed others knew exactly what you needed, only to find out later they didn't have a clue about your expectations?

People can do many things, but mind reading is not one of them. Not many of us are lucky enough to find others come to them and say, "We thought you wanted a promotion so here is one for you!" or "We can give you a 20 percent discount on this order".

Expressing your unhappiness or voicing your disagreement may be difficult for you. Childhood conditioning is a contributing factor. Cultural influences don't help either.

Down under, "She'll be right, mate!" is the prevalent attitude. Complaining, demanding and criticising (even constructively) is seen as un-Australian and will get you labelled a whinger[6]. Resist such unhelpful social pressures and fight for what you feel is right.

✓ CHECKLIST: The Seven Rules of Complaining

> "The world is disgracefully managed,
> one hardly knows to whom to complain."
>
> Ronald Firbank, novelist

Expressing your displeasure or complaining about a problem is infinitely better than suffering in silence, but it isn't enough. You can do better than that. Ask for a prompt, fair and specific compensation.

---

[6] a person who complains incessantly

Tell others exactly how you want them to resolve the situation and ask them to do it right there and then. Instead of waiting for them to offer you a solution that may suit their interests, take initiative and demand a solution that will suit your interests better.

1. *Explain before you complain.* The person you are talking to may not be aware of your problem or grievance. Be courteous and friendly. Don't criticise or attack the person.

2. *Complain as soon after the event as possible.* Strike while the iron is hot and memories are fresh.

3. *Ask to be compensated.* Tell them what would make you happy.

4. *If possible, go to see them in person.* The most difficult thing to get rid of is a body. A telephone call is second best. Writing, faxing or e-mailing is usually the least effective.

5. *Bypass the door-minders and authority-starved lackeys.* Negotiate directly with the manager who has the authority to give you what you want. Many of them have nothing better to do and would welcome the opportunity to show their underlings

6. *Explain the rationale behind your request.* Use "because" a lot, no matter how weak your argument may be. People are suckers for "because" and will seldom scrutinise the causality and merits of your explanation.

7. *Be firm and persistent.* If they refuse to correct the situation, warn them that you will seek satisfaction through other channels (courts, media, competitors). Despite their apparent self-importance, deep down, even top-level managers are insecure. Use threats and blackmail as a last resort.

Negotiating With Banks

When banks are mentioned, people fume about bad service, a myriad of unfair fees and inflexible attitude. The prevalent view is that all banks are the same. My personal experience is quite different.

QUICK STORY: All banks are not the same!

One month my credit card bill was unusually high. On the next bill, there was an interest charge of $77.25. Since I always pay my bills in full, I thought, there must be some sort of mistake.

A call to customer service revealed that instead of $5,230, I paid $5,220. Since I did not pay the bill in full, I was charged interest on the whole amount of $5,230. This rule was clearly outlined in the Terms & Conditions booklet, meaning that legally, the bank was entitled to charge me the full interest.

> I claimed an honest, typing mistake: Why would I not pay the whole amount, as I *always* do? The lady on the other end of the line sympathised with me but said she couldn't cancel the charge - the amount in question was above her discretionary limit. She advised me to outline my case in a letter to the bank's credit card section.
>
> I thought: "Here we go again, the standard 'Lack of Authority' spiel, together with the 'Put-it-in-Writing' trick." But, I wrote it anyway.
>
> After a week, I got a call from the bank: They'd cancelled the interest charge. Sure enough, there was a refund of $77.25 on the next statement.

I learned a simple but profound lesson from that episode: Negotiate even when you are clearly at fault. Don't simply accept your "fate" and pay the penalties. You have nothing to lose and a lot to gain.

Negotiate even when you are in the wrong; you may get lucky.

Anybody can penalise, prosecute or litigate. Forgiveness is the ultimate sign of strength. It displays goodwill, indebts and says, "We understand. To show you we care and to strengthen our relationship, we will forego the immediate benefits we are entitled to get from you, so we can both benefit in the long run."

Since that incident, I've established a few property loans and opened various term and investment deposits with that bank. By foregoing seventy or so dollars of income and by displaying goodwill, they've benefited a thousand-fold from my ongoing custom.

WINNING TIPS: WHAT I WISH I KNEW TWENTY YEARS AGO

- You cannot solve people problems by technical means.
- Don't try to fix the system or the other person. Fix the problem.
- We don't see things as they are, we see them as we are.
- The party that feels the need to justify themselves to the other side is perceptually in a weaker position.
- Don't just complain; ask to be compensated.
- Negotiate even when you are in the wrong; you may get lucky.

Aimless No More!

PROPER PREPARATION, POWERFUL PERFORMANCE

Preparation is the most important phase of any negotiation. Critical questions - why we should prepare, how to go about it, what to do and what not to - will all be answered for you here.

Coming up:

- How to set and prioritise goals
- How to identify and analyse your options
- How to develop your negotiating strategy
- Forward and reverse planning
- How to structure multi-party business relationships

THE POWER OF PREPARATION

The Nightmare on Negotiating Street

"Well begun is half done."

Horace (Quintus Horatius Flaccus), Roman poet

"The most common and most serious mistake poor negotiators make is their lack of preparation. As a result, they find themselves in situations they don't fully understand, with unclear goals, uncertain criteria for success and no knowledge of the other party. No wonder most people enter negotiations with fear and apprehension. Welcome to "The Nightmare on Negotiating Street!"

I see four main reasons why we don't prepare well. *Time* is the usual suspect. Preparation takes time, so when rushed, something has to give. What usually gets sacrificed is proper planning and preparation.

The personality factor is hard to overcome. When it comes to planning, there are two distinct mindsets. *Planners* spend days planning tasks and events down to the last detail. *Improvisers* dislike planning and advocate a situational approach, preferring to deal with developments as they happen.

Knowledge (or the lack of it) helps or hinders adequate preparation. Inexperienced negotiators don't know how to prepare well. Their planning process is haphazard - it lacks methodology, it's almost always inefficient and often ineffective.

Lack of information makes thorough preparation impossible. To prepare properly, accurate records are needed from previous projects and deals. In business, many organisations either don't have such information or it is disorganised and difficult to find when needed. A little information goes a long way ... towards failure.

Why Prepare?

"If I had eight hours to chop down a tree,
I'd spend six sharpening my axe."

Abraham Lincoln, American statesman

The prevalent belief is that preparation is about discovering all the information about the other side so that we know exactly what to do beforehand. That is not completely true. You will never get all the information you need. Even if you did, too much information could have a paralysing effect or it may confuse you.

Also, if you think you are completely prepared, you may go into the negotiation overconfident, and that is not a good thing anymore. You will not listen enough and will not ask the right questions.

Flexibility is the main outcome of a successful preparation. You should be *reasonably* prepared and *quietly* confident. That is achieved by having developed a strategy or plan flexible enough to survive the first contact with your negotiating counterpart. Preparation enables you to respond rationally rather than react emotionally.

Power + Preparation + Practice = Perfect Performance

How Long Should Your Preparation Be?

"In all things, success depends upon previous preparation, and without such preparation there is sure to be failure."

Confucius, ancient Chinese philosopher

Abraham Lincoln was once asked how long it took him to prepare a speech. "It usually takes me about two weeks to prepare a good twenty minute speech", he answered, "but I can write a forty minute one in a week or so. And I can give a two-hour speech on any subject right now!"

No sane person would start building a house by constructing the roof first. Foundations are the key. You may have noticed how deep the foundations are for high-rise buildings. The taller the building, the deeper the foundations.

Preparing for a negotiation is no different, and the results are equally obvious: Prepared negotiators perform in a more efficient manner, meaning their negotiations progress faster and smoother. They are also more effective, achieving mutually beneficial agreements that are closer to the ideal outcome for both parties.

The Foundations Rule

The taller the building, the deeper the foundations.
The more complex the deal, the longer the preparation required.

The shorter the time available to accomplish something, the better prepared you have to be. The higher your goals and the more complex the negotiation, the longer and the more thorough your preparation should be.

Plans Are Nothing, Planning is Everything

"It is a bad plan that admits of no modification."

Publilius Syrus, Roman writer of maxims

There seems to be confusion between plans and planning. A plan is an outcome or product, while planning is a process or skill. Plans are the result of planning. A plan is only a piece of paper; one particular combination of steps and events, frozen in time. The aim of planning is not to produce a plan, but to stay flexible, anticipate developments and seize opportunities.

We place far too much emphasis on plans, while not enough attention is paid to the process of planning. "The plan shows at this stage we should be here and not here ...", we protest and rigidly stick to the plan while ignoring developments and opportunities that don't feature in it. If the plan doesn't reflect reality, we disregard reality.

People often ask me what should a negotiation plan look like. That depends on individual preferences. Some negotiators keep everything in their heads, while others use a laundry-list of important issues. The visual types draw mind-maps, flow-diagrams and charts of various kinds. A plan can be a prioritised list of your goals or a mud-map of some sort, similar to an itinerary for a journey. In general, your negotiation your plan will consist of four major components:

- "Where are we now?" - Analyse your current situation.
- "Where do we want to be?" - Set your negotiating goals.
- "How do we get there?" - Decide on your negotiating strategy.
- "Are we there yet?" - Monitor your progress towards the goal.

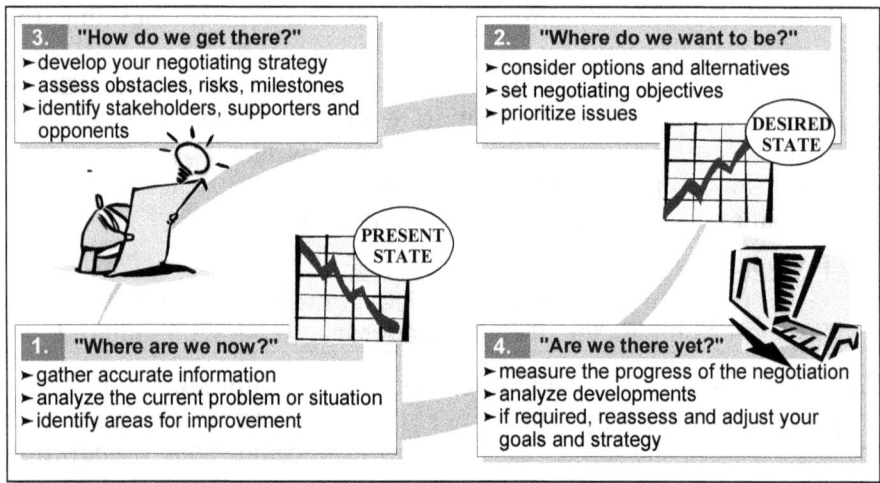

3. "How do we get there?"
► develop your negotiating strategy
► assess obstacles, risks, milestones
► identify stakeholders, supporters and opponents

2. "Where do we want to be?"
► consider options and alternatives
► set negotiating objectives
► prioritize issues

DESIRED STATE

PRESENT STATE

1. "Where are we now?"
► gather accurate information
► analyze the current problem or situation
► identify areas for improvement

4. "Are we there yet?"
► measure the progress of the negotiation
► analyze developments
► if required, reassess and adjust your goals and strategy

Expect the Best But Be Prepared for the Worst

"Don't worry, I'll think of something!"

Indiana Jones in "Raiders of the Lost Ark"

Self-improvement books are full of advice on how to motivate yourself, and how to develop learned optimism and a positive attitude. While this is all nice and laudable, all the motivation in the world will not be of much use to you if you don't do some thinking beforehand. Without preparation, all you can hope to become is an unprepared optimist.

The Nit-Picking Prescription
Expect the best but be prepared for the worst.

Hoping, wishing, praying or dreaming is fine, but it does not cut the mustard - planning, preparing and playing the game smart does! Preparation makes you feel confident (in your abilities), convinced (that you will do well), and creative (able to come up with new ideas).

The more you prepare, the more options you will identify and the more ideas you will get during the negotiation. And don't worry if they call you a nit-picker! Better to be perceived as a nit-picker *before* a problem happens than a sucker and a loser *after* it happens and catches you unprepared.

SETTING AND PRIORITISING GOALS

Goals are clear and concise statements of the accomplishments you are aiming to achieve in a negotiation, project, self-improvement effort, or any other undertaking. Goals are desired outcomes. They may be clear and concise, such as "I want a 20 percent discount!" or complex and convoluted. Clear and concise is better.

The Short & Sweet Rule
The longer and the more complex the objective you are trying to achieve, the more likely the negotiation will fail.

Make Your Goals Difficult, But Not Too Difficult!

The value of relatively ambitious goals has been demonstrated in various simulations. I sometimes do a simple experiment in my negotiation courses, a wage-negotiation between a union and an employer. Half of the participants playing the role of union negotiators are given a relatively easy goal, say, to achieve a two percent increase in average wages. The other half is given an ambitious goal, for example, to achieve a 15 percent pay-raise.

After the one-on-one negotiations are concluded, an interesting trend becomes obvious. Most of the negotiators with easy initial goals exceed expectations. The average increase achieved is usually around three percent.

Negotiators with difficult goals invariably fail to reach them. Instead of achieving the targeted 15 percent increase, on average, they manage around eight.

Negotiators with easy goals consider themselves winners, for they exceeded expectations. Those with difficult goals usually feel like losers. They failed to get even close to their goal. The goals anchored negotiators' expectations, and became reference points for evaluating outcomes.

This is what happens when we look at things in isolation. We can put things into perspective only by comparing the gains of the two groups: The "winners" achieved less than the "losers"! Labelling ourselves and others as winners and losers is often based on perceptions, not on reality.

This difference in outcomes between the two groups is called "the expectation bias" or "the expectation bias gap". The more you expect from yourself and others, the more you usually achieve.

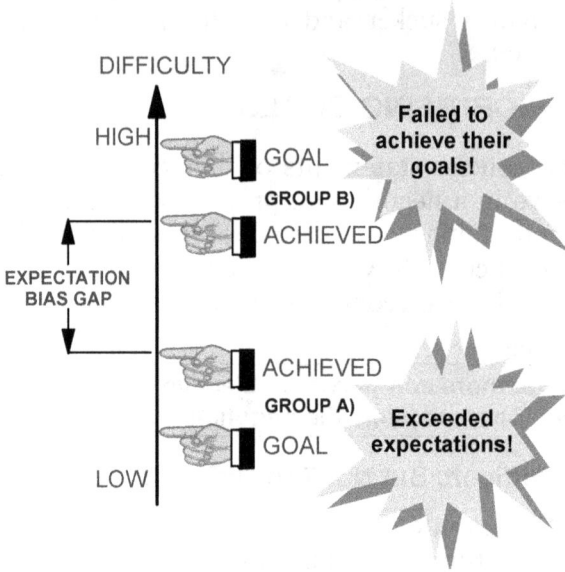

Expectation Bias
Ambitious goals usually result in higher gains compared to the outcomes of the same negotiation when easy goals were set.

How to Judge Success in Negotiation

"It's a silly game where nobody wins."

Thomas Fuller, churchman and historian

If we define success as the achievement of set goals, clearly the group with easy goals is more successful than the group with difficult goals. However, if we define success in terms of absolute gain than the group with difficult goals is by far the more successful one.

The most accurate way to judge your success or failure would be to compare it with how much others achieved under the same circumstances. That would hold all variables (situational factors) constant, except one: your performance.

Obviously, such evaluation is extremely difficult in research and next to impossible in practice, due to unpredictable influences of various forces beyond our control.

Since such an absolute way of measuring success is impractical, the relativist school advocates judging success against our own standards - the criteria that we set for ourselves. We define success as doing our personal or collective best, regardless of how it compares to the personal or collective best of others.

Let me suggest another way of measuring success in negotiation, based on the prize-price duality principle. Look at success as a prize and then ask, "Was the prize I got worth the price I had to pay?"

Is the prize worth the price?

Judge your success by the price you had to pay to get the prize.

Keep Prioritising Your Goals

"If we don't go for the higher tastes, we will settle for the lower ones."

Mortimer Adler, author and philosopher

Having a list of targets isn't enough. It is unlikely you'll manage to get everything you wanted, so prioritising your goals is a prudent strategy. Don't go overboard and have a dozen priority levels; three will usually do.

1. Highest priority: MUST HAVEs. These issues are non-negotiable. If you don't get all of those, there should be no deal and you should walk away.

2. Medium priority: NICE TO HAVEs. Try to get as many of these as possible.

3. Low priority: TRADE-AWAYs. These issues or goals are sometimes called "give-aways" because you could just give them to the other person. They are of low value to you, but may be more valuable to the other side. So, don't give anything away! You can trade them for something of more value to you. Always ask for something in return!

Neither the context nor the content of a negotiation are static. Our perceptions and expectations may also change, so it is perfectly normal to adjust our goals and priorities accordingly. An issue of the highest priority before the negotiation may be downgraded to a medium or even low priority goal. Likewise, something we were prepared to trade away could become a top priority.

Preferences are not carved in stone. Don't rigidly stick to your goals and priorities; change them as the situation dictates.

✗ The Three Lists Preparation Method

Whenever I have a project to manage or a deal to negotiate, I make three lists. I call them YES, MAYBE and NO. These can be for your eyes only, or you can even communicate them to the other side, if you think that would be in your interest.

YES is the list of things I want to get out of the deal, or a scope of work for a consultant or contractor on a project.

NO is the list of items I don't want, things I don't want to happen, or tasks I don't want the other party to do or perform.

```
YES - wanted, required
✓ _____
✓ _____
✓ _____  NO - not wanted or needed
✓ _____  ✗ _____
✓ _____  ✗ _____
           ✗ _____  MAYBE - unknown, uncertain
           ✗ _____  ? _____
           ✗ _____  ? _____
                      ? _____
                      ? _____
                      ? _____
```

If you open any formal contract, you will find a section called "Specific Exclusions". This is the legal equivalent of my NO list. By specifying what is *not* required, you minimise the possibility of misunderstandings, future disputes and costly conflict.

For instance, an electrician may say, "Remember when we were discussing this job, you asked me how much it would cost to run a separate cable back to the switchboard, including a dedicated circuit breaker? So, I've assumed you wanted it done. Here is the bill."

With just an informal agreement, without this list, you are in a weaker position. You did ask about it and now it's his word against yours. This way, you simply show him this section of the agreement and legally you are off the hook. You don't have to pay for that part of the work performed. If he wants to disconnect the cable and remove it all, he is free to do so. That will teach him to read the contract more carefully next time.

There will always be issues that need discussion and clarification. There are also tasks conditional on something else happening or not, as there are unclear or insufficiently defined goals. That's perfectly normal. Before you start discussing these grey issues face-to-face, write them down on the third list, the MAYBE list.

As you progress through a negotiation, you should keep crossing the items of the MAYBE list and moving them to one of the other two lists. They should either be done or agreed upon, or specifically excluded from the deal. The MAYBE list is like a short-term car park; to temporarily hold the uncertain or unresolved issues.

The Mind Mechanism at Work

> "Every game is composed of two parts,
> an outer game and an inner game."
>
> Timothy Gallwey, *The Inner Game of Tennis*

Goal setting works not just on a practical, but also on a subliminal level. Once you have a clear goal in your mind, provided you feel a strong desire to reach it, the goal becomes internalised. Your subconscious mind takes such an affirmation and self-programs it into its own "To do" list.

You think a thought. A feeling of some sort, positive or negative, gets attached to this thought (very few thoughts are emotionally neutral). The thought and the emotional attachment then act together as a magnet to attract the circumstance or the outcome.

The Wishcraft Curse

Be careful what you wish for, you may get it!

Genuine Needs or Irrational Greeds?

> "Perfection of means and confusion of goals
> seem to characterise our age."
>
> Albert Einstein, *Out of My Later Years*

The very nature of negotiation makes it easy for one or both sides to lose their cool. This doesn't just mean abusing the other side or being aggressive or obnoxious. It may mean losing sight of your real goals, abandoning the principle of rational thought and succumbing to emotions. Or, it could mean a distorted sense of proportion and a stubborn insistence on something you don't really need.

During long and tough divorce proceedings, a wife insisted on getting an exotic audiophile music system. She rarely listened to it during the fifteen years of marriage, but knew how much it meant to her husband. She used her irrational demand to emotionally punish and frustrate him.

Very few negotiators are greedy by choice. Being greedy is an irrational process, meaning that its mechanism is usually beyond the control of your logic and intellect. You can, however, try to confine and control your greed. Before deciding on a particular goal, ask yourself: "Do I really need this or do I simply want it? Is it a genuine need or an irrational greed?"

A question to keep asking yourself about anything you negotiate for:
Do I really need this, or do I just want it?

✓ CHECKLIST: Ten Attributes of Properly-Set Goals

- *Concise.* Keep it simple. Each goal has to be self explanatory.

- *Specific.* General statements, wishes and "nice to have" dreams won't do. The more detailed description of your goals, the better.

- *Written.* William Faulkner once said, "I don't know what I think until I read what I said." This may sound as a contradiction, but it is much easier to analyse and clarify one's thinking by writing it down. Plus, you'll avoid the danger of forgetting one or more of them, which is quite easy to do in a heated discussion!

- *Few in number.* Having too many objectives contradicts one of the prerequisites for success in any field: Concentration of effort and definiteness of purpose. It diffuses and weakens the impact.

- *Measurable.* To be measurable, goals have to be quantified in some way. Express them in terms of time, money or percentage.

- *Time-framed.* Positioning your goals in time makes it easier to measure your rate of progress towards achieving them.

- *Stable.* Once you set your goals, stick to them. Frequent changes of your goals are signs of poor planning and a lack of persistence.

- *Congruent and mutually compatible.* All goals set should have a common denominator; they should all lead you towards your ultimate purpose and shouldn't contradict each other.

- *Challenging and inspiring.* Your goals should be motivating, forcing you out of your comfort zone. Play hard, play to win.

- *Realistic.* Unrealistic goals are the main cause of frustration. Divide major goals into smaller ones, which are easier to achieve.

Examples of Properly Set Goals

For example, a goal for an IT group or a purchasing department may be: "In the next financial year we will reduce the IT purchasing costs by a minimum of 15 percent, compared to the current expenditure".

The goal is time-framed, they know when the financial year starts and ends. It is measurable and 15 percent is a specific figure. Notice that the goal does not specify *how* such a reduction in purchasing costs will be achieved. That will be determined in the next step, when an overall cost-cutting strategy is devised. For instance, all current IT supply contracts may be re-negotiated, or cheaper service providers engaged.

If buying a used car, your goal may be "By the end of March this year, I will buy a 2-year old Toyota Aurion, ATX model, with less than 40,000 km on the odometer, for under $19,000 cash."

HOW TO PLAN YOUR NEGOTIATIONS

✘ Forward and Reverse Planning

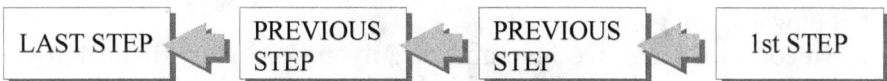

"Finis origine pendet." ("The end depends on the beginning.")

Latin proverb

There are two ways to plan a negotiation, a presentation, a project or even your life. In "forward planning", you start with where you are (NOW or CURRENT SITUATION), and finish with where you want to be (THEN or THE DESIRED SITUATION). Then, you outline steps and actions you have to take to get from NOW to THEN.
In "reverse planning", the sequence is designed backwards. You identify the desired end result or the THEN first (where you want to be, what you want to have), and then go back step-by-step until you reach your present situation (NOW).

FORWARD PLANNING

| 1st STEP | → | NEXT STEP | → | NEXT STEP | → | LAST STEP |

REVERSE PLANNING

| LAST STEP | ← | PREVIOUS STEP | ← | PREVIOUS STEP | ← | 1st STEP |

Some goals and situations lend themselves to forward planning, while others are more easily managed using the reverse method. In some more complex cases you may have to use the two approaches together by jumping forward and back a few times.

Let's say you are planning your retirement. Please, even if you are in your twenties or thirties, don't skip this example. As with any planning, the sooner you start, the better!

For the sake of simplicity, we will assume you can get an investment return of 10% per year, disregard inflation and ignore compounding interest. When you work with a financial planner, a similar planning process will be used, only in more detail, factoring in all these issues.

You may have defined your goal as "I want to retire on the annual income of $50,000 a year (in today's money) in 20 years time, when I'm 55." That is your last step. To figure out what the previous step needs to be, you have to ask yourself "How much money in the bank and other interest- or income-producing investments do I need in order to get $50,000 a year?"

That means your step before last is to have a minimum of $500,000 in investments, since 10% of half-a-million is the fifty grand annually for your retirement. You now have to go all the way back to your present situation and ask yourself "How much money do I have in investment right now?"

Let's say you have $150,000. So, in the next 20 years you have to accumulate $350,000. That will determine the steps you have to take along the way (now you are actually starting to mix forward and backward planning). Can you set aside $17,500 per year ? If not, you have to go back to the last step and set a more modest goal, say a $40,000 per year income, which will require $250,000 of a nest egg and only $12,500 annual contribution, instead of $17,500. Such iterative process is often used in planning.

Start With the End in Mind - Develop Your Exit Strategy

One goal of reverse planning is risk mitigation. I've noticed that very few negotiators formulate their exit strategy. To minimise the risk of a win-lose or lose-lose outcome, you have to know what to do if things stall, if deadlock happens or if crises develops.

Apart from starting a negotiation that should not be started at all, the biggest mistake you can make is to keep a futile negotiation going. Before you get into any deal, decide at what point will you walk away and how are you going to do it.

Negotiations are like love affairs. Anyone can start them, but to end them successfully and amicably requires a considerable skill.

The Climax Principle

How you start a negotiation (or anything else in life) isn't that important. What really counts is how well you finish.

If you like chess, you will recall that there are opening gambits, a middle game, and end gambits. The same can be said about negotiation.

The opening moves establish the agenda and the negotiating range. The middle game is where most agreements or disagreements happen, and the end gambits result either in one party walking away, or in the wrap-up of the deal.

🛠 The BOOO Tool: Is Your Best Deal Elsewhere?

The more options you have, the more powerful your negotiating position is. Obviously, not all of those alternatives are equally desirable. The most attractive one I call BOOO (Best Of Other Options). It sounds appropriate too, since one of its most common uses is to scare whomever you are negotiating with into giving you a better deal. When you mention your BOOO, they know you have other options and are prepared to exercise them.

BOOO (Best Of Other Options)

Your best alternative outside the current negotiation or deal.

You may have read books that talk about BOON (Best Option Outside Negotiation) or BATNA (Best Alternative To a Negotiated Agreement). These all refer to the same thing. BOOO may not be a better name, but at least it's mine. Why use somebody else's terms if you can invent your own?

As you negotiate, continuously evaluate the risks/rewards ratio of the deal and keep asking yourself, "How does this offer compare with my BOOO?" If it doesn't stack up, walk away!

When to Stop Preparing and Start Talking?

"Some people are making such thorough preparation for rainy days that they aren't enjoying today's sunshine," said William Feather. Indeed, too much preparation is clearly bad. But how much is too much? As most questions of importance, it does not have a clear-cut answer. It depends.

The ability to sense the right time for moving on comes with experience; it cannot be taught or demonstrated. Different negotiators in different situations stop at different points along the preparation curve.

Too much preparation analysis leads to negotiation paralysis.

I believe the preparation curve follows the S-shape. Initially, one is unprepared, or the preparation is done superficially. Then, as we think through the various issues and aspects of the negotiating task ahead, we reach the state of in-depth preparation. The more time and effort we spend, the better results we can expect. The results are in direct proportion to the time and effort invested.

However, the curve eventually flattens off, and we reach the point of diminishing returns. We keep going through various (usually wrong) assumptions, constructing different (mostly unlikely) scenarios. All that additional effort is making us more confused rather than better prepared!

A similar syndrome in management is called "paralysis-by-analysis". Instead of saying, "This will do!" and taking action, we are still talking, analysing and pontificating.

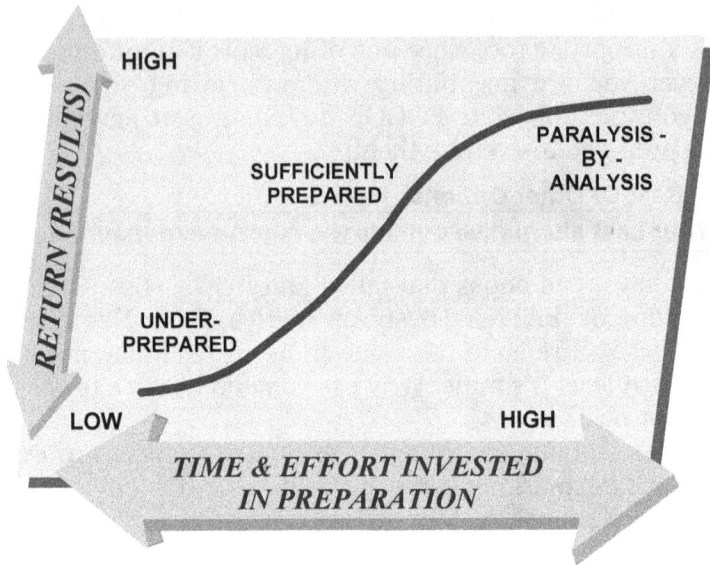

```
                                              PARALYSIS -
                                                BY -
              SUFFICIENTLY                    ANALYSIS
               PREPARED


    UNDER-
    PREPARED


  LOW                                   HIGH
```

HIGH / RETURN (RESULTS) / TIME & EFFORT INVESTED IN PREPARATION

How Deep is That Muddy Puddle?

You are in a hurry to cross the street, but there is a large puddle in front of you. Cars are parked on both sides, so you cannot go around it, and it's too big to jump over. You have to step into it. The water is murky so you cannot see how deep it is. What would you do?[7]

Preparing for a negotiation or a project is the same type of conundrum. You can't tell how deep the puddle is until you step into it, just as you can't tell if you are prepared until you start negotiating. Only then would you be able to step back and do some more preparation if required.

The Preparation Predicament

You can't tell how well you are prepared until you start negotiating.

How to Structure Multiple Business Relationships

As if the preparation stage wasn't difficult enough, negotiating with multiple parties complicates it even further. Let's use a construction example. You may be building a house or your company may have a construction project. How are you going to structure your contractual relationships?

---

[7]This is a rhetorical question, don't treat it as a problem to be solved.

Since this is not a book on negotiating construction contracts, we will limit our discussion to the two basic options. I've illustrated them for you in the diagram below.

Whenever you have a complex, multi-party deal or project, it pays to draw a map showing all the players and their relationships.

In Option 1, the client has one contractand one point-of-contact only; in this case with the builder. The builder has engaged the services of a building consultant or an architect and has hired sub-contractors (bricklayers, concreters, roof carpenters, plumbers, electricians). These contractors then have supply agreements with various suppliers of bricks, cable, concrete, cement, and other materials. The builder (or main contractor, as he is also called) manages and is responsible for the whole project.

If unhappy with the quality of bricklaying, the client does not have to deal directly with the bricklaying subcontractor; all he has to do is complain to the builder.

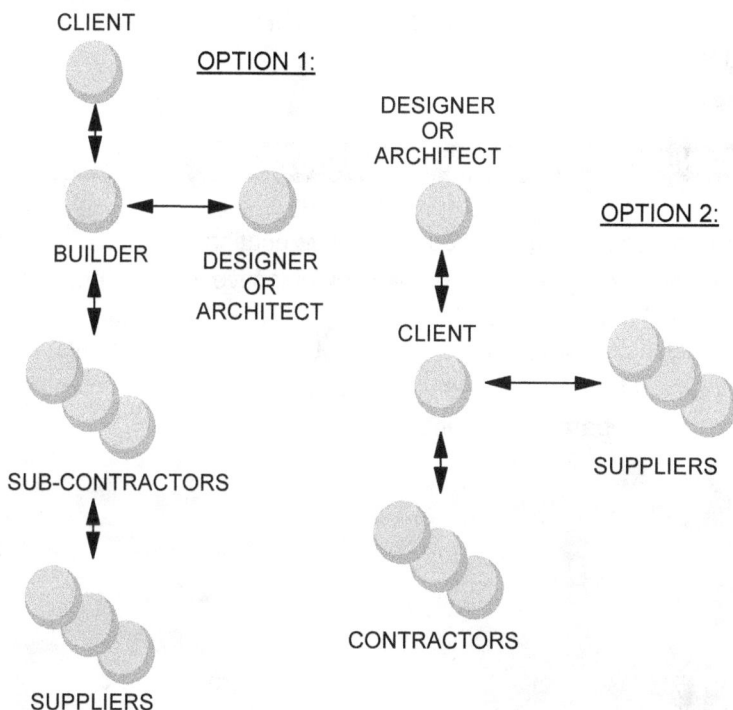

CLIENT

OPTION 1:

DESIGNER
OR
ARCHITECT

OPTION 2:

BUILDER   DESIGNER
OR
ARCHITECT

CLIENT

SUPPLIERS

SUB-CONTRACTORS

CONTRACTORS

SUPPLIERS

In Option 2, the client is managing the whole project himself. He has hired the architect and engaged various contractors through separate contracts as an owner-builder. Which of the two arrangements is better for you as a client?

In Option 1, if anything goes wrong, it is the builder's responsibility. He has to check and supervise, instruct and resolve ongoing issues. All the risk is on him, but he will price that risk, so this arrangement will usually be more expensive for you. He will add his profit margin on top of all hourly or unit rates. If a carpenter charges the builder $40 per hour, the builder may charge you $50 per hour.

Every risk has a price, and the party that assumes such risk should be adequately compensated for it. The more risk you take on as a client, the cheaper the price of a service should be.

If something goes wrong in Option 2, you (the client) have to fix it. You are the only link between the designer (or architect), the contractors and the material suppliers.

On the plus side, *if* negotiated properly (and this is a big if), this arrangement should be cheaper, but these savings can quickly evaporate in case of disputes, variations and claims. It may be the case of falsely economising.

The builder in Option 1 is (or should be) a professional. He has done many similar projects and knows where the traps are; you most likely don't.

WINNING TIPS: WHAT I WISH I KNEW TWENTY YEARS AGO

- Plans are nothing, planning is everything.
- Preparation is often more critical than execution.
- The longer and the more complex the objective you are trying to achieve, the more likely the negotiation will fail.
- Too much preparation analysis leads to negotiation paralysis.
- How you start isn't that important. What counts is how you finish.
- Power + Preparation + Practice = Perfect Performance

✘ Preparation Tool #1 - About the Parties

PREPARATION CHECKLIST - ABOUT THE PARTIES

My Goals   *Their Goals*

MUST HAVEs

☐ _____   ☐ _____
☐ _____   ☐ _____
☐ _____   ☐ _____

NICE TO HAVEs

☐ _____   ☐ _____
☐ _____   ☐ _____
☐ _____   ☐ _____

TRADEAWAYs

☐ _____   ☐ _____
☐ _____   ☐ _____
☐ _____   ☐ _____

Options & Alternatives

MINE   THEIRS

☐ _____   ☐ _____
☐ _____   ☐ _____
☐ _____   ☐ _____

Strategy

MINE   THEIRS

☐ _____   ☐ _____
☐ _____   ☐ _____
☐ _____   ☐ _____

⚒ Preparation Tool #2 - About the Deal or Situation

PREPARATION CHECKLIST - ABOUT THE DEAL

Critical Aspects Of the Deal

- ☐ _____
- ☐ _____
- ☐ _____
- ☐ _____

Previous Developments & Their Impact

- ☐ _____
- ☐ _____
- ☐ _____
- ☐ _____

Relationship Issues & Stakeholders' Impact

- ☐ _____
- ☐ _____
- ☐ _____
- ☐ _____

Ways of Increasing Value or Enlarging the Deal

- ☐ _____
- ☐ _____
- ☐ _____
- ☐ _____

Possible Misunderstandings, Conflicts, Roadblocks

What can happen and why	How to prevent it or correct it
☐ _____	☐ _____
☐ _____	☐ _____
☐ _____	☐ _____

Weak No More!

LEVERAGE YOUR NEGOTIATING POWER

Power is the central issue in any negotiation or relationship. Responsible use of power can make a deal, just as the abuse of power can break it.

Discovering your strengths and capitalising on them in your dealings with others will prove crucial for your success.

Coming up:

- Types and sources of power
- How power behaves in a relationship
- How to avoid making power-draining mistakes

IDENTIFY YOUR STRENGTHS (SOURCES OF POWER)

What Is Power?

"The secret of business is to know something nobody else knows."

Aristotle Onasis, Greek shipping magnate

Negotiation is the process of using our power to get what we want. But how do we define power itself? I see four types of power:

- *Power to get what you want from others.*
- *Power to make decisions.* If you have the ability or authority to decide what is to be done, how, why, where, when and by whom, you have the power. You are the manager or the leader.
- *Power to control behaviour.* If you can tell others what to do and how to behave, you are in a powerful position.
- *Power to change things.* Power gives you the tools to bring about, accelerate or sustain change. Such power is the power to get things done, to change ways of communicating, working, relating, organising, or producing. In his 1938 book, *Power, A New Social Analysis*, philosopher Bertrand Russell defined power as "the production of intended effects".

The Dirty Dozen: Sources of Power in Negotiation

Negotiators often fail to identify all of their strengths (or sources of power) and to leverage them in the deal-making process. Here is a list of dozen major sources of personal and organisational power:

- *Job title (position).* Also known as "Legitimate Power", although I would rather call it "Proclaimed or Bureaucratic Power". Comes from the position held in a corporate hierarchy, akin to the military command-and-control model.
- *Educational title or membership (Dr, Ph.D., MBA).* Just don't go overboard and list twenty seven acronyms after your name!
- *Association.* Sometimes also called "connection power". Based on your connections with powerful, influential, respectful and otherwise important people or organisations.
- *Knowledge or "expert power".* You know something others can benefit from, something they need or want to know.
- *Skills or "craftsmanship power".* You can do or make something others need or want. You may not have the theoretical and conceptual knowledge of why something works, but you do know how to get the results.
- *Personality.* People like dealing with you because you are friendly,

approachable and pleasant. Most people will do their best for you if they like you and feel you respect them.

- *Reputation.* You are respected as a person of high ethical, moral and business standards. You always do the right thing and you do it right.
- *Time, urgency or deadlines.* You are not in a hurry, you can afford to wait it out. Or, your negotiating counterpart is in a rush and has a real, imminent deadline looming.
- *Options and alternatives.* The more options you have, the less desperate you will be to conclude an inferior deal.
- *Scarcity.* You have something not many people have, something they want badly or urgently. The opposite is a weakness called abundance (everyone has it or can have it), or competition. The more competitors you have, the weaker your position.
- *Reward.* You have the power to reward others for doing things you want them to do. This is the "carrot" component of the infamous "carrot and stick" motivational method.
- *Punishment.* Coercive type of power, based on the fear of "the stick". It comes as reprimands, poor performance reviews, a blocked career path, transfer or retrenchment. Also used on kids (by parents) and on the general public (by governments).

I was once asked by a course participant who I thought had the ultimate power in the world. How would you respond?

The answer to that question depends on your beliefs and your world view. Some claim that God, as the ultimate authority in the Universe, has all the power. The capitalists believe in the power of so called free markets. Self-help gurus peddle the belief in yourself as the panacea for all personal problems. My personal opinion?

The ultimate source of power
Whoever has or controls the money makes the rules.

Expand Your Limits

> "A man must know his limits."
> Clint Eastwood as Dirty Harry in "The Magnum Force"

Pointing out shortcomings in others is not a difficult task and many of us are quite good at it. However, when the time comes to do the same to ourselves, we adopt a self-righteous attitude and start rationalising our weaknesses and turning them into quazi-strengths.

We can fool some people only some of the time, but astonishingly, it seems we can fool ourselves all of the time.

The first step on the negotiating journey is to recognise your limits. You may have limited time, options, knowledge or experience. The second step is to invest time and effort in expanding those limits.

The Limitations Rule

First, get to know your limits. Then, work on expanding them.

Good negotiators know themselves well. As they work on correcting their weaknesses, they are leveraging their strengths to achieve more with less. Identify your strengths and weaknesses. Then, capitalise on the strengths and compensate for the weaknesses.

🛠 The Power Analysis Tool

"Strengths can become weaknesses
when we rely too much on them, carry them to exaggerated lengths, or apply them where they don't belong."

Richard Farson, *Management of the Absurd*

Your sources of power fall into two categories. Your general strengths are always there. These are the qualities you possess as a person. For example, you may consider yourself to be friendly, trustworthy, a good listener or a resourceful problem solver.

Specific strengths or sources of power relate to a specific negotiation, relationship or business deal. These are situational strengths. Some of these specific strengths will come from your general strengths while others may come from your opponent's weaknesses.

For instance, you may not be a particularly persistent or patient person, so you didn't list those as your general sources of power. Yet, in this instance you are prepared to outwait the other person and to bide your time. This time you will persist until you get what you want. So, your list of Specific Strengths in this situation will have patience and persistence among your sources of power.

✎ EXERCISE: Power analysis

What are your strengths as a negotiator, your sources of power? How do you use them? What results do you get?

POWER IN RELATIONSHIPS

Aspects of Power

Apart from knowing your sources of power, it is equally important to understand how power behaves. Power is situational and dynamic. The balance of power changes over time.

For example, when you go for a job interview, your power is still relatively low. They are attracted, but haven't swallowed the hook.

Once you get invited for a second interview, you know you've got something valuable they want. The point at which your power is at its peak is just after they've made their offer. They want you. Now is the time to play hard-to-get and negotiate for more. Timing is critical; make too many demands too early, and you lose.

Power, like beauty, is in the eyes of the beholder. It's the perception that matters, not the real power. How negotiators perceive their opponent's and their own power determines the dynamics of negotiation. If they think you are in a strong position, then you are.

Power is almost always limited - no side has complete power over the other side. Usually there is at least one other option you could take, which automatically means you have loosened the grip the other side had on you.

Power can also be attained or lost by association. You will be judged by the company you keep (the people you work with) and by the organisations you represent. I remember a couple of situations where people from other departments were wary of me and didn't want to help me just because they hated my boss. I succeeded in gaining their co-operation once they got to know me better, after I distanced myself from my boss and his methods.

The transference of power is common in business and politics. This is where another party transfers authority to you and gets you to represent their interests. You are the "authorised representative."

You don't have to exercise or use your power to benefit from it. Power may be exerted without action. The mere thought that you have certain power may be enough for those you are negotiating with to fall in line.

Think Carefully Before Using Your Power

In discussions during my negotiation seminars, one issue that frequently gets raised by participants is unfulfilled obligations by a consultant, a contractor or a vendor. There is always a formal contract, so these clients could seek satisfaction through the legal system. The question is if such a course of action would be smart.

BUSINESS CASE: Construction contract troubles

You are the client. Your construction contract is late. The contractor asks for extension of time and a substantial progress payment (to help with their cash-flow problems), although they haven't completed all the required tasks. They underestimated the job's complexity and may even go bankrupt.

STOP & THINK! What would you do?

95

Your choice is between two non-optimal options. Legally, you can refuse to make the progress payment. Each day of delay costs you money in lost business and opportunity costs, so you may also be entitled to impose penalties on the contractor to compensate you for such delays. The law is clearly on your side, but exercising this power could be counter-productive.

The Power Conundrum

Just because you have the legal right to prosecute or some other type of power, does not mean you should actually use it. The exercise of power is costly, messy and risky.

You will have to pay lawyers and your case may drag through courts for months or years. In the meantime, your project will linger unfinished. You may even lose in the end. How many plaintiffs thought their win was a foregone conclusion, only to lose on a technicality or because the judge or the jury sympathised with the defendant.

You will not only damage but just about kill your relationship with this contractor. Even if they survive the threat of bankruptcy, they will never work for you again.

What is the point of taking them to court if you cannot get any money out of them? Internal satisfaction and a sense of psychological closure? Explain that to your boss when you ask for a six month extension so you can get quotes from other contractors to finish the job off, and a few more million in extra funds to accomplish that. Better start updating your resume!

Third, you can bet that the other suppliers and contractors will follow the case closely. You will get a reputation as a difficult client. Suppliers will quote higher prices on your projects as their insurance against risk, or may even refuse to work for you.

The other option is to authorise the (undeserved) progress payment, although the required milestone hasn't been reached. Apart from the obvious problem of such an approval being against the company's policy and the contract, there are future implications. You are setting a precedent. Next time a similar situation develops between the two of you, they will expect the same lenient treatment.

One of my clients, a manager from a large oil and gas company commented: "We never take anybody to court ...", and then the discussion followed the rationale above.

If your company doesn't legally protect what is theirs or doesn't demand that contractual obligations are met, its position in future deals will be seriously weakened. Contractors and suppliers will sign anything just to get the job: "Oh, don't worry about these clauses, they never take anybody to court ..." Sometimes you have to litigate just to send a message that you won't be taken for granted.

HOW TO AVOID MAKING POWER-DRAINING MISTAKES

A power-draining mistake is anything you say or do that works against your interests. It can even be something intangible, such as a counter-productive attitude or erroneous beliefs, anything you have control over that makes your situation weaker or the other person's position stronger.

☹ Mistake #1: Falling in Love

Poor negotiators fall in love with something they think they cannot live without. Winners still go after what they want, but in a different way. They don't want it too much. They know if you want something too badly, you are not likely to get it.

Women make this unfortunate mistake on a regular basis; after all, they do shop more than men. You can tell how people think and what they value just by looking into their shopping habits. Just as with cosmetics (praying on female vanity and procreation instinct), women think the more clothes and shoes they have, the more attractive they will be to men.

Men fall in love too, but with different objects. Some of their weaknesses are golf clubs, sports cars and power tools. These props help them in their self-perpetuating delusion that they are fixers, action-takers, exciting to women and fun to be around.

To cool your urges down, when tempted by a seemingly irresistible offer or when falling in love with something, repeat this mantra until you start thinking rationally again: "I don't really need this. I am happy without it. There are many other deals ahead."

When things get overheated and emotions rule over reason, apply the "fly-on-the-wall" detachment strategy. Imagine you are a fly on the wall, observing the whole situation. Detach yourself mentally and psychologically from the deal, conflict or argument.

☹ Mistake #2: Foolish Praise

It's a nice, sunny weekend. A husband and wife go house-hunting. Finally, after seeing five homes that don't quite match their expectations, the sixth one is a true find.

The husband likes it, but it's the wife who really falls in love. And it's love at first sight! "Oh, honey, just look at that games room, wouldn't the kids just love it? My, don't you just love these curtains... They must have spent a fortune on the garden, I can already imagine myself relaxing under that fig tree, reading a book."

The husband tries to dampen his wife's enthusiasm, his mind

working hard to find some faults with the property. Yet, he likes it too, and he has given up trying to control his wife's big mouth a long time ago. So, all he manages to utter is a string of grunts of the "Not bad" and "It's OK" variety.

And the real estate agent? He's just smiling, nodding after each compliment, his ego swollen with pride since he was the one who succeeded in listing this sure winner. The buyers are too excited to notice the agent's hazed look, with dollar signs flipping in his glazed eyes just like those readouts at a petrol pump. Ah, the sweet smell of full commission, earned in just one afternoon!

The Law of Foolish Praise

Don't praise something you want to buy!

⏳ QUICK QUIZ: How to recognise a serious buyer

A real estate agent is holding an open house. Who is a serious buyer? The one who ...

a) ... criticises the property, pointing to things that need fixing or replacing and how much all that would cost.

b) ... has a quick look, asks about the price and leaves.

c) .... mentions a few positive features of the property and how much she likes them, but never asks about the price.

✋ STOP & THINK!

a) WINNING THINKING! He already sees himself in possession of the property. He is already planning and calculating the cost of all renovations and changes he would like to do. Or, he may be simply trying to bring the price down.

b) NAIVE THINKING! Unlikely. People who like the property usually hang around for a much longer time than those who don't. She may be another real estate agent collecting information on her competitors (you), or a neighbour comparing the features and the value of her home to the one you are selling.

c) VERY NAIVE THINKING! People who praise your possessions in front of you or your agent are either very poor negotiators, or, more likely, aren't seriously interested in buying it.

☹ Mistake #3: Negotiating From an Inferior Posture

When interpersonal power is concerned, the biggest mistake you can make is to focus on and get intimidated by your opponent's strengths. Instead, identify and exploit their weaknesses.

Never deal with others from an inferior posture; assume a posture of power. Stay calm, confident and composed.

Hint that you are considering other options - you have many irons in the fire. If things start stalling, show them you are not afraid of deadlock. Be relaxed and patient; you are never in a hurry. Make them think that you are ready to walk away if you don't get what you are asking for.

Ultimately, it is not the real power that matters in negotiation, but the mutual perception of power. There are two aims of your perception manipulation process:

1. To change the other side's impression of the strength of your position, so it appears that you are in a stronger position than you really are.

2. To change the other side's impression of the strength of their own position, so they think they are in weaker position than they really are.

☹ Mistake #4: Disclosing Your Lack of Options

> "Necessity never made a good bargain."
>
> Benjamin Franklin

✈ QUICK STORY: How not to get a hotel discount

A travel-weary guest is fronting the reception in a busy Dubai hotel on a hot day. He wipes off the sweat from his forehead, catches a breath and says to the receptionist in an unmistakable Aussie accent: "Crickey, I've been running all over the city with all this bloody luggage, looking for a hotel room. There must be some bloody shopping festival or an exhibition going on, all the bastards are fully booked. You wouldn't happen to have any vacant rooms in this joint, would ya, love?"

"We have, sir", replied the check-in girl, with an understanding, yet slightly condescending smile.

"You have? Great!" he turned and smiled at me. I had just checked out and was waiting for my transport to the airport, but could not resist the temptation of witnessing this show.

"Now, I know you girls are always helpful," he leaned on the counter winking at the receptionist, "how much discount can you give me if I stay five nights?"

How much discount do you think the Aussie tourist got after making such a fundamental mistake? He disclosed his lack of options, so his demand for a discount was out-of-place.

A shrewd seller only gives discounts when asked and when not doing so would lose him a sale. So, even if you don't have any alternatives, behave as if you did.

☹ Mistake #5: Being Nice and Giving Away Too Much

> "You can't shake hands with a clenched fist."
>
> Indira Gandhi, Indian prime minister

Being nice and understanding is generally laudable. In negotiation, however, many people interpret being nice and understanding as a weakness, and exploit it for their own benefit. This is a typical example how generally positive qualities could work against your interests.

Giving away too much in order to conclude the deal is one strategy that never works. For as long as you are too accommodating or too generous with your concessions, others won't know where your bottom line is. They will assume you still have plenty of room to move and will keep asking for more.

The Insatiability Principle

**The more you keep giving away,
the more will others expect from you.**

Your meek attitude will set a precedent for future dealings, meaning you not only lose in the current negotiation, but in the long run, too. Unless you draw clear boundaries, they won't understand what is acceptable to you and what is not and they will see no end in sight.

WINNING TIPS: WHAT I WISH I KNEW TWENTY YEARS AGO

- Before each negotiation, take stock of your strengths and weaknesses.
- Get to know your limits so you can work on expanding them.
- Whoever has or controls the money makes the rules.
- Think carefully before using your power. The exercise of power is costly, messy and risky.
- Don't praise something you want to buy!
- Keep your options open. Even if you don't have any alternatives, behave as if you did.

Ignorant No More!

UNDERSTANDING PERSONALITIES & PREFERENCES

Negotiation is a people business. Get to know the other side. What is their dominant negotiating style? How do they see the issues to be negotiated? Why do they behave in a certain way?

Coming up:

- Three fundamental negotiating styles: aggressive, assertive (principled) and submissive negotiators
- What kind of negotiator are you?
- How to quickly establish someone's negotiating profile
- Specific advice for female negotiators

THREE BASIC NEGOTIATING STYLES

The Combative or Aggressive Negotiator

There are two characters I'd like you to meet. Foxy is the embodiment of a shrewd, calculated intimidator. He is cunning, he is smart and he knows it. I use the masculine gender for Foxy, although there are many female "Foxettes" lurking in the bushes.

Roger, a concerned client in need of reassurance

Foxy, his consultant, leaving his options open

You may have Foxy for a boss, business partner or a client. You may even be so unlucky as to work in a department or whole company full of Foxies. You may even be married to one!

For Foxy, every negotiation is a contest, a game. He wants to win at any cost, in every situation, and in every sense of the word.

Over the years, Foxy has learned that a strong opening demand gets you halfway towards getting what you want. His openings are extreme, designed to intimidate, to throw the other side out of balance, to make them question their assumptions and lower their expectations. If Foxy runs out of arguments, he attacks the other negotiator's credibility or personality.

The Opening Rule

A strong opening gets you halfway towards getting what you want.

Foxy isn't always openly aggressive. He knows when to keep quiet and when to appear nice and reasonable. Regardless of the fact that he may simply be bluffing, Foxy always sticks to his original demands, even if he knows they aren't realistic. He locks his thinking early in the negotiation along the lines of "either ... or": "Either you give me what I want or live with the unpleasant consequences of my wrath".

Only when it becomes obvious that the negotiation is breaking down will Foxy make a small concession or two. The prospect of deadlock does not worry Foxy too much. He actually does his best work under pressure and displays surprising ingenuity when cornered. This rare trait is a valuable quality of any negotiator and Foxy is justifiably proud of it.

The Extremely Co-operative or Submissive Negotiator

Roger is the living example of a frightened, insecure individual who awaits every negotiation or any other stressful and demanding situation with trepidation. He thinks others are smarter than him, have more options and power than he has, or deserve to win more than he does. He overestimates others and underestimates himself; he sells himself short.

Roger prefers not to negotiate at all. If there is a way to avoid negotiation, Roger is the first to take that path. He is the guy who pays the full price for everything. When forced to negotiate, either by his wife, mother-in-law or his boss, Roger negotiates in a submissive way. A champion of avoiding sticky, unpleasant situations, he not only runs away from conflict, he does everything to prevent conflicts from happening in the first place.

Roger craves approval from others. He wants to be liked. He doesn't want to offend or upset anybody, so he never asks for much more than he expects to get.

This is Roger's second mistake. His opening move is weak. To compound the problem, his following move is even weaker. Roger deviates too quickly from his initial position and makes large concessions too early.

Negotiation is not a popularity contest
Your aim is to be respected and treated fairly, not to be liked.

It comes as no surprise that people like negotiating with Roger. It doesn't take them long to realise that Roger is a very forgiving negotiating partner. He never explodes in a violent rage as Foxy does, he seldom says no, and he bends backwards to comply with their demands.

Roger knows the only advantage of being submissive - the absence of conflict. In short, Roger goes through negotiations quietly so he can lose safely.

The Relativity of Winning and Losing

If you had only two boxes of stickers, one printed with LOSER and the other WINNER, which one would you slap on Foxy's forehead? Some would consider Foxy a winner: more often than not, he gets what he wants. Others disagree. True, in the short-term, Foxy may get his way.

However, in the long run, nobody will want to negotiate or do business with him.

Both views are valid. Sometimes it pays to be aggressive, just as in some situations submission is a wiser choice. Foxy's negotiating style could be justified in some cases, primarily in the "Hit & Run" situations.

In most family and business situations, however, Foxy's approach would not win him any new friends, and he is bound to lose the old ones as well!

Roger's case is usually much easier. Most of us would label him a loser - he is too soft, too accommodating, too much of a pushover.

The Assertive or Principled Negotiator

"It is often easier to fight for principles than to live up to them."

Adlai Stevenson, U.S. politician, diplomat, two-time presidential candidate

The aggressive and the submissive negotiator are but the extremes on the continuum of styles. Generally speaking, these extremes are risky and usually counter-productive.

The main problem is that aggressive negotiators are always aggressive and that submissive types are always submissive. Both assume their stances out of habit, not choice.

AGGRESSIVE NEGOTIATOR	ASSERTIVE NEGOTIATOR	SUBMISSIVE NEGOTIATOR
■ Be tough. Never give up without a fight. ■ Intimidate, bully and attack the other guy. ■ Take a firm position and don't budge. ■ Win at all costs.	■ Be friendly, but firm on principles. ■ Fix the problem, not the other person. ■ Focus on interests, not on positions. ■ Expand the deal.	■ Be nice. ■ Modify your position to appease others. ■ Let them win to preserve the peace and the relationship. ■ Be liked.

The balanced position belongs to assertive or principled negotiators. Principled negotiators don't play games or use tricks and tactics, but negotiate based on principles of mutual respect, constructive dialogue and joint problem-solving.

Principled negotiators are friendly and polite, but at the same time, they assertively protect their interests and dignity. If insulted or intimidated, unwilling to compromise their values or principles, they are prepared to walk away.

�֎ Preparation Tool: Drawing Up Your Negotiating Profile

✎ EXERCISE: What Kind of Negotiator Are You?

For each statement choose *Yes* ("I agree" or "It applies to me"), *Maybe* ("It applies to me sometimes") or *No* ("It doesn't apply to me" or "I don't agree"), then write Y, M or N in a box.

Don't think too long; use your initial, instinctive response. There are no right or wrong answers in this exercise.

1. ☐ I can be impatient. When I want something, I want it now!

2. ☐ I often accept less than I wanted just to get the deal done.

3. ☐ There are many valid solutions to every problem.

4. ☐ In every dispute, one side is right and one side is wrong.

5. ☐ I don't mind accepting less in a negotiation if it means we'll all get along happily.

6. ☐ I have to fight for what I want or I won't get it.

7. ☐ People are not right or wrong, only different.

8. ☐ My worth and the strength of my negotiating position depend on what others think of me.

9. ☐ Others push me and boss me around, but I never do it to them.

10. ☐ I would rather walk away from a negotiation than compromise my values, beliefs or principles.

11. ☐ The end justifies the means (everything is allowed in order to achieve your goal).

12. ☐ I don't have the right to challenge authority figures.

13. ☐ I try to understand the motives and needs of the other party and come up with solutions they would be happy with, too.

14. ☐ I refuse to play manipulative games and always openly offer a constructive solution.

15. ☐ One should try to get as much money from the other side and not leave any value on the negotiating table.

16. ☐ Addressing a conflict or fighting back will only make it worse, so it's better to appease the other side.

17. ☐ I'll get a better deal by giving the other party a good deal too.

18. ☐ To preserve and improve my relationship with others I have to keep them happy and meet their expectations.

19. ☐ The more tricks and tactics I know, the better negotiator I'll be.

20. ☐ It is possible to satisfy both sides' needs in a negotiation.

21. ☐ You have to be tough with people to get what you want.

SCORING SHEET: For each statement move across to the right and find the "2 1 0" cluster. For YES, circle 2, for M circle 1, for NO circle 0. Then go down vertically and add-up all the circled numbers in each column to get a score for A, B, and C.

Question #	A = AGGR	B = PRIN	C = SUBM
1.	2 1 0		
2.			2 1 0
3.		2 1 0	
4.	2 1 0		
5.			2 1 0
6.	2 1 0		
7.		2 1 0	
8.			2 1 0
9.			2 1 0
10.		2 1 0	
11.	2 1 0		
12.			2 1 0
13.		2 1 0	
14.		2 1 0	
15.	2 1 0		
16.			2 1 0
17.		2 1 0	
18.			2 1 0
19.	2 1 0		
20.		2 1 0	
21.	2 1 0		
Totals:	/14	/14	/14

Some people score high on one and low on the other two columns. For example, A=2, B=12 and C=10. A balanced score is also normal, say A=6, B=7 and C=5.

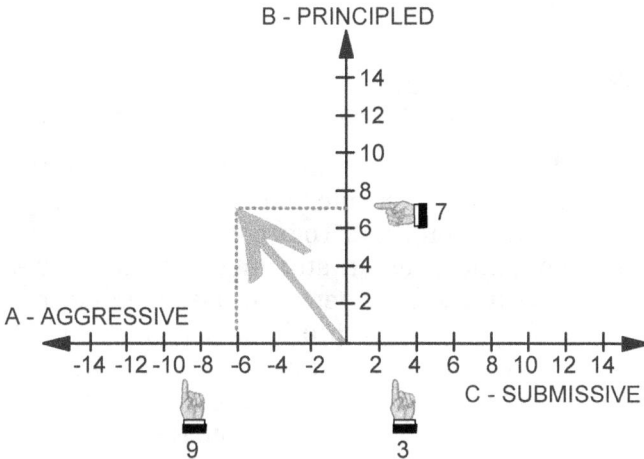

You can draw your negotiating profile by placing a dot or cross on each of the three axis. Then, subtract the A from C. If your A is larger than C, you are predominately an aggressive negotiator. If your C-A figure is positive, you tend to be predominantly submissive. Now you can draw your vector sum of figures B and C-A.

In the example illustrated above, you've scored 9 for A, a moderately high aggressive score, 3 for C (the submissive) and 7 for B (principled). C-A is negative (-6). We draw a vertical line upward from -6, and the intersection with horizontal 7 (principled) will be the tip of your arrow (your negotiating vector).

QUICK NEGOTIATING PERSONALITY PROFILE BUILDER

The Personality Behaviour Prediction Theory

"All men are frauds. The only difference between them is that some admit it. I myself deny it."

H. L. Mencken, essayist and satirist

One sure way to lose in a deal is to go into it without knowing what kind of person you are and what you want to get out of it. The other deadly mistake is not understanding what kind of person you are negotiating with and what he or she wants to get out of the deal.

You will get to know some of your negotiating counterparts quite well - their expectations, their motives and preferences, their idiosyncrasies, strengths and weaknesses. Others will be more or less unknown to you. You will have to quickly profile them, so you can decide how to approach the whole negotiation.

Knowing a few pivotal traits of an individual will enable you to predict most of their behaviour. You'll never understand anybody fully, and you'll never be able to anticipate all of people's actions. But knowing the main aspects of someone's personality will be enough to give you the edge.

Personality Behaviour Prediction Theory
People are predictable, therefore, they are controllable.

How much of an advantage will "reading" others bring you? Generally, the more you know about people you deal with, the higher the odds that you will get what you want. To become a truly successful negotiator, you should become an astute student of human nature.

Of course, there is always a danger of over-explaining someone's behaviour or of "reading too much into it" by ascribing motives and fabricating explanations. As always, experience helps. The better you get at it, the easier it will be for you to put together isolated and seeming unrelated pieces of someone's personality puzzle.

If you haven't negotiated with a particular person or organisation before, all you can do is ask others for their opinions and perceptions. Be careful in such situations.

You may be selective and hear only certain parts of the message - those that confirm your beliefs and expectations - while rejecting others. The source may be biased and deliberately misleading the listener. Or, they may simply be wrong.

I remember instances when I was warned about certain, supposedly unfriendly and troublesome individuals. Yet, when I met those "rogues", they turned out to be the exact opposite.

A Word of Warning

> "I buy expensive suits. They just look cheap on me."
>
> Warren Buffett, investment guru, philanthropist

The Personality Behaviour Prediction Theory is based on our perception of others, and perception is a funny beast. Be careful not to mistake politeness for weakness. What is laudable determination to one person may be labelled counterproductive stubbornness by another. Ambition may come across as greed, confidence as cockiness or arrogance. What is an assertive behaviour to one negotiator can be an aggressive attack to another.

Anything can be perceived the wrong way and used against you: what you say, what you do, what you look like, what you stand for.

The "Damned If You Do, Damned If You Don't" Conundrum
Anything can be perceived the wrong way and used against you: what you say, what you do, what you look like, what you stand for.

The "I'm OK you are not!" syndrome doesn't help, either. Greedy negotiators label generous ones as naive suckers. Aggressive deal makers consider those who don't use the same ways as wimps and sissies.

Shy or timid negotiators describe aggressive people as ruthless and unscrupulous. Impulsive, excitable types refer to methodological scrutinisers as boring nit-pickers, while they in turn label the creative types as dreamers or risk-takers.

MISTAKE	MAKING DECISIONS BASED ON APPEARANCES
	People who ...
	■ ... appear confident often aren't.
	■ ... emphasise their honesty are mostly crooks.
	■ ... threaten to walk out of a deal are unlikely to do so.
	■ ... say they have a better offer usually don't.
	■ ... say they won't change their mind often will.

How to Judge Someone's Character

"The best index to a person's character is
(a) how he treats people who can't do him any good, and
(b) how he treats people who can't fight back."

Abigail Van Buren, newspaper columnist and radio host

We evaluate and judge others in various situations; from formal and structured, such as negotiations and job interviews to informal or spontaneous, such as casual conversations, shared meals and social situations.

Whatever the setting, don't judge others by how they treat you. If they want something from you it is unlikely they will show their true colours. Watch how they treat other people, especially their subordinates. See how they relate to money (are they greedy) and how they behave in conflicts and in crises (can they take the pressure).

To evaluate their confidence and self-esteem, watch for two clues - if they can pay and receive a genuine, heartfelt compliment and if they can handle criticism.

Doers or Debilitators?

In negotiations as in business generally, you will meet two types of people. Doers do, take action, participate, and contribute. Doers value simplicity, efficiency and effectiveness. They are bottom-line focused: Something either works in a certain situation or it doesn't.

Doers are often clever, not from the intellectual point-of-view, but in a "street-wise" sense. Most are prudent and pragmatic.

Debilitators debilitate, disable, derail proposals and incentives, criticise, condemn and complain. Debiltators also appear clever, but in a more pontificating, high-brow way.

While doers simplify, debilitators complicate, intellectualise and use lots of "On the other hand..." and "Having said that ..." statements. Debilitators are fault-finders, opposers and barrier-builders.

Now, don't get me wrong, no self-respecting Libran would denigrate complexity, paradox and shades of grey, but debilitators argue and pontificate even in clear-cut situations. We could call that pseudo-cleverness or "cleverness-for-the-sake-of-being-cute", which is really a form of stupidity.

Deep down, lots of seemingly intelligent and knowledgeable people are actually quite dumb. I call this syndrome "The Appearance Delusion."

The Appearance Delusion

Many situations, things or people aren't what they seem to be.
Often they are completely opposite.

I've met a great deal of debilitators in my life, mostly in large corporations (some room to hide) and in government departments and agencies (heaps of room to hide). I am sure you have too.

Relaters or Closers?

When it comes to clinching a deal, there are two types of negotiators. Both types will ask you questions, but you can tell them apart by the types of questions they ask and by what they do in response.

Closers ask fewer questions than the Relaters. Their questions are designed to lead you as quickly as possible to their ultimate aim - to "close you"! Your answers give the Closers just enough information to make a sale or get the deal.

Closers are quite transparent. You can tell from the start that they are only interested in getting you to say yes. Whatever you say, they will counter with statements such as "Aha, we have just the solution for you ..." or "This is exactly the kind of problem our product was designed to solve!"

Relaters' main reason for asking questions is to understand you better - your needs, preferences, your business and your problems. Relaters understand that without correctly identifying the other negotiator's needs, the chances of reaching a mutually beneficial deal are slim. So, they spend more time probing and clarifying, and less time selling and persuading.

Who Are Better Negotiators, Optimists or Pessimists?

"The man who is a pessimist before forty-eight knows too much;
if he is an optimist after it he knows too little"

Mark Twain

The main problem facing pessimists in negotiation is their lack of persistence; they tend to give up too soon. On the positive side, pessimists are generally better in assessing the reality. They expect others to lie, cheat, stall invent obstacles, or ask for more money, which is what usually happens.

Optimists' outlook is too idealistic; they view the world through their rose-coloured glasses. They don't know when to quit and often keep trying for far too long, stubbornly hoping for a break. Their "She'll be right, mate!" attitude invites all sorts of dangers.

Adopting a win-win approach, the optimists naturally expect the same from the other side. If that does not happen, they find themselves in a weaker position, having to react to the unexpectedly adversarial attitude of the other side.

Optimists also tend to skimp on preparation. They prefer to play it "by ear" and don't see the need for serious, systematic planning. Believing in their capacity to control the negotiation, they end up in a reactive mode, where they have to play a constant catch-up.

OPTIMISTS	PRAGMATISTS	PESSIMISTS
■persist for too long, hoping for a break	■know when to quit and when to persevere	■give up too easily when facing adversity
■don't discriminate, not critical enough	■selectively, appropriately critical	■too critical and cynical
■like using new and untested methods and tools	■rely on tried & tested, but remain open to possibilities	■avoid even starting things - it will all turn out wrong anyway

The illusion of control is an interesting phenomenon. While optimists believe they have the power to get and stay in control, pessimists consider most developments to be outside their control. They advocate "prepare for the worst because it will happen" thinking.

What situation would you prefer to find yourself in? To expect the best and then get disappointed when problems happen and catch you unprepared, or to prepare for the worst and get a pleasant surprise when things occasionally turn out well?"

Would you rather appear smart or be successful?

You are not there to be cute, you are there to get what you want.

I've noticed that many negotiators pretend to understand an issue, rather than ask for clarification and risk being perceived as slow or uninformed. Big mistake!

You are not there to be cute, you are there to get what you want. You don't want to come across as a know-it-all, dominating, highly strung smart ass, either. All you want is the best deal for yourself.

The Battle Between Pragmatism and Creativity

> "Great leaders are pragmatists who can deal with difficult realities but still have the optimism and courage to act."
>
> Nitin Nohria, academic, author of business books

Pragmatists rely on tried and tested. If something is working and producing desired results, they keep doing it or using it. "Don't change the winning horse!' they say. While pragmatism is generally a prudent approach to negotiation and life, it can go too far. Generally, the older we get, the more we cling to the tried and tested. And, as a corollary, the more set in our ways we become, the less creative and innovative we get. I call it the "Experience Curse".

The Experience Curse

The more experienced you get, the more inflexible you will be.

This is why you see negotiators using the same tactics over and over again, whether such moves are called for or not. Just like mediocre poker or chess players who learn half-a-dozen openings and then start each game with one or the other, they have grown stale.

If you find yourself in such a rut, you have to refresh, renew and revitalise your thinking. By emptying your mind you will allow new ideas to come in and will reawaken the playfulness and spontaneity, two qualities necessary for a spirited mind.

In his book *A World Waiting To Be Born,* M. Scott Peck clarifies it for us, " ... the purpose of emptying the mind is not ultimately to have nothing there; rather it is to make room in the mind for something new, something unexpected, to come in."

Children as Negotiators

Do you consider children to be good negotiators? Do you think we could learn a thing or two from them. Or, should I say re-learn?

Sadly, as we grow-up, we tend to distance ourselves from lots of things we did as kids. We lose many positive qualities such as inquisitiveness, creativity and that uncanny ability to make a fool of ourselves in front of others without giving a damn about it[8]. To make

---

[8] If you happen to know the word for this impressive trait, please let me know.

things worse, not only do we lose the good traits, but, in order to fill the void thus created, we also acquire the bad ones.

One precious quality that gets lost very early is the willingness to do one's own thing. When kids decide they want something, there is no easy way of stopping them. As we mature, we acquire that nasty habit of following others and doing what others are doing. We trust other people's opinions and judgements more than our own. We jump on the bandwagons and follow trends. Herd mentality is alive and well. In short, we become conformists and lose our intrinsic uniqueness and individuality.

First and foremost, kids know what they want and are not afraid of asking for it. They tell you in no uncertain terms. Their goals are immediate. Long-range goals do not feature on children's wish-lists. Kids may not ask for something directly, they often start high and then gradually scale down their demands. If a pet lizard is their goal, they start by asking for a pony.

When kids get a "No!", they simply don't take no for an answer, but keep repeating and restating their demands.

Kids are also good at pushing hot buttons. Even toddlers know how to play the emotional card. Some become real masters of the "make the parent guilty" game. Older kids augment guilt with more advanced concepts, such as reciprocity: "Dad, if I wash your car, can I go to the movies with Angela?"

The question of timing is one of the most crucial aspects of any human endeavour, and negotiation is no different. The same proposal put forward at different times to the same person could invoke markedly different reactions, resulting in significantly improved or reduced probability of acceptance.

Just ask any kid how they decide when to ask their parents for something they want. "When mum is in a hurry..." or "When dad's team just won a game..." would be typical answers. Whoever comes up with answers such as, "In front of their friends ..." or "After a few beers ..." is showing an even greater promise to become a shrewd negotiator later in life.

✖ Building Personality Profiles

> "Everyone is kneaded out of the same dough
> but not baked in the same oven."
>
> Yiddish proverb

As social beings, we intuitively and automatically go through a quick evaluation process at the outset of every personal encounter. Dozens of questions race through our minds: Is he dangerous? Can he be trusted? She's friendly, is she genuine or just faking it?

When we meet others, we immediately scrutinise their looks, their behaviour and the things they say. We instinctively categorise and label people. Don't let anybody convince you that stereotyping is undesirable, unfair or just plain wrong. Stereotyping is a useful tool, and just like any tool it has its uses and limitations.

A quick personality profile checklist is presented here in a two-column table format. Of course, nobody is completely rational or totally emotional, or always trusting and always suspicious. These are just the ends of the spectrum. However, many times in life we have to simplify and make quick assessments of others.

✖ TOOL: Quick Negotiating Personality Profile Builder

❑ Extrovert (gregarious)	❑ Introvert (shy, quiet)
❑ Emotional	❑ Logical
❑ High discloser	❑ Low discloser
❑ Accommodating	❑ Dominant
❑ Optimist	❑ Pessimist
❑ Trusting	❑ Suspicious
❑ Big picture person	❑ Detail-oriented person
❑ Closer, short-term oriented	❑ Relater, long-term oriented
❑ Firm, controlling	❑ Flexible, permissive
❑ Decisive	❑ Indecisive (procrastinator)
❑ Impulsive	❑ Methodological
❑ Pragmatist	❑ Adventurer
❑ Planner	❑ Improviser
❑ Reckless, risk taker	❑ Cautious, risk averse
❑ Bargain seeker	❑ Value seeker
❑ Patient	❑ Impatient
❑ Team player	❑ Individualist
❑ Sequential (issue-by-issue)	❑ Linker (deal as a package)
❑ Constructive (Do-er)	❑ Destructive (Debilitator)

FIGHT LIKE A MAN, BUT FEEL LIKE A WOMAN

> "No man can be fully a man unless he comes to terms
> with the female double within him."
>
> Sheldon B. Kopp, *If You Meet The Buddha on the Road, Kill Him!*

Negotiation is a feminine concept, and, arguably, women do make better listeners, mediators and facilitators. I didn't say better negotiators, because the jury is still out on that one. While women posses some laudable qualities, such as the ones just mentioned, they sell them selves short when it comes to other aspects of negotiation. More about that later in this chapter.

If physical fights were allowed in business, a favourite male way of solving problems and settling disputes would still be by brute force or by the threat of brute force.

A typical male thinks he is a good negotiator. A typical female knows she is a good negotiator, because to get to where she is and to succeed in a male world, she had to be.

Some researchers claim that 10-15 percent of men have a "female mind". While this intriguing aspect doesn't seem to have anything to do with sexuality or masculinity, it has a lot to do with the way those men think, behave and relate to others.

I suspect I belong to this peculiar group. I've never liked typical male pursuits such as sports or pub crawling. I've also had lots of female friends. As most women would, I take things personally, especially when faced with aggressive and intimidating behaviour.

You may have seen two managers fighting at a meeting, blaming, shouting, intimidating, even insulting each other. Then, a few days later, you see them having lunch together. How is that possible?

If someone verbally abused me in a business setting (or any setting) our relationship would be dead to me. I would do my best to avoid that person at any cost and I would never forget the insult. Apparently, this is a typically female way of looking at conflict. Most men would think nothing of it; apparently it's considered normal in the "male world".

Men and Women as Relationship Builders

"It is, for instance, true that most women cannot read a map
as well as a man. But women can read a character better. And people are
more important than maps. (The male mind, at this point, will immediately
think of exceptions to this.)"

Anne Moir and David Jessel, *BrainSex*

Men form relatively superficial relationships at work. There may be lots of them, but very few intimate ones. There isn't much empathy and deep personal loyalty. Hierarchy is established and accepted through power dominance and the "pecking order". Men form gangs, with one leader and a few followers (three to five).

Unpleasant, aggressive and generally unlikable people (men only!) are tolerated, because they are either useful or too powerful to be challenged, so they have to be endured. We could say that male are relationships of function.

Women, on the other hand, form fewer relationships at work, but their relationships are usually deeper and more intimate. Women form either diads (two best friends) or small circles, through which they share experiences and support one another.

Theirs are relationships based on feelings. It all starts back in childhood, when boys form gangs and girls pair up with their best friend and form more intimate one-on-one relationships.

Interestingly, in some surveys, both men and women found women more understanding. When they need some empathy or a shoulder to cry on, men seek support from their female colleagues, rather than from their testosterone-laden male mates.

The Games Negotiators Play

> "Life is a game in which the rules are constantly changing; nothing spoils a game more than those who take it seriously."
>
> Quentin Crisp, *Manners from Heaven*

Organisational structures were created by men, for men. No wonder women struggle to find themselves in such a set-up. Playing a man's game, following the rules created by men and within structures created to men's liking is not easy.

Men do view work as a game. Male games tend to be competitive, of the "Mine is bigger than yours" type or "I'm the dominant male here!" variety. Men like making their own rules and showing off how they can deftly and tactically manoeuvre around the rules set by others.

Of course, women play games too, but their games are different and played for different reasons. Female games are usually submissive: "Poor Me" or "Guess Who is the Victim Here?". Women play games mostly due to their perception that to make it in "the man's world", they simply have to.

If you are a woman, I obviously cannot dispense advice to you from a female point of view. I couldn't possibly fully understand how it feels to be a woman or function like one. All I can do is advise you from my personal perspective, based on the principle that we are who we are and cannot or should not try to be anybody else. If you are a man, keep reading, the issues that follow are important for you to understand as well.

✓ CHECKLIST: Guerrilla Strategies For Female Negotiators

> "I don't know the key to success,
> but the key to failure is trying to please everybody."
>
> Bill Cosby, author and comedian

- *Whatever you do, don't try to behave like a man.* Be yourself. No matter how capable or determined you are to succeed, you will not win at a man's game. He's had much more practice at it!

- *Capitalise on your unique qualities, anything that can give you an edge.* Just as many men use aggressiveness, bluffing, intimidation and physical presence to their advantage, you can use your female qualities to your advantage. It may be sex appeal, intuition, or female connections.

- *Don't be overtly emotional.* Display your emotions openly and you will be speedily stereotyped along the familiar lines such as, "Told you women are too emotional to be in this business!" I know it isn't fair but that is the way it is. If you occasionally feel like crying or venting your rage on something or someone (and who doesn't?) don't do it in public.

- *Don't be jealous, bitter, shy or reclusive, either.* Most successful men are shameless self-promoters. Broadcast your capabilities and achievements. To be valued by others, you have to value yourself first.

- *Above all, don't be afraid.* Men will sense fear in you and will try to push you around and put you into a submissive position (where they claim you belong). This applies to timid and submissive males, too!

- *Stand up for yourself.* You'd be surprised how very little fighting back men need to leave you alone or to give you what you want! There are plenty of easier targets around. Just as in dating, men also use the numbers strategy in business. Sooner or later they will get what they want from someone.

The Androgynous Negotiator - Get to Know the Other You

There is a poignant one-liner in "My Fair Lady", when professor Higgins exclaims, "Why can't a woman be more like a man?" When it comes to negotiation, I think his question was wrong. "Why can't a man be more like a woman?" would be more appropriate.

Research shows that women are better judges of a person's character than men. Women are also perceived as more trustworthy before a negotiation starts, and both men and women would prefer to deal with a woman rather than a man in many situations.

Whatever the case may be, I hope you realise we are talking about balance here. Yin and Yang is not just some hippie concept for new age fanatics. The first step towards becoming a balanced person is to accept the duality within you. No matter what we are talking about, balance is usually the best state of affairs. Balancing the male and female qualities cannot be anything but beneficial.

I don't know you personally, so I have to use broad-sweeping brush strokes here. If you are male, discover and become comfortable with your feminine side. Pay more attention to your feelings and rely on your intuition more often.

If you are a woman and you consider yourself too emotional, excessively accommodating and overly passive, search for the little tough guy within. Let him out when appropriate. He will know how to demand and get respect, and how to relate to men on an equal footing. You deserve it.

If you are too serious, find a little child within, your long lost playful self. Learn from the child. Watch him do deals his way. Nurture your contrarian streak!

The Yin & Yang Rule

To become a balanced person and to capitalise on it in your negotiations, accept and nurture the male-female duality in yourself.

WINNING TIPS: WHAT I WISH I KNEW TWENTY YEARS AGO

- To anticipate the behaviour of the people you negotiate with, you need to understand their personalities first.
- People are predictable, therefore, they are controllable.
- Your aim is to be respected and treated fairly, not to be liked.
- You are not there to be cute, you are there to get what you want.
- Anything can be perceived the wrong way and used against you: What you say or do, what you look like, what you stand for.
- Get to know "the other you", your masculine or feminine side. Nurture your contrarian streak.

SPECIAL WINNING TIPS FOR FEMALE NEGOTIATORS

- The Cinderella story is a fairy tale (please read page 30 again)!
- Whatever you do, don't try to behave like a man.
- Don't be too emotional, jealous, bitter, shy or reclusive.
- Above all, don't be afraid.
- Capitalise on your unique qualities, those that give you an edge.
- Stand up for yourself. Don't let them push you around.

Ordinary No More!

DEVELOP THE MINDSET OF GREAT NEGOTIATORS

To become successful in negotiations, first you have to understand what makes a great negotiator. Then you can emulate their success by developing the same mindset and applying their lessons learned in your own life.

Coming up:

- 21 qualities of great negotiators
- How to acquire positive, productive and profitable negotiating traits and habits
- How to be a professional in anything you do

21 QUALITIES OF GREAT NEGOTIATORS

I Am Good, But Am I Really Great?

> "Then you shall judge yourself," the king answered.
> "That is the most difficult thing of all. It is much more difficult to judge oneself
> than to judge others. If you succeed in judging yourself rightly,
> then you are indeed a man of true wisdom."
>
> Antoine De Saint-Exupery, *The Little Prince*

One plucky participant in my negotiation course asked an interesting question: "Igor, would you say you are a great negotiator?" Now, I'm sure you can recognise that as a loaded question. A cocky trainer would answer in the affirmative, but you may have already guessed I'm not that type .

To complicate the matter further, notice the word *great*[9]. Had the more modest term *good* been used, I would most likely have answered positively, but after all, are there any truly great negotiators? Personally, I haven't met any yet. Even famous negotiators make mistakes; just read a biography (but not an autobiography!) of anybody famous, be it in business, politics, sport or entertainment.

✎ Exercise: Defining a great negotiator

Who do you consider to be a great negotiator? What qualities, personal or business traits make a great negotiator? List them in your notebook.

You may be married to a good negotiator, or you may be doing business with one. Perhaps you think you are a great negotiator. Sometimes, whole nationalities or professions are stereotyped according to the prevalent perceptions about their negotiating prowess. There are some interesting observations and claims raised in my seminars: The best negotiators are Lebanese and Armenians! Chinese are the toughest! It is impossible to outsmart lawyers!

When I introduced myself as a Yugoslav on a course I was presenting in the late nineties, when the bloody collapse of Yugoslavia was still fresh in people's minds, one participant commented half-jokingly: "It is unusual to see a Yugoslav teaching negotiation skills. I thought you guys shot first and asked questions later!" Hmm ...

To Understand Success, Study Failure

One way to understand success is to study its opposite - failure. Instead of looking at what master negotiators do and who they are, let's consider first what they don't do and what they are not.

[9]Paying attention to key words is an invaluable skill for a negotiator.

One of the prevalent perceptions is that successful people in general (and negotiators in particular) are successful because they are lucky. Sure, luck does play a part. Serendipity and synchronicity do exist and some people are blessed with a good fortune. But, in most cases, winners create their own luck.

You will see, the more thought you put into your actions, and the more time and effort you spend preparing for negotiations, projects or presentations, the luckier you will get!

Another myth is that success in negotiation comes from the use of specific negotiating techniques. Techniques can be either tricks (the games you play with others) or tactics (the moves you make in order to achieve your goal). Tricks are considered negative and unprofessional, while tactics are mostly regarded as legitimate and acceptable. However, the line between the two is very tentative. What is a trick to you may be an acceptable tactic to the other negotiator.

We will talk about these issues soon, in the chapter called *Manipulated No More!*, which discuses some of the most common tricks and tactics others may use on you. Once you recognise such moves, you can immunise yourself against them.

So, if neither luck nor tactics are crucial, what is? How about motivation? Yes, motivation is a necessary factor but not a sufficient one. Something more is needed. There are many motivated people who hardly make ends meet. If you are a loser and you motivate yourself, all you'll achieve is to end up a motivated loser.

Belief? There are many people who believe in various things - in life after death, in UFOs, in Elvis being alive and well, yet they aren't much better off than others who don't believe in these things!

Hard work also comes to mind. Hard work is a myth created and propagated by those who want you to work hard so you can make them rich. "Keep your nose down at the grindstone," they say, "and in another fifteen years, as a sign of our gratitude, you will get a Chinese-made retirement watch worth $49.95!" I know retired people who have worked hard their whole life, yet hardly have enough savings to pay for their own funeral.

The Hard Work Myth

Myth: "Work hard and you will eventually succeed." Reality: "Work smart, negotiate even smarter, and you may get somewhere."

Ethics? Sadly, no. There are many decent, ethical people who are struggling, just as there are many unethical people who are successful and rich beyond their wildest dreams.

Is it a friendly, personable approach? Well, I bet you know friendly folks who have never seen more than $50 in one lot, just as you may know those sour types who never smile and never say anything nice to anybody, who are successful in business or their profession.

Persistence? No. Many individuals and corporations are so persistent in their beliefs and actions, they stubbornly refuse to change. Yet, the values, ideas and methods they so vehemently cling onto cannot produce new, better results. I call them fanatics, because that's what they are. Fanaticism is basically a stubborn refusal to change or adapt, based on a blind, irrational belief in something.

There is no one aspect, quality or ingredient that will transform you into an instant winner in negotiation. Success is a multi-variate equation. The multiplicity of factors affecting the outcome of any life situation is mind-boggling. What is required is a comprehensive, holistic approach, the one we have adopted in this book.

Shortcuts and haphazard approaches sometimes produce results, but these are the long shots. You may as well keep buying weekly lottery tickets and spend the rest of your life hoping to win. The aim here is to proactively engineer yourself into a winner and your deals into winning deals, not to rely on blind hope or luck.

The Success Equation of Great Negotiators

"No matter where you are, make sure you are there."

Mahatma Gandhi, Indian political and spiritual leader

Each successful negotiator has his or her own recipe for success. We have and will continue to talk about many of them in this book. I have listed below the most important qualities or attributes of great negotiators. Not all of these qualities are equally important, and I would not even try to list them in the order of importance; so they are presented here in no particular order.

Great negotiators are:

1. *Fair and decent.* They use fairness and reciprocity as their main deal-making criteria. They truly aim for long-term, mutually beneficial agreements built on trust and mutual respect.

2. *Flexible and adaptable.* They have a planned strategy (or two), but don't rigidly stick to it if the situation warrants a change of plans. They remain open to suggestions and alternatives.

3. *Altruistic and amicable.* Genuinely interested in the other side, smart negotiators are able to quickly put others at ease and establish rapport.

4. *Discriminating and scrutinising.* They understand what others are saying, what they are not saying, what is important and what isn't. They are able to quickly get to the heart of the matter, claim or argument.

5. *Ethical and principled.* They don't play games or use tricks, deceit or intimidation. They are prepared to walk away if they are insulted or intimidated or if their values or dignity is questioned or threatened.

6. *Self-disciplined and patient.* They are prepared to forgo short-term gratification and go for long-term benefits instead. They invest time and effort to build trust and develop relationships.

7. *Dispassionate and logical.* They negotiate in a methodological, planned and structured manner, avoiding spur-of-the-moment decisions and controlling urges and impulses. They know their options and are prepared to walk away if there is a better option somewhere else.

8. *Reflective.* They continuously analyse their performance and aim to understand themselves, the other side and the deal. They don't overestimate their strengths or underestimate or hide their weaknesses. They have a realistic view of their assets and liabilities.

9. *Self-driven and ambitious.* They don't wait for external factors to force them into action. Instead, they push themselves out of their comfort zones, over the threshold of opportunity and away from the edge of complacency.

10. *Action-oriented.* Although they prepare well, great negotiators don't wait for conditions to be perfect, because they know they'll never be. They take timely and appropriate action.

11. *Politically savvy.* Before negotiating, great negotiators identify all concerned stakeholders and work on securing their agreement first. Likewise, once the deal is made, their job is not done. The deal has to be sold to people who have to approve it and implement it.

12. *Culturally sensitive.* They are aware of religious, cultural and other differences and sensitivities, and work their way around them.

13. *Persuasive.* Great negotiators express themselves well and convey ideas clearly and diplomatically.

14. *Calm and composed.* When under pressure, they maintain their professionalism and stay focused. Not easily distracted, they handle negative or hostile reactions of others with calm and composure.

15. *Comprehensive and bi-focal.* They see all sides of a problem or an issue to be negotiated, and recognise what's relevant and what is not. They are able to successfully deal with both macro

(large) and micro (small) issues. They understand the big picture, but also keep an eye on details that could derail the deal.

16. *Far-sighted.* They see and explore possibilities and opportunities before they become obvious. They can anticipate developments and act in an adaptive manner.

17. *Intuitive.* They don't rely exclusively on logic or on a formal problem-solving approach, but listen to their inner-voice and use their intuition. If something doesn't feel right, it most likely isn't!

18. *Fast thinking and acting.* Thinking on your feet is an invaluable skill. Master negotiators are skilled communicators, and clear communication comes from clear thinking.

19. *Prudent and pragmatic.* Master negotiators know what works and stick to it. They don't over complicate or try to be cute. They stick to the proven methods and approaches and avoid taking unnecessary risks.

20. *Professional.* They always do their best. For them, negotiation is more than a skill, craft or task - it is their way of life.

21. *Confident.* Great negotiators believe in themselves. Once inside the virtuous cycle of success, they can realistically appraise their odds of reaching the best possible outcome under the circumstances.

HOW TO BECOME AN EXTRAORDINARY NEGOTIATOR

Your Mindset is Your Key to Greatness

"And at this stage, Nature played the dirtiest trick imaginable. You grew up, but your self-image didn't. No wonder there are so many people who aren't achieving what they would like in their lives!"

J. H. Brennan, author

To be a truly effective negotiator, you first and foremost have to become a true person. A true person accepts responsibility for his or her life, for the decisions made and actions taken. A true person abandons the destructive psychological games lesser people play with others and with themselves.

True people do not allow others to control their life. They recognise the futility of blaming others for their own mistakes and failures.

The "Lock & Key" Principle

Your mindset may lock you out and prevent you from getting what you want, or it could unlock the doors to your success.

Be Confident and Constructive

"Confidence is the sexiest thing a woman can have.
It's much sexier than any body part."

Oprah Winfrey, talk-show host

The great quotation above does not apply to women only; the same can be said for men too. According to popular polls, women find confidence #1 quality in prospective partners. Dating and seduction could be considered a special case of negotiation.

Confidence in yourself, in your abilities and your actions is the very foundation of success in negotiation. The degree of confidence you have in yourself and the degree of confidence others have in you determines your chances of getting what you want. If you don't believe in yourself, how can you expect others to?

On the other hand, too much confidence borders on arrogance. As always in life, a balance has to be reached.

Some lucky people are born confident; others have to learn the ways of becoming more self-assured. These are some of the practical achievable steps in building your self-confidence.

First of all, you have to know what you do best and than concentrate on doing just that, instead of trying various other things. Second, you have to let others know of your abilities and promote yourself. Finally, put your confidence (or lack of it) in perspective. Don't just look up to people who "got it", consider those who "didn't get it", too. Nobody knows everything. We all make mistakes and have a flaw of some kind.

Instead of fault-finding and blaming yourself or others, be confident in your abilities and your ultimate success in every negotiation. Instead of behaving in a self-sabotaging or deal-breaking way, be constructive. Focus on the outcomes you want to achieve.

Fake it Until You Make it

"Acting is a nice childish profession - pretending you're someone else and, at the same time, selling yourself."

Catherine Hepburn, actress

Broadcasting my achievements was a foreign concept to me. I naively believed that no good deed would go unrewarded. Fighting for promotions or asking for what I wanted or deserved did not come naturally to me either.

Eventually, I realised such an approach to life wasn't doing me any good. Depending on others to recognise and reward you is a long shot, so I decided to improve my odds. I started practising the qualities I thought I was lacking, such as assertiveness and confidence.

In other words, I started by faking it. Just as some fake it at family gatherings ("These are marvellous socks, just what I always wanted, thank you, Grandma ..."), we can fake it in business and in negotiations. If afraid, act brave. If clueless, act confident. If embarrassed, laugh.

After a while, just by acting more confident, you will start feeling more confident too. And then it won't be acting or faking it any more, it will become the true you!

Fake-it-until-you-make-it Principle

By acting a certain way, you will gradually start to feel that way, too.
Just as feelings result in actions, actions can change feelings.

Then I started scrutinising and emulating successful people. Most of them were self-made and self-proclaimed. Many started their businesses without knowing much about the subject; they certainly weren't experts. After a while, they simply proclaimed themselves as such, and others believed them.

Encouraged by such audacity, I decided to do the same. Since I was already a published author, proclaiming myself a management expert wasn't a big stretch. I had intuitive confidence in my abilities, I believed I could pull it off, and I was right. Self-fulfilling prophecy?

The Aristos Principle - Professionalism Defined

"Don't join an easy crowd; you won't grow.
Go where the expectations and the demands to perform are high."

Jim Rohn, self-help philosopher

I define a professional as a person who does his or her best, regardless of surrounding circumstances, a person who continues and persists with an idea, project or undertaking long after the initial enthusiasm is gone.

Professionalism is not a qualification or occupation, but a state of mind and an approach to work and life.

Sure, there are professional negotiators, negotiating anything from hostage situations and family conflicts to business deals. But not all of those who negotiate for a living deserve to be called *professionals;* most are mere *practitioners.* To me, the crucial aspect of professionalism is situational: Professionals are able to achieve the best possible results under uncertain and often difficult circumstances.

My favourite TV cooking program is "The Surprise Chef". The star of the show is Aaron Papandroulakis, a.k.a. Aristos, a restaurateur from Perth. Aristos is a West Australian of Greek origin and a genuinely nice guy.

Aristos in Greek means "best under current circumstances", and that is precisely what the show is all about. He meets shoppers in supermarkets and offers to cook them a dinner using only the ingredients found in their fridge, pantry and shopping trolley.

Apart from being original, this is a very brave approach. Busy people's pantries and fridges often contain only a few basic items such as baked beans, canned tomato, frozen peas, minced beef and one or two pasta packets. How is that for a gourmet challenge?

In many ways, negotiations are like Aristos' cooking. You have to make the most out of your limited resources and achieve your best under trying circumstances and multiple constraints. It could be the lack of time, or incomplete information that is available, or perhaps conflicting demands being imposed on you by various stakeholders on whose behalf you negotiate.

A sign of a true chef is the ability to create a gourmet meal out of humble ingredients. A sign of a master negotiator is to maximise the desired outcomes under adverse and unfavourable conditions.

The Aristos Recipe For Success

Do the best you can, where you are, with what you've got.

Don't Gossip, Criticise or Insinuate

🕸 TRICKY TRAP: Tell me about them

Client: "We have carefully reviewed your and your competitor's proposals. Although their fee is lower than yours, we have some reservations of using them for the first time. In confidence, do you think they are capable of managing this important project?"

As with all tactics, there are two possibilities here. The client is either really concerned and is asking this contractor for his opinion on competitor's personnel, or, he may be hinting to the contractor that a price reduction would probably win them the contract.

Now, two kinds of responses are possible. Some sellers will take the bait and attack their competitor's lousy service, poor workmanship, unreliable supply, shonky business practices or anything else that makes the competition look bad, hoping they will look good by default.

Others will say the competitor's people, products and service are OK, but will emphasise that theirs are even better. They will deflect the inquiry from the competition's weaknesses onto their own strengths.

Personally I think the first approach is unprofessional. Criticising your competition will reflect poorly on you. You may have heard this one from your parent or grandparent: If you have nothing nice to say about somebody, don't say anything at all.

Banish the "Black & White" Thinking

> "I contradict myself. I am large. I contain multitudes."
>
> Walt Whitman, poet

Black & white thinking is any thinking resulting in one of the following thoughts or statements:

- Right - wrong: "I'm right and you are wrong!"
- Love - hate: "I hate your proposal but I love my own ideas!"
- Us versus them: "You are either with us or against us!
- I'm OK, you are not: "I am honest and fair, but you are not. You are selfish and unreasonable! Why can't you be more like me?"
- Win - lose: "For me to win you must lose!"
- Take it or leave it: "It's either my way, or the highway!"

Negotiators from individualistic, action-oriented cultures, such as the American one, tend to see the world through black & white glasses, and oversimplify things as a result. Reflection, concensus-building and teamwork don't come naturally to managers and negotiators from those cultures, and action without reflection is a recipe for disaster.

The Shades of Grey Continuum

Life is not black and white. Learn to live with shades of grey.

Why is "Black & White" thinking so common? It is the simplest and easiest way of classifying people, options or situations. We don't have to agonise over pros and cons, or consider nuances or exceptions. We simplify and then we simplify some more! It's quick and easy.

Unfortunately, "Black & White" thinking is usually wrong. It leads to positional and confrontational negotiation, instead of co-operative and integrative problem solving.

Be a Contrarian (When Others ZIG, You ZAG)

> "If any young man comes to me and asks how to make his fortune,
> I tell him to do the same. Don't follow everybody else.
> Get off the beaten track. Be a little mad."
>
> Jeno Paulucci, *How It Was to Make $100,000,000 in a Hurry*

After reading biographies and autobiographies of successful people, be it in business, politics or arts, one common trait stood out. Many, if not most, became successful not by taking the well trodden path or by thinking in conventional terms, but by doing exactly the opposite of what the majority was doing or thinking at the time.

They were contrarians who went against the prevalent opinions and fashions. They advocated unusual options and unpopular measures; some even took risks deemed foolish by others. They certainly didn't take the easy road.

The Zig-Zag Principle (The Contrarian Mantra)

Buy swimming pools in winter and gas heaters at spring sales. When everybody zigs, you zag.

Be Bold, Surprising and Different (Anything But Predictable)

"To make a lot of money, you will have to decide to become somewhat abnormal. Normal people are rarely successful."

Stuart Wilde, *The Trick to Money Is Having Some*

Remember my claim that negotiations are predictable and therefore controllable? The same applies to many other interpersonal situations, such as job interviews, court trails, and marriages, for example. You know what such situations are all about, what the other person wants, how you are expected to behave, what you are supposed to do or say, and what you aren't.

The more you get to know the other negotiator, the easier it should be for you to get what you want. After a while, you should be able to read them "like an open book". Such is the power of familiarity. Anything consistent is predictable and therefore controllable.

Of course, predictability is a two way street. Just as it works for you, it can as easily work against your interests. When you negotiate with the same people over and over again, you disclose lots of information about yourself: What is important to you, the way you think, how you make decisions, your values and attitudes. Sooner or later, they will form a fairly accurate picture of you, and if they are smart, they will use that valuable information to get what they want from you.

That is why it pays not to be too predictable. Don't make it too easy for others. Surprise them. Do different things and do them differently.

Question your own assumptions and beliefs

"Sceptical scrutiny is the means, in both science and religion, by which deep insights can be winnowed from deep nonsense."

Carl Sagan, astronomer turned author

Good negotiators often exhibit contradictory qualities. Although outwardly confident and self-assured, they often question their ways and search for their own weaknesses. They ask themselves: "What if I'm misinformed? What if I'm mistaken?" It's better for you to discover a shortcoming of yours, and do something about it, rather then allow the other negotiator to discover it first and exploit it for his gains.

Good negotiators are scrutinisers. They scrutinise not only the other side, but also their own assumptions, beliefs, goals, methods and plans. Close and constant scrutiny will help you minimise the possibility that your approach will fail or backfire. It will give you an opportunity to fine-tune your strategy, to change it significantly or even to abandon it completely.

Furthermore, such an exercise is your best preparation before you face the other person. If they are worth their salt as negotiators, they will try to prove you are wrong, mistaken or misinformed. Or that you are inferior, undeserving or unreasonable. You better have some aces up your sleeve.

WINNING TIPS: WHAT I WISH I KNEW TWENTY YEARS AGO

- To improve the quality of your results, you have to improve the quality of your decisions and actions first.
- Your mindset is the key. It may lock you out and prevent you from getting what you want, or unlock the doors to your success.
- Professionalism is not a qualification or occupation, but a state of mind and an approach to work and life.
- Do the best you can, where you are, with what you've got.
- Life is not black and white. Learn to recognise shades of grey.
- Be contrarian. When they zig, you zag!

Selfish No More!

NEGOTIATION AS RELATIONSHIP BUILDING

Two processes happen simultaneously during negotiation. Problem-solving deals with the content (the issues to be negotiated) and relationship building is about the context (trust, the history and the future of the relationship). While negotiators pay attention to the first, they often overlook this second, equally important aspect of deal-making.

Coming up:

- How to get what you want by helping others get what they want
- Trust as the foundation of any deal or relationship
- How to develop long-term, mutually beneficial relationships

THE RELATIONSHIP SIDE OF NEGOTIATION

Negotiation as a Relationship-Building Process

"I love mankind ... it's people I can't stand!!"

Linus in comic strip *Peanuts* by Charles Schultz

Negotiation is the art of managing relationships. You constantly negotiate and re-negotiate the nature, purpose and rules of these relationships as you struggle through life. The most important is your relationship with yourself. If you fail to establish a comfortable and productive relationship with yourself, it will be impossible for you to establish strong, mutually beneficial relationships with others.

**To be able to trust and respect others,
you must trust and respect yourself first.**

To negotiate with another person, you need some sort of a functioning relationship and some degree of trust. If your relationship is so damaged that you cannot stand the sight of the other person, or that neither side wants to have anything to do with each other, negotiation will not work.

All relationships are based on the simple principle of give and take. We negotiate when we need something from each other. The goal of negotiation is not to prove we are right and the other side is wrong. It is to achieve our aims while working together with the other side and helping them to achieve their aims.

All negotiations are interpersonal.

We cannot negotiate with a company, country or government; we can only negotiate with people, with individuals. So, in essence, there are no international, inter-organisational or interdepartmental negotiations - all negotiations are interpersonal!

Negotiation as a Dance

"He who cannot dance will say 'The drum is bad!' "

African proverb

Would you rather negotiate with a tough but fair negotiator who has a clear goal or with a nice person who doesn't know what he wants? Or, phrased in a slightly different way, would you rather face a good, experienced negotiator or prefer to negotiate with a confused and inexperienced negotiator?

When I ask these questions at my negotiating seminars, a typical answer I get is: "Why, of course I would prefer to deal with a poor negotiator, it would be easier for me to get what I want." This view is based more on wishful thinking then on reality. Perhaps paradoxically, I think you are much more likely to get what you want from an experienced negotiator.

True master negotiators will understand your needs and requirements and aim for the optimal deal. They will correctly identify your priorities and clarify the things that can be traded in the quest for the optimal deal, such as those that are important to one side, but are not important to the other. Of course they will always try to satisfy their interests first, but they will also work hard on giving you as much as possible. A win-win solution is the most likely outcome. Sure, sometimes they may get a bit more than you, but you will win nevertheless.

A poor or inexperienced negotiator would most likely take a firm, inflexible position. They usually look at things from "either-or", or "black and white" perspective, as we have already discussed.

You cannot negotiate effectively if the other side does not want to or know how to work with you on enhancing the deal. In either case, it is unlikely that all options would be fully explored and that an optimal deal would be engineered.

Even if the experienced negotiator has a win-lose mentality (he wins, you lose), all is not in vain. What is the worst thing that can happen to you if you negotiate with a good, albeit a win-lose negotiator? Even if you fail to get what you want, you can still benefit by learning from this experience. They usually tell you what they want in no uncertain terms, so they are predictable - at least you know where you stand and you don't have play the "guess what she's thinking" or "what does he want me to do now?" game.

On the other hand, lots of nice, friendly negotiators don't know what they want. That makes your negotiating task infinitely more difficult. You not only have to take care of your own needs, but to get to an agreement, you also have to help them discover and clarify their needs - and that's hard work.

Just ask any consultant or vendor who had to deal with an unprepared, confused, and suspicious client, who didn't know what he or she really wanted. In a sense, you are negotiating for two people!

The Double-Trouble Principle

Negotiating with an unskilled, unprepared or uncertain negotiator, who doesn't know what he or she really needs, requires you to double your efforts and negotiate for both of you.

Negotiation is an interactive process, just like dancing. You need to adjust to the other person. You may be dancing with a clumsy, inexperienced partner, who steps on your feet and is often out of sync with the music. The whole experience is far more enjoyable with a good, experienced dancer.

✓ CHECKLIST: Evaluating the Relationship

> "I respect only those who resist me; but I cannot tolerate them."
>
> Charles De Gaulle, French general, later president

Marriage and relationship experts advocate an ongoing assessment of our marriages, friendships and other relationships. Just as we work on our lawns and gardens at home, we should work on our relationships in personal and business life. Since relationships do change with time, so should our attitudes and approaches to resolving issues within them. As a negotiator, to decide on the best way to improve or terminate a relationship, you have to evaluate its aspects and premises. I use a simple, five-factor framework. It's easy to remember and makes intuitive sense:

- In terms of POWER: Is it a master/servant relationship (unequal power) or a relationship of equals?
- In terms of TIME: Is it a short-term (one deal) relationship or a long-term one (partnership)?
- In terms of PURPOSE: Is it professional (business), personal (pleasure and friendship) or mixed?
- In terms of EXCLUSIVITY: Are we the only partner (supplier, consultant, client) on this deal or are there others involved? Is it an exclusive or a non-exclusive relationship?
- In terms of STRENGTH: Is the relationship growing, getting stronger and deeper, or is it weakening and deteriorating?

TRUST AS THE FOUNDATION OF ANY DEAL

Gullibility and Paranoia - Pitfalls at the Extremes of Trust

> "I have made a ceaseless effort not to ridicule, not to bewail, not to scorn human actions, but to understand them."
>
> Baruch Spinoza, 17th century Dutch philosopher

There are two principal sources of misery in communication and negotiation. The first is gullibility: Believing a lie, not recognising a falsehood, falling for pretences, being convinced by a smoke and mirrors show.

Negotiators who trust too much usually believe that people are basically honest and decent, only to realise (when it's too late) that many aren't. This type of judgmental error causes all sorts of win-lose deals to happen; deals that are unfair, inequitable, immoral and often even illegal.

The second type of error negotiators make is not trusting enough, not believing the truth, or rejecting the genuine because they are convinced of its falsehood. This usually happens when we overreact as a result of bad experiences; a sort of "once bitten, twice shy" frame of mind. Such over-generalisation culminates in statements such as "all men are the same" or "big corporations can't be trusted".

As a result of such overly-suspicious attitudes, deals that should happen, don't. Trust is the bottom line. There is nothing more crippling for a deal than the lack of trust. There is no contract, no matter how detailed or comprehensive, and no amount of due diligence that could substitute trust.

FEAR	TRUST
They will ...	They will ...
■ rip me off.	■ do the right thing by me.
■ lie or withhold information.	■ tell me the truth.
■ promise a lot, deliver little.	■ negotiate in good faith.
■ ignore my needs.	■ consider my interests.
■ deliberately hurt my interests.	■ try to satisfy my needs.

Tough Question: "What is Your Budget?"

"Every sale has five basic obstacles:
no need, no money, no hurry, no desire, no trust."

Zig Ziglar, self-help author and motivational speaker

Let's consider a common exchange between buyers and sellers, in this case a client and a consultant. After the client's brief description of the problem and the outline of his needs, the consultant asks a straightforward question: "What is your budget for this project?"

What is going through the client's mind at this point? Thoughts like, "Why is he asking this question? Danger! This is a trick question! I'm not supposed to answer this ... If I disclose my budget, he will propose more expensive solutions and unnecessary services ... ".

Now, put yourself in the seller's position. He is trying to place this client and the project in a box, to classify them in some way. To frame the conversation and take it forward, the consultant has to know more. How big is the project? It may be too big or too small for his consulting firm. How profitable could the deal be? How risky is it? How committed is the client? How serious is he, how realistic?

The answer to many of these questions is the client's budget. If the client mentions an unrealistically low figure, the consultant will have to question the client's commitment and seriousness. Or, it could be a warning sign that he is facing a tough and demanding client, maybe even a time-waster who wants a lot for very little money.

If the consultant has a genuine interest in the client and wants to deliver the best service possible, the budget question is not only perfectly reasonable, but absolutely necessary. If, however, the seller wants to maximise his income and charge the client as much as possible, then the question is a trick one and should not be answered by the client, or answered vaguely and evasively.

So, we see again that trust is the pivotal force in any conversation and negotiation. Trust determines the level, the depth and the timing of disclosure.

How Committed is the Other Side?

You can judge the other person's commitment to the deal by the amount of time, money and effort they put into it. Say you wrote a book and are negotiating with a publisher who offers you an advance of $3,000. How committed do you think they are? What if they offered you $30,000? Would that change your answer?

Money indicates confidence and commitment

The amount of money, time and effort each side puts into a negotiation is the best indicator of their commitment to the deal.

Perhaps you are not familiar with publishing deals. An advance is an upfront payment by the publisher to the author, made after the contract is signed, usually months before the book is published.

The good news for authors is that an advance is non-refundable. If the book doesn't get published or if it sells so few copies that the author's royalty is less than the amount advanced, the advance doesn't have to be paid back.

The amount of the advance offered is a reflection of the publisher's confidence in the book's success. The more of an advance they pay you, the more committed they will be to the whole deal and the harder they will work in promoting and selling your book (so they can get their investment back as quickly as possible).

If you are author, this is the main reason why you should insist on a substantial advance during your negotiations with publishers. Just as in job interview, once they make you an offer, your power is at its peak; that is the time to be demanding. Once you sign on the dotted line, your power dwindles to just about nothing!

The same applies to negotiating any licensing deal with a manufacturer. Say you've got an idea or invention and someone is interested in buying it or licensing it from you. The amount of up-front payment they offer you is the best indicator of their seriousness and commitment to the whole deal.

HOW TO GET PEOPLE TO NEGOTIATE WITH YOU AGAIN

Don't Violate Implicit Understandings

Implicit understandings in negotiation are expectations of reciprocity, fairness or honesty. Nothing disappoints people more than when these expectations are violated.

Think about instances when you picked up another parent's kid from school. Then, once when you were in a tight bind and needed her to pick your child up, she said no and put up some lame excuse. Or when you loaned money to a friend, who later let you down when you needed a favour from him. I bet you were annoyed, at the least, or more likely seriously enraged. I would also bet you did no more favours for that person from then on.

Not returning a favour or not helping those that helped you in the past is the surest way to disappoint people, erode trust and damage relationships.

The same dynamics play out in negotiation. One person makes a concession but the other doesn't. The goodwill gesture is not appreciated and there is no return favour.

Many negotiators start in a win-win frame of mind, but if the other negotiator displays a win-lose mentality or does not reciprocate, they change their approach, thinking: "I gave you a chance to work together co-operatively and constructively, but you blew it. You want to play tough, OK, I can play tough!"

The other school of thought advocates disregarding the absence of reciprocity and continuing in the same co-operative frame of mind.

If the other negotiator does not reciprocate or gets aggressive, that doesn't mean that we should stop negotiating in good faith or that we should suddenly become aggressive in return. You don't fight fire with fire, you fight fire with water, these negotiators say. Which point of view do you subscribe to?

The Fire-fighting Rule

Don't fight fire with fire. Fight fire with water.

Move From Selfishness to Synergy

"Greed obscures judgement."

Frank W. Abagnale, *The Art of the Steal*

In the short term, greed, guile and gluttony often pay off. That is why there are so many greedy, selfish and inconsiderate people around. In the long run, they don't. Sooner or later this approach backfires, and there is a price to be paid at the end. In business, such a price is usually very high: Bankruptcy, public shame and humiliation, even jail. In our personal lives: divorce, broken families, loneliness.

The difference between the two approaches is evident from the outset. When winners meet other people to do deals with, they ask two simple, yet profoundly important questions: "What would I want if I were in that person's position?" and "How can I get them what they want so I can get what I want?"

Losers think differently, so as a result, their questions are very different: "What's in this for me?" and "How can I get what I want from them without giving much in return?"

The quality of questions you ask will determine the quality of your outcomes. A positional, selfish attitude is a trademark of win-lose negotiators, whose only question is "What can you do for me?"

Self-reliance or self-mastery is a level at which more developed negotiators operate. By asking "What can I do for myself?" they assume responsibility for their own actions and don't base their wins on others' losses.

Then comes empathy for the other person and a desire to serve others by asking: "What can I do for you?"

Teamwork and synergy are at the highest level of negotiating mastery. The ultimate question in negotiation is "What can we do together to enhance the deal and create additional value?"

Give Them the Best Deal You Possibly Can

Exercise: How would you define a good deal?

To me, a "good deal" means:

_____

_____

_____

_____

If you are a win-win type negotiator, your definition of a good deal will probably be based on the concepts such as fairness, reciprocity, mutual benefit and long-term commitment.

We can also use efficiency and effectiveness in our definition: How much time, money and effort have we invested in the deal (efficiency) in order to achieve our goals (effectiveness).

I judge deals and agreements by the following three criteria:

The Deal Evaluation Formula

Parties are happy with the deal, committed to it, and ready for new deals.

Create Profitable and Pleasurable Experiences

"They may forget what you said,
but they will never forget how you made them feel."

Carl W. Buechner, writer and lecturer

We can look at shopping from two different viewpoints. The utilitarian way is to concentrate on saving money, which means finding a store with the cheapest price.

Think about instances where you got a great deal, and by great deal I mean you got what you wanted cheaper than in other stores. Did you enjoy shopping there?

My guess is that in most cases your answer would be no. The store was crowded, the atmosphere was noisy, rushed, or it was too warm or too cold. The staff were not around to help you when you needed assistance or they lacked knowledge. Perhaps they were stressed out, brusque, even rude. Checkout queues stretched for miles. In short, you just went there to save money.

The alternative is to shop at "exclusive" stores and boutiques to increase our shopping pleasure. There is only one problem with shops that provide a nice shopping experience: They are expensive. All those plush carpets, smiling "sales executives" oozing sex-appeal, free colour catalogues the size of a phone directory and other high class props cost money, and in the end, you and other buyers have to pay for it.

Negotiations can be looked at in the same way. Most are unpleasant, strained encounters with people we don't really like or care much about. We are suspicious of their intentions, the surroundings are far from ideal and we are under pressure from the stakeholders (wife, kids, boss, client).

Yet, we still go through it all, thinking in the end it will all be worth the trouble. We wouldn't even dream about having a pleasurable experience; that would be far too much to ask.

There are two ways to make people come back for more: You either give them such a good deal that they would be mad not to come back, or you make them feel good some other way.

TIP	THE LAWS OF REPEAT BUSINESS
	■ Give them such a good deal they would be mad not to come back for more. ■ Make them feel good about you, the deal and, most importantly, about themselves.

The first path leads to diminished benefits for you. The second path is usually more cost-effective. A cappuccino, pleasant ambience and friendly disposition don't cost much; most pleasantries are free. Since most other people they negotiate with make them feel inadequate or miserable, they will come back to you to feel good again.

☹ WHAT NOT TO DO: How to Kill a Relationship

People will not negotiate or do business with you when you ...

- ... don't keep your promises or commitments.
- ... show lack of respect for them, their values, ideas or efforts.
- ... play the friendship card to extract unreasonable concessions.
- ... don't reciprocate after a favour.
- ... fail to support them in tough times or critical situations.
- ... use double standards, one for them and another for yourself.
- ... blatantly put your interests ahead of theirs.
- ... criticise them, belittle or denigrate.
- ... intimidate, threaten or cajole them into submission.

WINNING TIPS: WHAT I WISH I KNEW TWENTY YEARS AGO

- All negotiations are interpersonal.
- Trust is the foundation of every deal and every relationship.
- To be able to trust and respect others, you must trust and respect yourself.
- Negotiating with an unskilled, unprepared or uncertain negotiator, who doesn't know what he or she really needs, requires you to double your efforts and negotiate for both of you.
- The amount of money, time and effort each side puts into a negotiation is the best indicator of their commitment to the deal.

Stingy No More!

NEGOTIATE VALUE INSTEAD OF PRICE

This is one of the most important chapters of this book. It can literally save you thousands of dollars! Instead of mindless bargaining, we should negotiate long-term benefits.

Coming up:

- Three levels of negotiating mastery: price-, principled- and value-negotiations
- How to maximise value for both parties
- How to trade concessions
- Negotiating strategies for buyers and sellers
- Negotiating with car dealers
- Real estate negotiations

DO WE GET WHAT WE PAY FOR?

Three Levels of Negotiating Mastery

I divide negotiations and negotiating mindsets into three levels. Price negotiation applies mostly to single-issue negotiations, those of the 'Hit & Run" variety. Tricks, tactics and bluffs abound, the atmosphere is competitive, and both sides drive a hard bargain.

Sadly, judging by what I hear on my in-house courses and consulting assignments, price negotiation is still practised by purchasing professionals world-wide. To accept the cheapest quote is still a bedrock requirement of most purchasing departments, even in many large and supposedly world-class corporations.

Principled negotiation is, as the very name suggests, based on a set of principles such as reciprocity, mutual respect and searching for win-win outcomes through a constructive dialogue and collaboration; no hiding, pretending, acting or intimidating. Before discussing the substance we should agree on these rules that will govern the whole negotiation, so all parties have a clear understanding of each other's needs and expectations. We have already discussed this step and called it "setting the negotiating table".

Myth: "You get what you pay for!"
Reality: "You get what you negotiate."

Purchasing price is only one of the factors in negotiation, and may not even be the most important one. While price negotiators take a short-term view ("Gimme the lowest price NOW!"), value negotiators look at the deal holistically and in the long-term. Value negotiators are not power- but achievement-driven.

Let's say you are buying a car. Value negotiators consider factors such as the resale value, the cost of servicing and spare parts, the insurance premiums and other life-cycle costs. Then there are issues such as reliability and dealership network's service quality, safety features, fuel consumption or environmental impact.

The Prize-Price Compromise or the Trade-Off Principle

The term pricing doesn't refer to money only. It is about determining what price you are prepared to pay for the prize you desire. Accountants call it "cost-benefit analysis". The Prize - Price compromise is a fundamental concept in life. There is no such thing as a free lunch; sooner or later you will pay the price. Ask yourself, "What trade-offs am I making here? Is my gain worth the pain?" This is the bottom line of your cost-benefit analysis.

Keep your eyes on the PRIZE and your mind on the PRICE.

💣 QUICK STORY: Beware of your contract requirements!

A HR manager from a large oil & gas company approached me to run a series of negotiation training courses for hundreds of their managers, engineers and other professionals. She accepted my fees without negotiation. This was a good sign - they needed to improve their negotiation skills after all. It was also a bad sign - I obviously quoted too low.

It was March; the first courses were scheduled for early May. Then I received a formal contract from their legal department. It was a standard long-term agreement for site-based contractors. Most sections did not apply to our project at all. Instead of 25 or so pages, two would cover everything nicely, I told them. They refused to change anything. Big companies want to play by their own rules, I found, and don't want to accommodate a little guy.

A few clauses imposed conditions and penalties for certain aspects of the deal and asked for reports, guarantees and various types of insurance. The larger the company, the longer their contracts and the more paranoid they are.

One clause stipulated that the training course in question would automatically become their intellectual property. To me, that was not negotiable. I refused to budge and the deadlock ensued. I openly asked the training manager if she wanted the ownership of the course. She didn't, so I got her to instruct the contract people to remove the offending clause.

Due to all the additional contractual terms, I increased the original price by half and they grudgingly accepted. By then it was too late to reschedule the courses or to find another provider, even if she wanted to. She imposed an arbitrary deadline on herself and didn't have an alternative consultant. No fallback options, no power.

Their unwillingness to modify or to simplify the agreement, and their insistence on the use of their standard contract increased their costs by half. They won on the points of the contract (except the one on intellectual property), I won on the price.

The Buyer's Curse

Be careful what you ask for - you'll have to pay for it. The more details you specify, the higher the price gets!

The Haggling Ritual

"There are two fools in every market:
one asks too little, the other one asks too much."

Russian proverb

Haggling about a price is a ritual expected in many cultures. You must have seen it in markets, souks, and other places where there are no fixed prices and where values are uncertain.

The ritual is usually started by the seller, who either names the price first or invites the prospective buyer to make the first offer. Some sellers claim that when buyers make first offers they get higher prices, especially if the items for sale are highly desirable and of such nature that prospects can fall in love with them. Artwork, rare cars, books and antiques fall into this category.

Inevitably, the seller starts high. The buyer then tries to bring the price down by using all sorts of justifications: It is too small, too big, too heavy, it is blue while he would prefer red, it is scratched, chipped, faded, or in some other way affected or imperfect, his wife is against the purchase, his budget is limited, he bought a similar one recently and it didn't work, and so on. Any justification, no matter how improbable or silly it may sound, is fine - neither the seller takes it too seriously nor the buyer himself fully believes in it.

Sellers, on the other hand, like to quibble, to educate and to resist. They like to play the "I've never sold it so cheaply!" game. The aim is to keep talking, but without giving in too quickly.

The main benefit is the self-satisfaction resulting from the hard work both sides put into it. The haggling ritual involves offers and counter-offers, arguments and refutations, bluffs and counter-bluffs. All that posturing, fault-finding, sales puffery and exaggeration serves an important purpose - both sides feel more satisfied with the deal, because they had to work hard to achieve it.

The Effort - Appreciation Law

The harder people work or negotiate to get something, the more they will appreciate it and the happier with the outcome they will be.

The Top Three Bargaining Rules

Some buyers dislike bargaining rituals and aim for the bottom price. They say, "Look, I don't want to waste your time or mine. Why don't you give me the absolutely lowest price you would accept? If it is within my budget, I will pay it without quibble." While such a strategy may save you time and even work in some situations, it violates The Effort - Appreciation law.

Imagine a buyer who pays the named price without a word, takes the goods and departs. How is the seller feeling? He is chastising himself for not asking for more. No matter how big their profit margin is, people are greedy and always want more. And when the buyer gets home to his wife, how is she going to view her husband's bargaining aptitude? Useless! He didn't even try to reduce the price! What did she do to have such an inept provider for a husband? In short, the acceptance of the first offer leads to unhappiness on both sides!

The First Rule of Bargaining

Never accept the first offer.

I primarily blame the "system" for this widespread avoidance of negotiation. We get conditioned to go quietly about the business, without asking for much or making waves along the way.

The dogma of fixed prices prevails in many cultures and industries. If you try to bargain, you get a condescending look and are told in no uncertain terms that the price is fixed.

Despite all this pressure to conform and al those years of negative conditioning, don't ever feel guilty for negotiating! Don't let sellers condition you into submission. Keep negotiating regardless.

The Second Rule of Bargaining

There is no such thing as a fixed price.

Anxious buyers tend to discuss price very early in the negotiating process. They don't realise how difficult it is for sellers to provide even a price range, let alone a fixed quote for something poorly defined and even more poorly communicated to them. If buying, make sure you discuss your functional needs first (what the equipment or service you are buying has to do), then its technical aspects or features that may or may not be needed, and finally the price for the agreed configuration or scope of work.

The Third Rule of Bargaining

Negotiate price last. Money does not solve all problems.

✓ CHECKLIST: Why People Haggle

- They are just practising their newly acquired negotiation skills.
- They are stingy and want something for nothing.
- They are ready to buy but are just testing your firmness.
- They want it, but cannot afford it, due to a limited budget.
- They enjoy the bargaining just for the sake of bargaining.
- They want to impress the boss, the family or the subordinates.
- Their culture mandates haggling. Accepting an offer without negotiation would be strange and unnatural to them.
- They are expected to get the lowest possible price; it is their job as a purchasing agent or procurement manager.
- They don't intend to buy from you, but need your low-ball quote to use it as a leverage tool against their preferred supplier.
- They don't know how to say no to you, so they haggle as an excuse to get out of the deal.

THE RECIPROCITY PRINCIPLE

The Principle of Indirect Effort: Give First and Get Later

Negotiation has been labelled as a "give and take" process. Notice the order. You give something to the other side first. This starts the relationship on a positive note. It sets a precedent and displays goodwill. Once you've done that, the other side knows you care about their needs too, that you are a reasonable person and that you are prepared to work hard to achieve a mutually beneficial outcome.

I still don't like that word "take". Taking is selfish and aggressive. You don't just take lemons from your neighbour's tree, or help yourself to your friend's lawnmower. You ask and then you may get it.

It pays to approach most relationships as servants. "Servant" in this context does not indicate a submissive or subservient attitude. It means doing your best to help others get what they want out of a deal or situation, in return for something you need. Taking alone never gets you as much as giving first and taking later!

The Principle of Indirect Effort

Help others get what they want and they may help you get what you want. Put service to others first and your rewards should follow.

You may have noticed my use of "may" and "should" in the definition above. The other person may or may not reciprocate - there is no guarantee that your goodwill will be returned.

Get Something You Want for Something You Don't

"I needed a drink, I needed a lot of life insurance, I needed a vacation, I needed a home in the country. What I had was a coat, a hat and a gun."

Detective Philip Marlowe, in *Farewell, My Lovely*

Instead of "give & take" I use the Reciprocity Principle. Reciprocity is a better term to use than concession, which has negative connotations. Don't view concessions as giving up something valuable, or something you are entitled to. Look at it simply as an exchange. Trade what you have for what you want.

The Reciprocity Principle

Don't just give things away - ask for something in return.

A conditional "if ... then..." proposition is the most powerful tool in negotiation. Even kids are familiar with issue linking. How many times have they heard Grandma's healthy-eating deal sweetener: "C'mon honey, finish your veggies first, and then you can have my delicious apple pie!"

The Law of Relative Importance

The beauty of the Reciprocity Principle lies in the fact that you give up something not too precious to you, something you never really wanted in the first place, in exchange for obtaining something you do really want or need more.

To get something of value does not mean you have to give up something of value to you. Value is relative. Just like beauty, it's in the eyes of the beholder. Something of relatively low importance to you may be extremely important to somebody else. The whole concept of sales and marketing is centred around finding people who value what you've got and will gladly exchange their cash for something you have plenty of!

The Law of Relative Importance

We want different things and in a different order of importance. If something is precious and desirable to you, do not automatically assume it will be precious to and desired by others, and vice versa.

⧗ QUICK QUIZ: Management & unions

You are a manager of a mining company. Leaders of one of the five unions representing your employees present their demand for a ten percent pay-raise. How do you respond?

a) Offer them five percent, take it or leave it.

b) Offer five percent now but conditional upon the achievement of the ten percent productivity increase within 12 months.

c) Offer two percent now, two percent in 12 months time plus another two percent in two years time.

d) Ask them to show you how the company can afford a ten percent rise.

e) Tell them that awarding a pay-raise to members of one union wouldn't be fair to the other unions involved. Ask them to agree amongst themselves on who deserves how much and then to present a unified proposal to you.

✋ STOP & THINK! What would you do?

a) LOSER MOVE! Offering half of what they demand is fine, but you've made the concession too quickly. Plus, the ultimatum is a no-no. "Take it or leave it!" should be outlawed. Get ready for continuous trouble.

b) BETTER THAN a)! Conditional offers are wise. However, now you have another, more complex negotiation on your hands. How will such productivity improvement be defined and measured?

147

c) SO-SO! By offering staged concessions you are playing a delay game. It is better from your cash-flow perspective, but you've forgotten to attach conditions. What are you getting in return? Strengthen your position by linking this option with b).

d) RISKY! You are inviting legitimate grievances and may be weakening your position significantly. If you've just awarded top management a 25 two percent pay-raise or bonus, or if you've paid out a significant dividend to shareholders, the unions will demand the same!

e) GREAT MOVE! Seems risky, but knowing human nature, they will never agree amongst themselves. If they eventually do, this will buy you months or years of peace. Hopefully, by then, you will have moved up (or out) and some other poor sod doing your old job will have to deal with this problem.

HOW TO TRADE CONCESSIONS

Don't Make Premature or Unnecessary Concessions

Before we consider the issue of *how* to trade concessions, we have to be clear on *why* we are making concessions at all. As I see it, there are only three situations when a concession is justifiable:

1. *To reciprocate* - when the other side makes a concession and asks you or expects you to follow suit.

2. *To keep the negotiation alive.* You've reached a deadlock or they are about to walk away, so you want to prevent the deal from collapsing.

3. *To finalise (sweeten) the deal* - make one last concession to get the deal over the finishing line.

Premature Concessionalitis (making concessions too early) is a debilitating ailment that afflicts many inexperienced negotiators.

You want to demonstrate you mean business, so you give them something of value immediately. You worry that your proposal won't be accepted as it is, so you quickly throw in a couple of freebies. You want to be seen as a nice, reasonable person who is prepared to compromise so you concede on something just to start the trend and display goodwill. Generally, these are bad opening moves.

The preliminary negotiating stages set the scene for later discussions. You should not make any concessions during that time. The bargaining has not started in earnest and there is no need to jump the gun. You may ask hypothetical questions for the purpose of exploration, but without committing to anything.

By making premature concessions you signal to the other negotiator that you are needy and anxious, perhaps even that you feel insecure and powerless.

Only make concessions once you fully understand the needs, the aims and the aspirations of the other side, or you may be unnecessarily giving things away you could safely keep otherwise.

The Premature Concessions Trap

Don't make any concessions during the first three stages of negotiation (Preparing, Probing and Proposing).
Trade them only during the final stages.

Concessions Should Indicate Your Bottom Line

Imagine this negotiation: I name my price, you seem unhappy, you flinch, so I drop my asking price two percent. Then we negotiate, you put me under pressure and I drop my price a further five percent. I am desperate; I need my monthly sales bonus.

You are still not happy, so you intimidate me with stories about my competition, some invented complaints about my service, and the influence of global warming on the depressed market for my products and services. I get the message and cut my price to the bone by offering another three percent drop in price.

How has our little negotiation progressed? Quite well for you, but quite badly for me. There is no sense of closure. I haven't created a natural settlement point. My concessions were all over the place, up and down like a yo-yo.

As a buyer, you would be delighted and confused at the same time. You got a total of ten percent reduction in price, but you still don't know how close you are to my bottom line.

To create a stable settlement point and to send you a strong signal about my bottom line (real or arbitrary, it doesn't matter), my concessions should be rapidly diminishing. Once you get a three percent discount, you cannot expect my next concession to be seven percent!

First concession: five percent for bulk order, demo model, or any similar reason. Second concession: two percent from my manager (so you cannot play the "I want to see the Boss" trick on me). Third concession: half a percent if paid in cash (instead of paying by credit card) now (instead of the usual 60 or 90 days smart buyers demand), in return for helping me with my cash flow.

Now you know I am not prepared to give you another three percent reduction even if you beg, bribe or marry my ugly sister. My pattern of concessions has led us towards a natural and stable settlement point *I* would be happy with. Now, it is for you to decide if that point is the one *you* are happy with.

The optimal concession pattern

1. THE BIGGEST	2. SMALL	3. SMALLER	4. TINY

149

This is not to say that you should always make four concessions. There could be two, three or any number of steps. Just make sure each concession is significantly smaller than the previous one, so a clear trend is demonstrated.

TIP	THREE WAYS TO MINIMISE YOUR CONCESSIONS
	■ Boost the significance (to the other side) of your concessions, no matter how small they may seem to you.
	■ Downplay the significance (to you) of their concessions, no matter how big the other side claims they are.
	■ Keep reminding them of all the concessions you made at point: "Look, I gave you ..., and I agreed to ...., I met you half-way on ...., I am already below my bottom line here ...".

NEGOTIATING STRATEGIES FOR SELLERS

How a 10% Discount Turns Into 67% Reduction in Profit

They would like to do business with you, but your price is over their budget, they claim. Reduce it by ten percent and the contract is yours. You think about it for a while, agree and shake their hand.

What have you just done? Let's assume a relatively modest profit margin of 15 percent of the selling price. You have reduced the price by ten percent, which means you are left with a five percent profit, a very slim profit margin in anyone's books. Your ten percent reduction of the total price is actually a whopping 67 percent reduction in your profit: You've given away two thirds of it!

Sure, there are times when such a move could be warranted. They may be a new client, and you want to add such a reputable name to your client list, so you get more business from other clients. Or, there may be more large projects where this one came from. You may be going through a quiet period so any profit is better than no profit at all if you lose the sale.

Discounting on price is the worst way to get business. Any undertaking with a minuscule profit margin is a risky one. Any difficulty, delay or cost increase can take you into the red. It is like driving a fast racing car only a few inches from an abyss. You are either a very brave and capable driver or very crazy.

The Profit-Percentage Predicament

Before you are tempted to reduce your price, think in percentage terms - not percentage of the total price, but of your profit.

Selling Move: An Alternative to Discounting

"PRICE, n. Value, plus a reasonable sum for the wear and tear
of conscience in demanding it."

Ambrose Bierce, *The Devil's Dictionary*

There are three alternatives to discounting the price. Firstly, we could *reduce the quality*. CEO of the petrol-station chain: "What is the highest level of ethanol we can mix into our petrol before the motorists start noticing degraded performance and having engine trouble?" Generally, this option is way too risky. Once you start cutting corners in the quality area, you are doomed. Luckily, there are better options!

Secondly, we could *reduce costs by doing the job faster*. Management training company: "If we train your managers in two instead of four days, would you be happy with the investment in this negotiation workshop?"

Finally, we could *reduce the scope or the number of features*. Consultant: "Your funds don't allow for a full-time support expert on site, but we can provide you with telephone support."

Let's say the buyer is trying to negotiate down the price of a luxury model. Seller's response? Instead of savagely discounting the top-of-the-range model, switch to a basic model. Seller: "This advanced model is priced way above your budget, and since you don't need most of the extra features, the standard model is perfect for your application." To fix the price, reduce the package!

Fix the Price, Reduce the Package

To protect your profit margins, instead of reducing the price, reduce the scope or the duration of your service (but not quality!)

How to Avoid Time-Wasters and Comparison Shoppers

Sales experts advocate the process of "qualifying" prospective buyers. Qualifying is about finding the answers to questions such as, "Can they afford it? How serious are they? Do they have the intention to buy or are they just doing comparison shopping?"

You can use a similar system. Ask questions such as, "Are you getting other quotes?" and "Have you invited any other suppliers to quote on this supply contract?" Of course, they may not answer truthfully. Distinguishing between true prospects and tyre kickers is never easy, but you will get better at it with time.

One approach sellers find useful is the "see me last" invitation. Having the last opportunity to quote your price may give you an advantage over your competitors: "By all means talk to other suppliers, and then come and see me. I will do my best to beat any genuine quote you may get."

NEGOTIATING STRATEGIES FOR BUYERS

Pick & Choose Buying Strategy

> "Price is what you pay. Value is what you get."
>
> Warren Buffett, investment guru, philanthropist

Pick & Choose is a simple yet effective approach. First, get a few item-ised quotations. Then, identify the most favourable items to you in terms of the criteria you set (price, quality, functionality, support, de-livery) in each of the bids. Finally, contact each vendor separately and offer them an opportunity to revise their offers by improving on the points (items) where their rivals' offers are superior.

Alternatively, you can pick and choose the most favourable indi-vidual items from all quotes, select the preferred vendor (based on previous dealings, overall impression, responsiveness, quality of the proposal, etc.) and ask them to match or beat the most favourable items from other vendors.

Let's say seller #2 gives you a free delivery. Seller #3 gives you free training. However, you prefer to buy from seller #1. Tell him about the free delivery and free training offers from his competitors and hint that if he offers the same, you will buy from him!

The Itemising Law

If selling, provide a package price. If buying, get itemised quotes.

Smart consultants and service providers try to avoid point-by-point comparison shopping and the Pick & Choose trick by not itemising their fees in a proposal. Most sellers prefer lump-sum, all-inclusive prices, because it is much easier to hide certain charges from buyers. The more information they provide on their quotes or invoices, the more likely that buyers will challenge certain charges!

Negotiating With Car Dealers

TRUE STORY: Buying a second-hand car

You are in a used car yard. You've found the car you like - a four year old Ford Fairlane in immaculate condition. The car costs $46,000 new, and the sticker price is $19,990. It has just been traded in by a large company. Your budget is $15,000 but you can go up to $16,000. What would you do?

a) Since you really like the car, go and borrow $2,000 more so you can offer $18,000.

b) Forget about the car, it is priced far above your upper limit.

c) Ring or visit other dealers and compare the prices for similar or identical cars. Then, if you still like this deal, come back.

d) Offer the dealer $14,000 cash.

e) I need more information, this case is quite complex.

STOP & THINK! How would you proceed?

a) LOSER MOVE! The sticker price is the dealer's wishful thinking. No sane person would pay even $18,000 for that car.

b) ANOTHER LOSER MOVE! How do you know how low they can go? Never voluntarily eliminate yourself from the contest.

c) RISKY MOVE! Visiting other dealers is a good move, but you should have done that beforehand. Once they see you coming back, they know you couldn't get a better deal elsewhere.

d) WINNING MOVE! Your offer is probably close to his cost price.

e) SMARTASS MOVE! Life is messy and often you have to make decisions without having all the information.

This is a true story from my brother's experience. Prior to negotiating with this dealer, we ascertained the prices for similar vehicles in four other car yards. We also checked private sale ads in the Saturday's paper. We even negotiated with another dealer for an almost identical car, with the sticker price of $17,990.

The lowest he would accept was $16,000, so we walked away, hoping that we would get a better deal elsewhere. However, that gave us the bottom line against which to compare similar cars.

My brother wanted to offer $15,000. I advised him to start even lower, at $14,000 or thereabouts. The salesman claimed he had no authority and went to see his boss, the used car manager.

About 15 minutes later (intimidation on their part?) the manager emerged out of his office and told us that his cost price was $14,600. If my brother could pay the additional $600, the manager said, we had a deal. My brother accepted the counteroffer.

We made one mistake, though - we didn't ascertain the market value of that car. One way to do that is to call one or more insurance companies and get some insurance quotes. They have the most accurate valuation figures for every conceivable make and model.

After the purchase, when we rang a few places to get quotes for a comprehensive insurance, we were told the car's market value was between $15,500 and $17,000, depending on its condition. As it turned out, by paying only $14,600, we hadn't done badly after all.

The danger of aiming too low

If you are getting all you are asking for, you are not asking enough.

Most of the time you aren't sure how well or how poorly you've done in a negotiation until something else happens. You may find an identical item for sale cheaper elsewhere, or you may learn that your colleague doing the same job as you earns ten percent more.

No matter how happy you were with the price you paid or the salary increase you negotiated, such developments would certainly impact your perception of and satisfaction with the outcomes you've achieved.

In our car buying example, we could evaluate the price paid against a valid anchor (the insurance value), but we still didn't know for sure how low the dealer was prepared to go. What if we had offered $13,000 instead of $14,000, and the boss came back with the same story, saying that his cost price was $13,600? We'll never know.

I am not sure about happiness, but there is a proven recipe for misery. It's finding whatever you've just bought cheaper somewhere else.

To ensure you are reasonably happy with a deal, once you've concluded it, move on and stop looking for the same item in other shops! This especially applies to products whose prices keep dropping, such as computers and TVs. You will always find it cheaper elsewhere, but that does not mean you got a bad deal *at the time*.

The Buyer's Remorse Avoidance Rule

To be happy after a purchase, once you've bought it, stop looking.

QUICK QUIZ: How special is the "special" price?

You are buying a dishwasher. The model you like is normally priced at $999 in your favourite store (part of a nation-wide chain). In their new specials catalogue it is on sale for $899.

How much do you expect to pay for it?

a) $999, since they always tell you the catalogue price was a misprint or that the catalogue has just expired.

b) $899, they say they cannot reduce the price any further, since it is already on "special".

c) $829, since I am a regular customer and they want my business, while still making some profit on this sale.

STOP & THINK!

a) PESSIMISTIC THINKING. Ask, "If you could sell it at that price three days ago, surely you can sell it today?" Or, ask to speak to the manager. If you get no satisfaction, go to another store. You'd be surprised how different their attitude may be.

b) ORDINARY THINKING. Anybody can walk in and buy at that price. You should be able to do better!

c) WINNING THINKING. Yeah, baby, kick ass!

REAL ESTATE NEGOTIATIONS

If you read personal profiles of the rich, a large percentage of self-made millionaires made their fortunes in real estate. In a booming or appreciating real-estate market, your superior negotiating and deal-making skills can make you quite wealthy, quite quickly.

I remember one participant in my negotiation course in Dubai. Although he lived in Bahrain, he wanted to invest in the booming Dubai market. After the second day of the course he purchased two off-the-plan apartments. The next day he brought the plans and contracts in and proudly showed us all the concessions he got from the developer and all the savings he made.

How to Find and Negotiate Profitable Real-Estate Deals

"Caveat emptor." ("Let the buyer beware.")

Latin proverb

There are two schools of thought when it comes to getting rich in real estate. The common wisdom says you make money when you sell. The "new age" wisdom says you make money when you buy. They claim it is easier to buy low than to sell high. Personally I dislike artificial dualities. You make money both ways - when you buy low *and* when you sell high.

Let's talk for a while about buying low. Of course, the following discourse applies not only to real estate but to anything else people buy or sell.

The easiest way to make fast profits in real estate is to find motivated sellers and get unwanted properties of their hands. Motivated sellers' highest need is to unload their property. Maximising the selling price and making a profit is not high on their list of priorities; urgency is. Selling quickly usually means having to sell low, and the lower they sell it to you, the more profit you will make as a buyer later on, when you sell it to someone else.

The Prosperity Prescription
Buy cheap cars and expensive houses.

Don't Be Scared of Complex, Difficult or Risky Deals

Just as they avoid hard work (physical laziness), many people would do anything to avoid hard thinking (mental laziness). They would happily delegate those unpleasant tasks to their lawyers, advisors, consultants or accountants. There is nothing wrong with such a principle - delegating specialist tasks to specialists is fine, but completely placing your fate in other people's hands is downright stupid.

In negotiation, one consequence of such sloth is the avoidance of complex or risky deals or anything that appears difficult, demanding or dangerous. Deals that scare people off often hide an opportunity for significant profits. Real estate is a very illustrative case.

Neglected or repossessed properties hide quick gains for astute buyers. That crack in the front wall may indicate serious structural problems, so nine-in-ten potential buyers don't even look past it.

Astute investors go beyond appearances and pay $200 or so to a structural engineer to inspect the house. Those $200 plus a small cost of repair could result in $30,000 of profit, if you get the house for a bargain price. After all, that ominously-looking crack in the wall could be many years old, there has been no recent movement or settlement, and the repair is quick and cheap.

Even if it proves to be more serious and you don't proceed with the deal, you could consider the inspection cost a price of an informal training course. You've stayed close to the inspector, asked questions and learned as much as you could. In future, you may be able to accurately asses the structural condition of a property yourself, without paying for such service.

You would think most owners would do the same exercise before they put their house on the market. Surprisingly, many don't. It could be a stingy attitude, or simply the idea never crossed their minds. Or they may be afraid of finding out the unpleasant truth, so they are practising the ostrich strategy. Such indolent attitude will ultimately cost them money, when they sell way below the market value, just to get rid of what they perceive as a "problem property". Their problem, your profit!

The Five Ds: How to Find Motivated Sellers in Real Estate

The first question to ask when buying anything is "Why are they selling?" The next is "Who am I dealing with, a motivated seller or a reluctant seller?" Life is too short to deal with reluctant sellers, it is much easier to get what you want from a motivated seller. The only challenge is to find them!

Who do you ask? Anybody who can shed light on the seller's situation and motivation: agents, relatives, neighbours, friends, even sellers themselves.

There are five main reasons sellers may be in a hurry to sell. These forces are in play when people sell vehicles, equipment, shares (stocks), even businesses. They are debt, doubt, down payment, distance and distress (such as death, disease or divorce).

1.   *Distance:* A homeowner gets transferred and has to sell to buy property in the new location. If an investor, he lives too far from the property; inspections take long time, lots of long-distance

calls, travel expenses, tenant problems. Gradually the out-of-sight-out-of-mind syndrome takes place. True, distance makes hearts grow fonder, but not when it comes to owning and maintaining an investment property in a far away land.

2. *Debt:* The seller has to sell his assets, or the bank may be selling on behalf of the "owner". All the bank wants is to recoup the outstanding debt. As soon as that price is exceeded, the bank will sell. Many speculators and investors made a fortune buying bargain-priced properties at foreclosures and auctions.

3. *Doubt:* Investing is not for the faint-hearted or for the impatient, and many investors are just that. Others are greedy and are never happy with their returns. Or they may have unrealistic expectations, and when those expectations are not met, they want to move on. They doubt property's long term prospects and want to sell. This is where you come in. You are everything they are not: composed, patient and realistic.

4. *Down payment:* The seven-year-itch is an interesting phenomenon. Statistics show that on average, Australian families sell their homes every seven years. The change is often for the change's sake. Bored, people start looking around, find another property, fall in love with it and make on offer subject to sale of their existing property. They now have a limited time to sell (30-60 days), otherwise they will lose the new property. By making a purchasing offer before they've sold their existing property, they have imposed a deadline on themselves and have to negotiate the sale under the dark cloud of urgency.

5. *Distress (Death, Disease or Divorce):* I've lumped these together because they are all fire sales. Maximising the selling price usually isn't one of the sellers' priorities. The property is too big for the surviving spouse, they cannot afford to keep it (asset rich but cash poor), or the owner has large medical or other bills to pay. Time for you to make a low-ball offer.

The Money Myth

Money is not the root of all evil, the lack of money is.

Should You Benefit from Other People's Problems?

"Were it not for the misfortunes of our friends, life would be unbearable."

Francois, duc de la Rochefoucauld, 17th century French author

Some of the situations just described involve unhappiness and suffering, even misery, on part of the sellers. You may ask yourself "Is it right for me to benefit from other people's troubles?" I am not here to pass moral judgement on you, you'll have to decide for yourself.

Most people make a living from other people's ignorance, problems or suffering. Lawyers benefit from individuals and corporations in conflict with the law or with each other. In most cases it does not matter if their client wins or loses - they still get paid. Doctors make their fortunes from the sick and dying, as do undertakers. Handsomely paid management consultants assist companies in dire straits.

If they all prosper due to the troubles and misfortunes of others and don't feel guilty, why should you? Many of these predicaments people find themselves in are self-inflicted. They cannot blame their lawyer or accountant for the troubles they find themselves in as a result of doing something stupid or illegal.

Most of the concepts and strategies that I teach participants in my training courses they could learn by themselves. Yet, they don't. Unwilling or unable to invest time, money and effort in self-study, they prefer someone else to research it for them, package it in a concise yet comprehensive whole, and present it in an entertaining and motivating way. This is where I come in

This book is no different. You could have collated most (but not all) of the information here from various sources, yet it's much easier to read it from a neatly packaged book. Plus, you would miss out on my quirky sense of humour!

WINNING TIPS: WHAT I WISH I KNEW TWENTY YEARS AGO

- Be careful what you ask for; you'll have to pay for it.
- If you are get all you are asking for, you are not asking enough.
- We want different things and in a different order of importance.
- The harder people have to work or negotiate for something, the more they will appreciate it.
- To avoid buyers' remorse, once you buy something, stop looking.
- If unsure, let the other side make the first offer.
- Never accept the first offer.
- There is no such things as a fixed price.
- If selling, provide a package price. If buying, get itemised quotes.
- Buy cheap cars and expensive houses.
- Money is not the root of all evil, the lack of money is.

Rushed No More!

USE TIME & TIMING TO YOUR ADVANTAGE

Negotiation is a dynamic process. It has its speed and momentum, milestones and deadlines. Things need to be rushed through or delayed. Time is usually of essence, so an accurate sense of time and timing is crucial.

Coming up:

- How to negotiate with multiple parties
- What to do when the other side is stalling the deal
- How to keep the negotiating momentum going
- How to use deadlines wisely

TIME AND TIMING IN NEGOTIATION

Be Patient: Don't Expect Too Much, Too Soon

"Dear God, I pray for patience. And I want it right now."

Oren Arnold, writer and editor

When it comes to the pace of negotiations, we assume steady progress and continuous achievement of goals. Nothing can be further from the truth! The time has come to look at the Italian job.

Vilfredo Pareto (1848-1923) was an Italian economist who concluded that the distribution of wealth in the Italian society at the time followed a logarithmic formula. This has been popularised as a claim that 80 percent of wealth is in the hands of 20 percent of people (the affluent). Pareto's principle (also called the 80/20 rule) has since gained universal popularity due to its validity in other situations.

In time management, we spend 80 percent of our time on insignificant issues and activities, those contributing only 20 percent to the desired results, while devoting only 20 percent of the time to the significant tasks that bring about 80 percent of our income or results.

In negotiations, we tend to spend 80 percent of the time discussing the 20 percent of issues (the critical aspects of the deal). The negotiating pace also follows the rule: 80 percent of issues on the agenda are usually resolved and agreed upon in the last 20 percent of time allocated for a negotiation (before the deadline).

The 80/20 Rule (Pareto's Principle) in negotiation

80% of issues will be resolved in the last 20% of the allocated time!

Buy Time: If in Doubt, Delay

"Time and I against any two."

Spanish proverb

From the days of Spartacus and Attila The Hun, to modern day corporate battles, the element of surprise has been attackers' best ally. However, it is possible to defend yourself against the shock and awe ploy. Delaying and time-buying tactics are the most efficient weapons against being pressured into making a decision on the spot.

Don't allow the other side to push you into making a negotiating move you will later regret. Leave yourself plenty of time. Have as few deadlines as practical and make your arrangements as flexible as possible. Obviously, this is the main benefit of proper planning and thorough preparation.

Only shallow, impulsive or over-confident people make important decisions on the spot. You don't want to be seen as shallow or impulsive, do you?

Delay is the cruellest form of denial.

The best way to condition the other negotiator not to expect instant decisions and commitments from you, is to use the following phrase: "What you are proposing is very interesting and deserves a careful consideration. Let me look into it and get back to you with my answer."

TIP	DELAY IS JUSTIFIED WHEN:
	■ the environment (interest rates, exchange rates, commodity prices, technology) is changing rapidly.
	■ you need more information or more preparation.
	■ you have to think about the proposal or consider your options.
	■ you are in a sub-optimal emotional or physical state - hungry, tired, jet-lagged, ill, horny, confused, depressed or stressed out.
	■ a low priority deal is delayed in favour of a higher priority deal.
	■ you have to consult with your team, stakeholders or superiors.
	■ the balance of power is shifting in your favour.

Sleep On It!

> "Give yourself time and room; what reason could not avoid,
> delay has often cured"
>
> Seneca, Roman philosopher and statesman

When you name you price outright, you take a significant risk. If you are asking for much more than the other side is expecting to pay, they may walk away. If your price is lower than what the buyer is prepared to pay, you are depriving yourself of additional income.

"Sleep on it" is a "nice & easy" alternative, a simple, yet powerful way of naming your price without committing to a specific figure. "For this type of service, other clients budget from $35,000 to $45,000, depending on the exact scope of the work. How does that sound?" You are probing by dropping a couple of anchors using a third party reference.

Of course, even the lowest figure mentioned is higher than the price you really want on this deal - leave yourself plenty of room. If they object, don't push for an immediate YES or NO. Ask them to sleep on it and think about it. That will give them time to get used to your proposed price.

Beware of pushing the other side to give you an instant answer, because in most cases the answer will be NO!

When Others are Stalling the Deal

"Delay always breeds danger
and to protract a great design is often to ruin it."
Miguel de Cervantes Saavedra, author of 'Don Quixote'

You've talked and you've listened; you've made offers and counter-offers; you've traded concessions. At the end, the other side told you to leave it with them. They will think about it, pass it onto their management for approval, consult with the project owner, consider wider implications ...

... and that was the last you have heard from them. Now, you worry. You want the deal. Why are they stalling? The first thought enters your mind: "They are intimidating me, playing hard to get. They want me to call and appear desperate. Well, I am, but I don't want them to know that!"

You could be right, many negotiators use delay as a weapon of intimidation. In this kind of impasse, the first person who makes contact displays neediness and loses power. Or, are you just a bit paranoid? There are other equally plausible reasons for their silence and lack of contact. Let me suggest a few:

- *They may be busy.* Your project or deal is not high on their priority list so it is sitting in the "Non-urgent" basket.
- *They've forgotten all about it.* Faced with another urgent, "drop all" issue, project or deal, they have simply forgotten about it.
- *Lingering in limbo.* Your contact is on a holiday or has left the company and forgot to hand your deal over to his replacement.
- *Inter-office black hole.* Your proposal got lost in-between various desks. The number of handlers, minders and approvers increases proportionally with the deal's importance and the size of the organisation.
- *They may be shopping around.* After eliciting your bottom line, they are now negotiating with your competitors, using your offer as an intimidation tool to get better terms. Or, they simply need this time to think it over, to consider their options and to devise their immediate strategy.
- *An intervention from above.* I'm not taking about the so called "Acts of God" (or force majeure, lat.), although those things happen, too. I'm talking about your counterpart's boss, or his boss' boss. Someone higher up has either killed the deal or the boss is stalling, possibly playing some political game. Either way, your negotiating counterpart doesn't know how to break the bad news to you and is therefore avoiding you.

HOW TO MANAGE THE NEGOTIATING MOMENTUM

Sequential or Simultaneous Negotiations? Choose Wisely!

Imagine you are buying a high priced item such as a car or a house. Or, perhaps you are negotiating with consulting companies who are bidding on your engineering or construction project. How would you sequence your negotiations?

Would you talk to the most promising supplier first, then move to the next best option if there is no agreement? Or would you keep all your options open and negotiate with all of them concurrently?

Proponents of the sequential approach advocate its efficiency and simplicity. You only negotiate with one party at a time, therefore saving time, effort and costs involved.

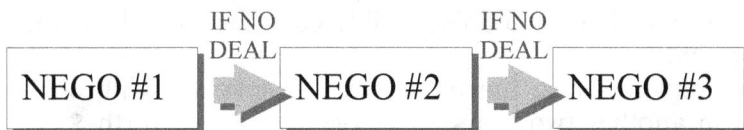

SEQUENTIAL NEGOTIATIONS

Advocates of the simultaneous approach argue that by negotiating with only one party we unnecessarily limit our options. Although the first option looks most promising after the initial evaluation of offers or proposals, it is possible that another party (not our first choice) could prove to be more flexible in negotiation and give us a better deal at the end. Had we concluded the deal with party #1 we would never know.

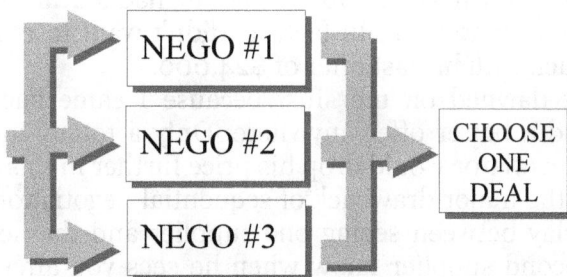

SIMULTANEOUS NEGOTIATIONS

Can you identify any disadvantages of the simultaneous approach? Imagine spending two months negotiating with all three bidders, without them knowing about one another. They are all investing a lot into these negotiations. Finally, you reveal you have been "courting" the other suppliers as well and that only one of them is getting the business. The two unsuccessful contenders won't be very happy, that's for sure. All their investment will go to waste.

It would only be fair to let them know that you will conduct multiple simultaneous negotiations. If one or more want to pull out of such arrangement, that is their choice.

Of course, we used three competitors in this example - negotiating with five or six suppliers is quite common on large deals.

Sometimes You Have to Make Decisions on the Spot!

I remember very well one of my car purchases. The dealer had three identical demonstrator vehicles, all six months old and with about 9,000 km on the odometer. New, they cost $36,000. The sticker price was $29,990.

I liked the car, but kept saying to the dealer that my budget was $20,000 and that I couldn't possibly pay more. I lied - I could, but I didn't want to[10].

He kept lowering the price and I just kept saying no. He even threw in another two years of factory warranty (worth $2,000) and stopped at $24,000.

I was in a dilemma. I hadn't considered that model, and did not have any feeling how much it was worth on the market. One of the prudent negotiating rules says if you haven't done your research on what you are buying, you should not make a decision on the spot. Walk away, do your research and if the offer is still better than the alternatives, come back.

That's exactly what I did. The next day I visited all other Toyota dealers in Perth, and nobody could match that deal.

So, I came back, hinting I was ready to negotiate. If he was prepared to come down to $22,000, I said, he had a deal. Well, he wasn't prepared to do that at all. In fact, he didn't want to move one single cent and stuck with his last offer of $24,000.

Then, it dawned on me. Just because I came back, he knew I couldn't find a better offer anywhere. Only a totally incompetent or desperate negotiator would drop his price further in this situation.

This is the major drawback of sequential negotiation: the inevitable time delay between seeing one supplier and the next one. What does the second supplier know when he sees you after a week, or a month? That you couldn't agree with the first supplier, and that now he is your best bet. You are in a weak position here.

Between the two, I prefer the simultaneous way. Keep your options open. Let them invest their time and effort into the deal; that should strengthen your position even further.

[10]Don't feel guilty lying to car dealers, real estate agents or politicians. They lie to you with impunity and don't feel a slightest remorse!

The Investment Quagmire

The more time, money and effort they invest in negotiating with you, the harder it will be for them to walk away from the deal.

Play by Your Own Rules

"The young man knows the rules, but the old man knows the exceptions."

Oliver Wendell Holmes, American physician, academic and author

The morale of the car-buying story is that rules should sometimes be broken. Perhaps, had I continued to negotiate during the first visit, without walking away, he would have dropped his price further and we would have concluded the deal there and then. By walking away and then coming back, I implicitly told him he was my best option and I paid the price.

Although I call them negotiation rules, in reality they are just guidelines that may or may not be followed. Deciding if, how and when to break a rule is a crucial life skill.

Rule-making as the ultimate level of mastery

Poor negotiators always follow the rules; mediocre negotiators decide when to break them; master negotiators make the rules.

Go First and Go Strong

"When they say you're ahead of your time, it's just a polite way of saying you have a real bad sense of timing."

George McGovern, historian, author, U.S. politician

There are two ways to manage the process of negotiation. The first I call "one-step-ahead". The proactive negotiators go first and go strong. They believe the best way to control the direction, flow and timing of a negotiation is by presenting their proposal first.

When you put an option on the table first, you anchor the negotiation at a particular point that suits your interests. You frame the negotiation by presenting your case in the way that serves your purpose best.

The other person is thus lead down the path you have mapped and charted. He or she now has to deal with the situation defined by your framework and is following your initiative. They now have to justify themselves to you if they don't like something you are proposing.

This will make them appear defensive, perhaps even recalcitrant or unreasonable. Since they have to find and rationalise the negatives in your proposal, it is much easier for you to hold the moral high ground. Now they not only have to disprove the merits of your claim or proposal but to present a counter-offer.

However, there are also difficulties in using this approach. It requires a well-prepared plan and an even better execution. Just as in warfare, defending is easier than attacking. That is why "one-step-ahead" strategy requires special skill and aptitude.

Just as playing chess is based on the ability to determine the opponent's intentions and predict his next moves, the "one-step-ahead" strategy is about predicting how the whole negotiating process will play itself out. When you are one step ahead, the other negotiator is relegated to playing a constant catch-up with you.

The One Step Ahead Principle: Success by Design

> "I skate to where the puck is going to be, not to where it has been."
>
> Wayne Gretzky, ice hockey player

During my university days the prevalent "wisdom" was to attend lectures but to study only a week or so before the exam. Gallons of coffee would flow, little sleep would happen and formulas and concepts would be memorised, although seldom fully understood. Later I noticed that people approached negotiations and projects in the same, haphazard manner, madly rushing towards the end.

My approach was different. By studying a few hours every day, from the very start of the semester, come the exam time, I would be ready. Then I discovered an even more powerful technique. The key to success was to study *before* each lecture, not *after*!

I would read about the upcoming subject in textbooks before the next class. While others were hearing the material for the first time, and could not tell what was important and what was not, I would focus on the few points I didn't fully understand. If the lecturer failed to explain them properly, I would ask for a clarification.

I quickly built a reputation for myself. Imagine if somebody asked you a smart question or two at every lecture. Would you remember them? Of course you would.

Apart from written tests, we also had to pass verbal exams. Some professors would pass me as soon as I stepped into their office! I had already demonstrated how much I knew by my questions during the semester, plus many of the academics considered exams a gross waste of their valuable time. What better way to save time than to pass or fail students as quickly as possible?

The One-Step-Ahead Principle

Being one step ahead of your counterpart is usually enough for you to control the negotiation.

The same approach could be used in project management, problem solving and negotiations. Being one-step-ahead of others will bring you just that needed bit of an advantage.

The "Lesser Fool Theory": Success by Default

"Eighty percent of success is showing up."

Woody Allen, writer, actor and film director

Remember the scene from the movie "Forrest Gump" when dumb Forrest and not-so-dumb Captain Dan go shrimping? Day after day they catch nothing and return dejected, utter losers. Then, one day, a typhoon wipes out their competitors' entire fleet. From that day on, Forrest and Dan return with a huge catch every time and make a fortune in shrimping.

This would be a bit far fetched, but otherwise plausible example of success-by-default. Forrest and Dan did nothing different, better or smarter. They simply managed to get their boat to survive the storm, while all their competitors didn't.

The "one step ahead" is an example of success-by-design while "playing hard to get" illustrates success-by-default, a passive, patient, let's-see-if-I-can-outlast-you approach. You overtake the competition by making less blunders and damaging mistakes. In many industries the major players are not particularly smart, innovative or resourceful. They succeeded primarily because they've made less dumb mistakes then their competitors.

The Lesser Fool Theory

It isn't always necessary to do everything right. Just making less dumb mistakes than your opponent may be enough for you to win.

Start With Mutually Agreeable Issues

A question I get asked most often is about the order in which we should negotiate a deal. Should we start with small, easily agreeable items, or with significant, usually conflicting aspects of the deal?

When you start with difficult issues, what do you get back? NOs. NO, we aren't happy with that. NO, this is way above our budget. NO, we need it urgently, we cannot wait that long. The whole negotiation starts on the wrong footing and stalls pretty much immediately.

Avoid opening a negotiation with important issues, those likely to be disputed or that can lead to an early conflict or a stalemate. This is a typical mistake of inexperienced, eager-beaver rookie negotiators. Instead, get the negotiation rolling by picking the low hanging fruit - small agreements that positively frame the negotiating momentum. Start at the bottom of your list of priorities, where the easy issues are likely to be found. Get some initial YESes under your belt.

Pick the low hanging fruit

Secure agreement on easy issues first. Start your negotiation with common interests and easily agreed upon items.

Of course, sooner or later you will get your first NO, but you have already established some positive track record, so you can use it as a momentum-booster: "John, we have agreed on so many issues so far, it would be a pity to get stuck on this one item!"

YES, YES, YES, YES, NO, ... is better than NO, NO, NO, NO, YES. With so many initial NOs, you may never get to that first YES!

USE DEADLINES WISELY

The Impact of Deadlines on Negotiators' Behaviour

> "I love deadlines.
> I like the whooshing sound they make as they fly by."
> Douglas Adams, author of *The Hitchhiker's Guide to the Galaxy*

What do you do when time is running short and when imminent deadlines loom? Some say crises, emergencies and deadlines bring out the best in negotiators, while others say they bring out the worst. What do you think?

Deadlines time-frame the negotiation by giving negotiators a temporal goal to aim for. Research shows that deadlines have a significant impact on the progress and momentum of negotiations. As we have seen in Pareto's Principle, most agreements are reached just before the time allocated for negotiations runs out.

So, if you desire a speedy conclusion of your negotiation and have any control of the deadline, bring it as much forward as possible.

The Shorter, The Sweeter Rule

Myth: Good deals take time to negotiate.
Reality: Protracted negotiations result in compromised outcomes.

Some deadlines are real, meaning they will happen no matter what, others are man-made. These arbitrary deadlines are determined by the negotiating parties and not by the events and developments. When you proclaim that you have to buy that new big plasma TV before your big party on Saturday evening, that is an arbitrary deadline. It is self-imposed and entirely within your control.

Imminent deadlines are those outside negotiators' control. A trade minister from one political party continues negotiating with his foreign counterpart after the election his party just lost. Both ministers know that there will be an imminent change of government, and if the deal is not concluded by then, the negotiation will probably have to be restarted with his successor. That is the nature of the political beast. Many deals that the previous government had in the negotiating and ratifying pipeline will be scrapped while others will be significantly changed.

TACTICS: Fait Accompli

> "This is like déjà vu all over again."
>
> "Yogi" Berra[11]

Deadlines are a two-edged sword. They may help you, work in your favour, or they may hinder your progress and work against you. We too often underestimate the time and effort needed to reach a deal and don't allow ourselves enough time to engineer the best deal possible.

On one project I managed a long time ago, approvals were required from various stakeholders. By the time I got everything signed, the whole project was three weeks late. The paperwork sat on various desks and in-trays for weeks!

I only had three days left to select the consulting company to do the engineering design or the whole project plan would have to be changed. That would again require top management approval, since any change would impact the schedule, including the plant shutdown timing.

Between two unpalatable choices, I went for one that minimised my further dealings with upper management. Other people's tardiness and incompetence limit the quality of your own performance.

TIME & TIMING TACTICS: Done Deal

Supplier: "I am pleased to tell you that we have already delivered the equipment to your plant. Our engineers are setting it up with your operators right now. By working over the weekend we've saved you a considerable time, so you can start production by the end of the week. Here is the invoice!"

The supplier realised that time was critical for the buyer and did his best to deliver, install and commission the equipment before the deadline.

We have no information on the contractual side of the whole deal. Perhaps there was a purchase order, or even a formal contract, but, due to the urgency of the whole purchase, it is equally likely that the final price and various charges have not been discussed, let alone approved by the customer.

Now, the supplier is saying: "We did the right thing by you, (worked over the weekend, paid our workers overtime, rescheduled other commitments), now you do the right thing by us!" Meaning, sign the invoice and pay the full amount without haggling.

Fait accompli is a powerful tactics and there isn't much that the buyer

---

[11]Lawrence Peter "Yogi" Berra, born 1925, a former American Major League Baseball player and manager, also known for his tautologic witticisms, known as Yogiisms.

can do. Sure, if there was no prior agreement, the buyer has the legal right to reject the delivered equipment and to ask the supplier to take it back. But, the buyer needs it very soon and hasn't got enough time to negotiate with other suppliers.

One mistake - failure to allow enough time for the purchase and installation of equipment - was enough to put the buyer in a weak position. With an imminent deadline looming and a lack of other options, the buyer is now forced to accept seller's terms.

WINNING TIPS: WHAT I WISH I KNEW TWENTY YEARS AGO

- Decide up-front if sequential or simultaneous negotiations would be more advantageous to you.
- Secure agreement on easy issues first. Start your negotiations with common interests and easily agreed upon items.
- Poor negotiators follow the rules; mediocre negotiators decide when to follow them and when to break them; master negotiators make the rules.
- Being one-step-ahead of your counterpart is usually enough to control a negotiation.
- It's not necessary to do everything right. Making less dumb mistakes than your opponent may be enough for you to win.
- The more time, money or effort invested in a deal, the harder it is to walk away from it.

Afraid No More!

MANAGE YOUR FEARS AND MITIGATE RISKS

Every decision you make as a negotiator should include some form of risk assessment. Questions such as "What can go wrong?" and "What should I do to prevent it from happening?" should always be on your mind.

Coming up:

- Control your fears and capitalise on them, instead of allowing your fears to control you
- How to deal with silence
- How to minimise risks and safeguard your sanity

WHAT ARE WE AFRAID OF IN NEGOTIATION?

"Humility is a virtue; timidity is a disease."

Jim Rohn

Fear is a shadow of every negotiator. It clouds judgement and inhibits action. Negotiations are emotionally-charged encounters, and as such naturally involve various degrees of fear. You may be afraid of saying something you shouldn't, of violating some unspoken rule or offending the other side. The other person may be afraid of commitment, of being cheated or failing in the eyes of those whose interest he represents - boss, spouse or clients.

The Fear of Unknown

"No passion so effectually robs the mind
of all its powers of acting and reasoning as fear."

Edmund Burke, *The Origin of Our Ideas of the Sublime and Beautiful*

The fear of unknown is the mother of all fears in negotiation. This is especially so in situations where negotiators don't know each other well or at all. As an umbrella concept, the fear of unknown includes the fear of unpleasantness or conflict, and the fear of loss. We may lose more than money, the loss may be psychological, such as the loss of face or confidence, or professional (losing confidence your clients or your boss have in you, as a professional or a team player).

The fear of unknown is best overcome through experience. The more you negotiate with various people and in various situations, the more you will realise that the fear of unknown is like the fear of dark many kids feel. You are not actually afraid of the dark, but of what your imagination suggests could be lurking in the dark. Just like most fears, the fear of unknown is seldom realised.

The Fear of Intimacy

Intimacy is the deepest level of communication between two people. We are not talking about physical but psychological intimacy here, getting to know the other person's thoughts, fears, ambitions, values and preferences.

You may be intimate with your work colleague or a boss. When negotiating in a business setting you don't have to excuse yourself to the other party, so you can discuss the proposal with your boss or team mate. One look at him and you will instantly know if he likes the proposal or not. That is psychological intimacy. You know how he thinks, what he values, likes and dislikes.

When we negotiate, we express our opinions, demonstrate our personalities, disclose lots of personal, sensitive and important information about ourselves to those we negotiate with. Such disclosure could be unsettling. The "inner you" feels vulnerable, exposed. We fear that the other side may use such knowledge of our soft spots to our detriment.

Indeed, the more you deal with a person or a company, the more they will get to know about you, but the more you will learn about them, too. Disclosure is seldom a one way only affair.

Reading people's minds would be a sort of instant intimacy. Would you like to be able to read other people's minds? I often pose this hypothetical question to participants in my seminars.

Initially, they say they would, for it would bring them a huge advantage in negotiation and any interpersonal dealings. However, when I add that others would be able to read your mind, too, their enthusiasm wanes. What would be the eventual outcome of such a situation? I predict that everybody would end up hating everybody else, for as soon as someone had a negative thought about us, we would take it personally and hold it against that person. Perhaps our inability to read other people's minds is a natural protection of our most intimate core.

The Fear of Silence

> "The tree of silence bears the fruit of peace."
>
> Arabian proverb

Remember Roger, our archetype of a good, decent negotiator, but one who nevertheless loses much more often then he wins? Well, Roger may be a quiet, unassuming rabbit, but he is also afraid of silence.

You would think that only talkative people cannot stand those pregnant pauses during negotiation. Many quiet people cannot deal effectively with silence either. Roger somehow confused silence with deadlock or impasse, a situation when negotiation doesn't move either way and parties are unwilling to budge from their last stated positions. Roger fears the prospect of a deadlock and would do anything to get the negotiation rolling again.

🕸 TRICKY TRAP: Silence is golden

Roger: "Well, to summarise, our best offer based on your specified quantity is $1,249 per unit."

Foxy says nothing, stares at Roger with his shifty eyes.

Five seconds later, although to him it seemed more like five minutes, Roger starts talking again:

Roger: "Look, Mr Foxy, I understand, the price does seem a bit high, but the value is definitely there, it includes all the features you've requested and confirms to all your specifications."

> Foxy is still silent, staring at the rabbit.
>
> Roger (his coolness gone, his whiskers trembling): "Well, if you are unhappy with the price, let me talk to my boss, I'm sure he can sweeten the deal with a discount. How does that sound?"

Roger made a common mistake. He made an offer, but then started talking again, hinting that his boss may make further concessions. In a sense, he negotiated on Foxy's behalf, against himself.

How to Deal With Silent Treatment

> "Drawing on my fine command of the English language, I said nothing."
>
> Robert Benchley, columnist, author, actor

The best antidote to silent treatment is to wait without offering any concessions while the silence continues. De-centering makes the wait more bearable. Don't look at the other negotiator - focus on a object or an activity instead. Inspect your nails, your shoes, your mobile phone, or the intricacies of your ball point pen. If you find these silly, here are some more constructive options:

- *Take notes.* Make your offer, shut up and start writing in your diary. They don't have to be genuine notes, you can just doodle, providing your counterpart cannot see it. This will arouse their curiosity and may make them start talking again.
- *Go get a drink.* Say something like "While you are thinking about it, let me get a coffee. Would you like one, too?"
- *Sip your drink.* When you return, if they are still silent, your job was just made easier. Now you have a prop to focus on for ten or fifteen minutes. You will definitely outlast their silence!
- *Ask neutral questions.* "Is there anything that I can clarify for you?" or "Have you got any comments or suggestions?"
- *Avoid negative questions or comments that may hand the initiative to the other person,* such as "Is there anything in my proposal you are unhappy with?" It makes you seem unsure in what you are proposing and invites a complaint, a negative comment or a demand for you to improve on your offer.

Confront Your Fears

> "I'm very brave generally," he went on in a low voice:
> "only today I happen to have a headache."
>
> Tweedledum, in *Through the Looking-Glass* by Lewis Carroll

Some of us were born brave, others will have to learn to be brave. Many start pretending to be brave; they act the way they see brave men act. They fake it until they make it. Bravery can be learned and practised.

No matter what you are afraid of and how likely your fears are to materialise, the trick is not to ignore fear or fight it, but to channel it into productive actions. Personally, I've used ambition to overpower my fears. It worked for me and it can work for you too.

The Fear Busting Principle
_____

Make your desire for success bigger than your fears.
_____

People often ask me how come I'm not afraid of or uncomfortable speaking in public, especially knowing that English is not my native language.

I tell them that once I remind myself how handsomely I'm being paid for my talks, all my fears disappear and all those butterflies in my stomach start flying in a beautiful formation! Using greed and fear to fight it out? Why not? No matter how strange it may sound, two wrongs sometimes do make a right!

The F.E.A.R. exercise

Choose a reasonable period of time, a month or two will do. Whenever you are afraid of something, write it down in your journal or notebook. It doesn't have to be related to your negotiations, write down *everything* you feel afraid of or apprehensive about.

Then, at the end of your chosen period, go back to your list and mark all the fears and concerns that actually happened.

I'd bet that very few of your fears ever materialised. Most of us worry excessively and unnecessarily. Remember, F.E.A.R. is an acronym for "False Expectations Appearing Real".

Help Others Overcome Their Fears and Reservations

"You can discover what your enemy fears most
by observing the means he uses to frighten you."

Eric Hoffer, writer and philosopher

Knowing how to deal with your fears is only a half of your worries. The other half is finding out what people you deal with are afraid of. You will not be able to successfully negotiate with others or persuade them to see things your way until you determine why they are reluctant to accept your proposal or an idea.

In other words, behind every objection or other symptom of resistance, there is a root cause, an underlying fear or concern. To address objections and to overcome resistance, you need to allay this underlying fear.

175

RISK MINIMISATION STRATEGIES

Risk Has a Price

"When you go in search of honey you must expect to be stung by bees."

Kenneth Kaunda, Zambian leader, first president

The first step in my dealings with prospective clients in my training and consulting business is to understand their business and then discuss their training or consulting needs. Then we submit a formal proposal, including the estimate of the costing.

Some clients, mostly large corporations, want a formal contract to be signed. The contract is always drafted by their contract department and contains numerous clauses that clearly pass the risk to us, the service provider.

When I object, they usually refuse to remove the most troublesome clauses (to us), while conceding on the ones they don't consider important (to them). If I want the business I accept the contract document, including the offending clauses, but increase the price of our services, to reflect the risk.

Inevitably, the client is unhappy with the price hike. I then have to explain that the more points they include in the contract the higher our price gets. They want to win on all the points and to get the cheapest price possible. So, I give them a choice: remove the contractual points in dispute and keep the old package with (cheaper) price, or keep the points in the contract (new package) but accept the higher price.

The Package (Points) - Price Rule

Don't let them win on both the package (points) and the price. Smaller package (less service) or less risky points - lower price. Larger package (more service) or more risky points - higher price.

How to Avoid Last Minute Disasters

"Have faith in Allah, but tie your camel regardless."

Arabian proverb

Many years ago, when I was starting in the seminar business, I flew to Brisbane late on a Wednesday evening and reached my hotel about 9 PM. A conference room in the same hotel was booked for my seminar by the training organiser.

After the unpacking, ironing of the shirts, and a quick shower, I retired for the night. Gradually, a feeling of unease started to descend on me. Intuition, premonition, sixth sense, call it what you will. I got up, got dressed and decided to go and inspect the conference room.

The surprise I got was an unpleasant one. The room was too small to accommodate twenty or so participants, it had no natural light (no windows of any kind) and its shape was irregular. As if that wasn't enough, it had two distinctive features. There was a bar in one corner, which was very distracting, but maybe it wasn't such a bad idea after all. If participants got bored they could knock down a few stiff ones and the spirit of learning would be rejuvenated.

More importantly, there was also a huge round pillar, positioned right in the middle of the room, probably by some hallucinating architect high on drugs. It was in the very spot where the laptop and projector table had to be, a few meters from the projector screen. In other words, the room was totally unsuitable for my purpose.

I also noticed that at 10.30 PM on the eve of the seminar, the room was totally empty - it hadn't been set-up for the event. How was that for "just-in-time" management?

I had a problem on my hands. Booking the venue and inspecting it were not my responsibilities. That was the job of locally based employees of the training company that organised the seminar. Obviously, they didn't do their job properly, or not at all. I doubt they would have chosen that particular room had they bothered to inspect it in person. As it happens, other people's problems become your problems when they start impacting your performance.

The Problem Ownership Paradox

Problems created by others become your problems when they start impacting your performance or hurting your interests.

How did I negotiate my way out of this mess? Well, the hotel had only two conference rooms. This lousy half-storeroom, half-cocktail-party joint, and a nice, big, airy, all glass penthouse conference room which could accommodate 30 or so people in a U-shaped seating arrangement. That penthouse was exactly what the doctor ordered and would have made me very happy.

However, just as it happens with other desirable things such as beautiful women, plum jobs and free parking spaces, this penthouse was already taken. In fact, by sheer coincidence[12], the client who booked the penthouse for his one-day sales meeting, was inspecting it the very moment the manager and I walked in.

After some inquiries on my part and my insistence that the manager checks his booking sheet, for there must had been a mistake, for this was obviously my room, the unexpected happened. The other client, noticing my profuse sweating, a generally unhappy facial expression and a dangerous twitch in my right eye simply said: "No worries, mate! We only have eight people anyway, why don't you take this room and we will use yours!"

[12]Or providence?

I could not believe my luck. I went to bed hoping that he doesn't go and have a look at the room from Hell and that he doesn't change his mind. He didn't. Don't you just love those easy going Aussies?

In the years that followed, I have faced a whole repertoire of mis-understandings, crossed communications, wrong bookings, missing materials, improbable coincidences and numerous other setbacks that would make even a perfectly normal, rational and relatively sane seminar presenter into a nervous wreck.

Luckily, I haven't gone go crazy (yet!), I just seasoned a bit. Now my New Self assumes nothing and checks everything! What I call "The Paranoid Presenter's Prescription" doesn't only apply to seminar rooms. I found it of immense value in any endeavour, project or nego-tiation. Remember it well and practice it diligently. It will keep prob-lems of your back and save you from lots of grief.

The Paranoid Presenter's Prescription

It is better to be paranoid than sorry.

✓ CHECKLIST: How to Demand and Get Satisfaction

To make "The Paranoid Presenter's Prescription' more user friendly, I have expanded it into a checklist for you:

1. Trust your intuition. If something doesn't feel right, it most likely isn't.

2. Never assume that you were understood or that your instruc-tions have been followed. In fact, assume nothing.

3. Arrive early. Check everything immediately and thoroughly.

4. If there is a problem, describe it without blaming or lecturing. Get the other party to agree that there is a problem.

5. Ask for an immediate and specific remedy.

6. Persist. Don't go away until you see the problem fully rectified.

7. Use the Nice & Easy way. Be nice to people involved. When you are in trouble, you need them more than they need you.

When Enough is Enough

"First they ignore you. Then they laugh at you.
Then they fight you. Then you win."

Mahatma Gandhi

Early in my training career I run a series of public courses for a major Australian training provider. The events were well received and al-most fully booked, meaning the organiser made lots of profit.

A few months later, I received their brochure promoting a series of courses with the same name (my course's name), but by another presenter. I got suspicious and asked to see the course materials, which they, surprisingly, promptly mailed to me. Surely enough, about 25 percent of the material was taken verbatim from either my book or from my course manual.

I sent them a "please explain" e-mail, and was given some lame excuse, blaming the manager in charge of training (the guy I negotiated the contract with), who had left the company in the meantime. How convenient.

After briefly considering legal action, I decided against it. Proving financial loss as a result of their actions would had been almost impossible. At that time I was presenting courses on a part-time basis only, and the amounts in question did not warrant any investment in legal fees. Plus, they had their in-house lawyers and the whole litigation would have been too risky for me.

So, I asked them to remove the stolen material and, once done, to send me a copy of the revised course manual, which they did.

I considered that a valuable lesson for the future. My title was not trade-marked, so they could use it with impunity. But by then proceeding to steal my content as well, they crossed the line.

The Enough Is Enough Rule
You can't prevent others from shitting on you, but you should under no circumstances allow them to rub your nose in it.

No matter how tight and detailed contract you may have, don't rely on it for protection. If somebody wants to shaft you, no contract will protect you.

By the same token, with people who can be trusted, no contract is necessary. They will do the right thing by you anyway, so there is no need to waste time, money and effort in drafting a water-tight agreement. The only problem in life is to know who is who.

Contracts are next to useless
You don't need them with people you can trust, and they won't protect you from those who want to shaft you.

✖ RISK MITIGATION: Watch and Listen for the Warning Signs

Things rarely just go wrong suddenly and without warning, and this case was no different. Going back to my dealings with the training organisation that stole my title and 25% of my material, I recall that early in that negotiation, my counterpart asked for the ownership of the course. " It is our policy to own all the courses we market!" he said. I politely refused to even discuss the possibility. Would you just

179

give your intellectual property away, after all your years of experience and months of effort that went into its design? I was neither stupid nor desperate, so they removed the offending clause from the contract.

That was the crucial warning sign I'd overlooked. They didn't give up their ambitions, and in the end achieved the same goal by more devious means.

I still had a full-time job at the time and my availability to run in-house courses was very limited, especially not at a short notice. They used that as a pretext to get another consultant to present my course on a temporary basis, under a licence. Finally, they bypassed me completely by getting him to quickly put together his materials (of which, as I said, about a quarter was actually mine), so they wouldn't even have to pay me the licensing fees.

Things rarely just go wrong suddenly; usually there are warning signs along the way. Keep your eyes and ears open.

☹☹ The Risk of a Lose - Lose Outcome

"War: first, one hopes to win; then one expects the enemy to lose;
then, one is satisfied that he too is suffering;
in the end, one is surprised that everyone has lost."

Karl Kraus, Austrian writer and journalist

As negotiators focus on that elusive dream of "win-win", they often overlook the ultimate risk in any negotiation - the prospect of both sides losing on a deal. Win-lose sounds plausible and makes intuitive sense, but when I ask participants in my seminars to consider all possible negotiating outcomes, "lose-lose" seldom comes to people's minds. How is the heartbreak of "lose-lose" possible?

A sub-optimal deal is reached. If you haven't done your homework properly and you've failed to identify that you did have a better option somewhere else, then any deal you reach will be a sub-optimal deal. You would have missed the opportunity to maximise your gain. If that happens to both parties and the deal is concluded, such a deal could be seen as a "lose-lose" outcome.

There is no deal when there should be one. Due to intransigence and lack of flexibility, there is no deal, although a compromise would be the best option for both parties. This is what usually happens when two stubborn people negotiate. Once each side is entrenched in their position, and convinced they are right and the other person is wrong, it is almost impossible to break such stalemate or impasse. As a result, both walk away with nothing.

There is a deal when there should not be one. This usually happens for two reasons. The first reason we've already discussed. A sub-optimal deal means that both parties had a better alternative somewhere else.

Secondly, when negotiators invest lot of time, money and effort into clinching a deal, the more they invest, the more reluctant they are to walk away. So, the investment biases their attitude towards the deal, and even if it is a sub-optimal deal, they still want to conclude it, just so they can show something for all those efforts. Walking away with nothing and starting the whole ordeal all over again with someone else is a hard thing to do.

🛠 RISK MITIGATION: Keep Your Guard Up at All Times

A loose tongue has probably killed more deals than any other mistake negotiators make. A casual remark in an elevator or a hotel's toilet may be enough for the other party to figure out what's really going on. What if they don't understand our language, you may ask? Simple: behave as if they do. Do not let your guard down, someone is bound to speak your language.

COMMUNICATION CASE: The language advantage

During one of my negotiating courses, a commercial negotiator for a large Saudi Arabian oil & gas producer, told us about a project negotiation with a Japanese engineering team. While the actual negotiation was in English, both teams spoke amongst themselves in their native tongues, often in front the other team.

The crucial advantage to the Saudis came from the fact that one of their negotiators understood Japanese, but concealed the fact from the Japanese team who didn't even consider such a possibility. How likely was it for an Arab engineer to speak Japanese? Not very likely at all, but one did understand enough of it to gain a significant advantage.

🛠 RISK MITIGATION: No Sex or Alcohol, I'm a Negotiator!

A favourite hospitality tactics of many nationalities is certainly "get them drunk and listen carefully." It is based on the ancient Latin saying "in vino veritas", truth is in the wine. Less cautious negotiators, even some professional deal-makers, fall surprisingly easily for this ploy.

When alcohol starts flowing, it is amazing how quickly all the caution is thrown away and how easily crucial details and sensitive information are blurted out.

The Drunk & Horny Trap

"In Vino Veritas" + the Mata Hari Effect = Disaster

I remember an interesting radio interview with a former high ranking Australian intelligence officer. She claimed that good looking, seductive women were the most valuable spies[13] because they were the most effective in extracting secret information from men. She didn't say if she was speaking from her personal experience, but her claim sounded plausible.

Many social and business situations involve both alcohol and women - a lethal mix, a double-dose of the truth serum. Hormones are tough enemies to beat, but there is a solution you can try.

When away on a negotiating trip, put your chastity belt on, ask the hotel management to remove your mini bar and lock yourself into your room after working hours. Or, even better, have your spouse with you at all times. If he or she cannot make it, your mother-in-law will do just fine!

WINNING TIPS: WHAT I WISH I KNEW TWENTY YEARS AGO

- Make your desire for success bigger than your fears.
- You cannot have it all, like get high returns from a low-risk deal. Decide which is more important to you.
- Risk has a price and somebody must pay for it. Make sure it's not you.
- It is better to be paranoid than sorry.
- Watch and listen for the warning signs.
- No contract and no amount of due diligence can be a substitute for trust.

---

[13] Mata Hari (real name Margaretha Geertruida Zelle), Dutch exotic dancer and courtesan, accused of spying for Germany during World War I and executed in 1917 in France.

Manipulated No More!

PROTECT YOURSELF FROM TRICKS & TACTICS

At best, tricks work once or for a short while. In the long run, they always backfire, hurt negotiators' interests and damage relationships. The primary aim of this chapter is not to teach you how to use them yourself, but to protect yourself when others use them on you.

Coming up:

- How to deal with negotiating tricks and traps
- Golden favourites - top 12 tricks & tactics
- How to protect yourself from being tricked or ripped-off
- How to negotiate with trades people and service providers

13

TRICKS & TACTICS - WHY OR WHY NOT?

"With foxes we must play the fox."

Thomas Fuller, churchman and historian

I remember an interesting assertion made by a cookbook author many years ago: "Show me the spices you use, and I'll tell you how good a cook you are."

We apply the same variety principle to many of our other activities. The more tools we have in our toolboxes, the better tradesmen or handymen we think we are.

Do you really need to know 29 different ways to make love to make your partner happy? Do you even have to use negotiating tricks and tactics in order to be a good negotiator? I don't think so. You should be able to recognise them if used against you, but that doesn't mean you should automatically use them yourself.

The Herbs and Spices Myth

The more tricks and tactics I know, the better negotiator I'll be.

Tactics are little techniques, ways of manipulating the situation or the other negotiator, to increase the likelihood of a favourable outcome. The problem with tactics is that while some work some of the time, most don't. There is no technique that works in all situations and for all negotiators.

Strategy is about the big picture. It broadly defines what you want to achieve and how. Tactics are the specific manoeuvres undertaken to achieve these goals. So, your first task as a negotiator in a particular situation is to make sure you got your strategy right. No matter how powerful your tactics are, they cannot possibly compensate for a lousy strategy.

Before Using Any Tactics

There are four main criteria to help you analyse the suitability and appropriateness of any technique. Ask yourself:

1. *Is it plausible?* If it isn't, it will be obvious to the other side that you are playing a game. When you say "I have to talk it over with my wife," the seller cannot tell if you are playing a delaying game or if you really have to do it. Most people have to involve their spouses in decision making, so such a tactic is plausible and believable.

2. *Is it congruent with your values and personality?* You want to bluff, but you are an honest person. You are not a good liar, people "see through you". Your bluff is likely to be seen for what it is. Or, you think a Good Guy, Bad Guy ploy could help you get a

better price from a supplier. You have a partner, but both of you are genuinely nice guys. Who should play the bad guy? Unless you posses extraordinary acting skills, forget it. Your performance will be anything but convincing; pathetic, more likely.

3. *How will the other side react to your tactics?* When one side plays games or uses tricks, the other is likely to resort to the same. Or, they may get disappointed. They've been expecting a constructive approach on your part, and now you are trying to manipulate them by using text-book tactics.

4. *What are the risks and consequences if this tactic fails?* If such a failure would make your situation or position worse, don't use such tactics. You may weaken your position, be exposed as a bluffer or liar, or the person you are dealing with may lose faith in you. The risks associated with manipulative tactics usually far outweigh the potential rewards.

The Best Tactics is No Tactics

"At a time of universal deceit telling the truth is a revolutionary act."

George Orwell, author and journalist

Inexperienced negotiators read a book or two on negotiation, discover a few tricks they like, and off they go to try them out in real life. Some tricks work once or twice while others fail on the first try. So, our rookie negotiator concludes that the tactics that worked twice in row should be adopted and used whenever possible. Don't change the winning horse, they say.

Ideas and possibilities are fine, but real life is real life. The horse soon gets tired and the tactics wear off. You are now riding a dead horse, and that won't get you very far. People those tactics are used on soon realise what's happening. You can make almost anything work once, but to make it work consistently and predictably, you are pushing your luck.

If you really feel you must use tricks or tactics, make sure you never use the same tactic on the same person twice.

When I was a kid, an unexplained and sudden sickness was the most common excuse from missing school. However, the teachers caught up with it very soon, and one had to bring a note from a parent or a doctor. Then we discovered the Grandma's Funeral ploy. Nobody checked if one's grandma really died and if her funeral had to be attended. The ploy worked well for while, but, as more and more students indiscriminately used such an excuse, the teachers got suspicious. We made the same mistake rookie negotiators make - we used the tactic way too often. Finally, when some students' grandparents allegedly died three or four times, the teachers put a stop to that sham by demanding to see official death certificates.

Once you find tactics that work for you, give them up. Use them only if you are convinced that without them, the deal would not happen. If you overuse them, people will associate you with the tactics and will think "Oh, no, here comes Mr Nibble-Me-To-Death. What is he going to ask for this time? ", "Well, well, if it isn't Miss Pay-Me-First!" or "I'm sick of this pompous Dr Look-at-My-Crisp-White-Coat & Stethoscope and his Respect-My-Authority tactics!"

Master negotiators transcend tactics. Tactics are for unimaginative or lazy people, unable or unwilling to face each situation on its own merits. Once you learn the tricks, leave them behind. You'll never look back.

TOP 12 GOLDEN HITS: TRICKS & TACTICS GALORE

#1: Good Guy, Bad Guy

> 🕸 TRICKY TRAP: I'm on your side!
>
> "I'm sorry about Kevin's outburst. He's been under lot of pressure, so sometimes he loses his temper. Don't take it personally.
>
> Look, I'm on your side here, I want you to get this contract, but you have to tell me your bottom line! I'll do my best to get him to sign the purchase order."

You have probably seen this plot numerous times in B-grade movies. It is also known as Good Cop, Bad Cop. Kevin shouted at the seller and stormed out. The seller is under emotional pressure, and now the "good guy" is stepping in, trying to elicit the lowest possible price ("bottom line").

I call this approach the Japanese Sauna trick. While the alternating hot and cold baths put you under physical stress, the Good Guy, Bad Guy treatment is its mental equivalent, a kind of warm-me-up, cool-me-down treatment.

This example actually uses two tactics together. The primary tactics is the Good Guy, Bad Guy and the supporting tactics is The Principal. Kevin (the bad guy) is the boss and has the final say. If the good guy was the boss, this trick would not work. This way, the two tactics work in synergy to the detriment of the seller.

You can use the Good Guy, Bad Guy in various creative ways. If you don't want to play the bad guy or are too nice for such a role, find someone else to do it - your boss, spouse, agent, business partner, accountant or lawyer.

Simply mentioning some higher authority that awaits you at home or back at work is often enough to intimidate the other negotiator into a more reasonable position. Of course, the bad guy doesn't even have to be a person. You can use rules and regulations, law, government, or any concept that supports your case.

COMPLAINING TACTICS: The Big Brother on your side

You: "I bought this _____ last week, but it doesn't _____ (work properly, meet my needs). I'd like a refund."

Store: "We can only give you credit towards future purchases in our store, we don't give refunds."

You: "That is illegal under the Trade Practices Act. I will have to lodge a complaint with the Ministry of Fair Trading!"

How to protect yourself from this trick? Simply, stick to your position, don't offer any further concessions, and be prepared to walk away (or at least threaten to).

#2: The Principal or Higher Authority

🕸 TRICKY TRAP: Higher authority

Client: "I'm sure you understand that I have get your proposed terms and conditions approved by my boss. I am not authorised to make strategic decisions such as this one. Unfortunately, he's not always as understanding and reasonable as I am, but I'll try my best and present your best offer to him!"

Here you see a reversal of the first case. The Principal is the primary tactics, supported by the Good Guy, Bad Guy plot.

This defensive tactic works well against door knockers, religious zealots, obnoxious tele-marketers, demanding clients and employees asking for undeserved pay rises. All it takes is a simple sentence: "I never _____ (whatever they are asking of you)".

For example, "I never sign anything on the spot. I always get my accountant and my lawyer to check it out." Or, "My wife would never allow me to do that!" Just make sure you don't start your sentence with "I'm sorry, I never ...". You are not sorry because there is nothing to be sorry about.

The Principal plot is even easier to use in business: "We don't give discounts, our prices are kept low at all times", or "We are not allowed to reduce our fees." If they challenge you, you can always fall back on the power of policies or procedures: "That's the Policy!" It is hard to argue against people's principles or corporate policies, even when they are clearly wrong, inappropriate or even if they simply don't make any sense.

The principal doesn't have to be a person, it could be a rule, a policy, a committee or even a whole department. Legal departments, contract people or purchasing sections all come handy here.

Even if you don't have a principal (a boss, a spouse, a business partner), simply invent one. Just make sure yours is plausible. If you are a manager, a director or a CEO, and a certain decision is obviously within your authority levels, it will be next to impossible for you to use the principal defence successfully.

#3: Take it or Leave it!

NO NEGOTIATION: Lame excuses, feeble justifications

Store manager: "Our store buys in bulk quantities and passes those savings directly to customers. Also, our catalogue prices are fixed for the whole year, so we don't give discounts."

There are two kinds of department stores (or any type of supplier for that matter). The first kind displays fixed prices and doesn't negotiate at all - the Take It Or Leave It approach. The second kind also displays fixed prices but is prepared to negotiate *if* you ask.

How do you tell which kind a particular store is? Offer them 25 percent less than the sticker price and see what happens. They will either repeat the mantra from their public relations manual "Our store buys in bulk ... thy kingdom come ..." or they will say "Let me see what I can do ..." and you are laughing all the way to the bank.

#4: Bait and Switch

TRICKY TRAP: A donkey or a horse?

You: "I noticed your advertisement for 2009 Paragon with 22,000 km on the clock for $15,995, so I came straight here, but I can't find the car. Can you help me?"

Dealer: "I am very sorry sir, but we just sold it an hour ago. It surely was the bargain of the year. However, we have other great deals in the yard for you. How about this lovely one-owner 2007 Octagon for $18,995?"

Another favourite trick of used-car dealers. The advertised bargain deal is always of the "too-good-to-be-true" variety, and the alternative on offer is not a bargain at all.

The name of the game is to attract as many people as possible into the yard, and then let his sidekicks loose on the unsuspecting prospects. Many people are lazy and inert. "Well, since we are all here, we may as well buy something ..."

Advertising goods for sale is an offer to trade and if the goods are fictitious, it is an offence to do so. Report them to authorities for misleading advertising. That should teach them a lesson or two.

A recent Australian legal case involved a fictitious BMW used as a low-priced bait. When the car dealer couldn't produce any proof that such a car was ever sold by him, the prospective buyer took legal action and won. The dealer had to buy an identical car and sell it to the plaintiff for the advertised price. Rejoice, you cheated masses, some justice at last!

#5: The Precedent

ⓘ INFORMATION POWER

Client: "I've heard from reliable sources that you waived this requirement from your last contract with another client of yours. Doing the same for us here will significantly influence our decision to engage you as the provider of our training services."

The precedent is a potent tactic, since it makes plausible sense: "Look, you've done it for them, why can't you do it for me? Or, maybe you don't want to do it for me? It's just not fair!"

Here a client somehow learned that the consultant he's negotiating with didn't insist on a certain standard requirement from another client of theirs. We don't know what that requirement was. It could have been a mandatory deposit payable by the client before the agency starts a project.

If a precedent works in your favour, ask for the same. If it doesn't, argue that your case is different or special, that it should not be considered of the same type or ruled by the same principle as the unfavourable precedent.

#6: Plumbers, Call Girls and Seminar Presenters

"Nothing is as good as it seems beforehand."

George Eliot, *Silas Marner*

NEGOTIATING HYPOTHETICAL

Something happened to your plumbing and your house is rapidly flooding with water. You call Emergency Plumbing Services, whose fridge magnet you've kept just in case. You congratulate yourself on such a wise decision. They inform you that one of their plumbers will be at your place in ten minutes.

a) Are you going to negotiate their fees while on the phone?

b) Are you going to ask about their call-out and hourly rates?

c) How much would you be prepared to pay?

STOP & THINK!

Participants in my negotiating seminars usually answer NO, NO and A LOT. Since "a lot" is not a precise figure, I probe further and get figures between $100 and $1,000. So far so good. Now the plumber comes in, checks around and in five minutes finds the source of the leak. He gets his tools, removes a faulty pressure relief valve and installs a new one. In ten minutes flat, he starts writing your invoice. It looks like this:

Crazy Don's Plumbing - A Division of Rip-off Merchants Inc.

TAX INVOICE

1. Emergency call-out fee: $75
2. Sunday and/or public holidays surcharge: $45
3. Labour: $90 per hour or part thereof
4. Replacement valve: $24.00

   Sub-total: $234.00

   GST or VAT tax at 10% $23.40

   Total payable: $257.40

Let me guess what you are thinking right now. $250 for a 10-minute job? You must be kidding me! You have just fallen victim of the dreaded Call-Girl Syndrome. Why do you think call-girls charge upfront? Training organisers use the same tactics. Hey, we are in a great company here!

The Call-Girl Syndrome
Once the service is delivered, the perception of its value is lower than the perceived value before the consumption of the said service.

We do have a valid reason for requiring pre-payment, though. Some participants register for a public seminar and then don't show up, which costs seminar organisers money. Unless they pay upfront, many "tourists" don't take these training events seriously.

#7: Peanuts or Funny Money

TRICKY TRAP: Funny Money

Car dealer: "Let me congratulate you on your smart decision to purchase this great car. Before we do the financing papers, did you know that for just $4 per day more you can enjoy the top model, with all those luxury options. Surely a lady of your status deserves life's little luxuries. And what is $4 anyway? You cannot even buy a nice cup of coffee for $4!"

Another favourite tactic of car dealers, insurance companies, banks and other widely loved and respected institutions. "The daily interest rate on our *Financial Loser Forever* credit card is only 0.1 percent." Wow, that's low, where do I sign?

How does it work in this case? Car loans are usually for a 5-year term. By paying $4 per day, over 5 years, these extras would cost you $7,600. $4 per day looked insignificant. However, for most people, $7,600 doesn't look funny any more.

The "Funny Money" can also work for you. If you are selling, break the charge down to the lowest plausible figure per unit, so it seems as cheap as possible. Don't say "This bulk purchase of 280 laptop computers will cost you $279,720." Say something like, "I am sure you will appreciate the very attractive unit price we are offering you, a small investment of only $999 per laptop."

If you are buying, as in our car financing example, do the opposite. Calculate the total purchase cost and try to bring it down since it seems such a large figure. Sellers' margins on "luxury" models are much higher than on "standard" models. The cost of those "luxury" add-ons are marginal, yet they command a premium, since buyers perceive them as expensive. So, tell the dealer: "Eight grand? No way. I'm sure you can do it for four!"

#8: The Puppy Love

"People don't ask for facts in making up their minds. They would rather have one good, soul-satisfying emotion than a dozen facts."
Robert Keith Leavitt, advertising copywriter, non-fiction author

Sellers may not know exactly *why* something works, but they do know what works and what doesn't, and the Puppy Love close works well most of the time: "Just leave your old car in our yard, Mr Suckerstein. See how you like the new Flasher 4WD, enjoy it over the weekend, take your family for a nice long drive. Best of all, if you decide not to go ahead with this deal, just bring it back on Monday."

Pet store owners use this ploy so much they even had the honour of naming it: "Look Mr Tooughbottom, just let the kids take little Rusty home for a day or two. If you change your mind you can always bring him on Monday!"

The father thinks he's got nothing to lose; he can always bring little Rusty back. What he's forgetting to consider is how difficult it would be to do so. The kids will spend the whole weekend playing with Rusty and get hooked for life. Taking Rusty back would break their hearts and, in their eyes, make poor Mr Toughbottom worse than Hitler's and Saddam's love child. Such is the power of emotional commitment.

The Way-out Delusion

Just because there is a way out, that does not necessarily mean you'll be able or willing to take it!

#9: Next Time (If You Get Another Chance) You Have to ...

COMPLAINING TACTICS: To make me happy again ...

Customer: "We've had lots of problems with your service department. We liked dealing with you and thought we had a true partnership going, but their attitude was really disappointing. We expected more commitment and flexibility from them."

The customer is expressing her displeasure with the supplier's performance. She makes sure the supplier does not take the criticism personally by pointing out how much she liked dealing with them.

She's either really disappointed by the service support or she may be trying to lower the salesman expectations. She could be priming him psychologically to offer a lower price and better terms next time around. The seller is now in the damage control mode, and that is exactly where the client wanted him to be. The message here is "Next time, *if* there is next time, and that is a BIG IF, you'll have to do much, much better!"

There isn't much the seller can do to change the perceptions of the customer. He can promise an improvement in the after-sales support and service, but the damage has already been done. The customer will be suspicious and empty promises will not satisfy her. If she is a good negotiator, she will be pushing for measurable indicators of quality and penalties for sub-standard performance.

#10: The Nibble

🕸 TRICKY TRAP: The Nibble

"As discussed, the supply of the network equipment and its installation comes to $116,000."
Client: "Fine, that is within our budget..."
IT firm: "There are also delivery costs of $1,950."
Client: "Well, we do need it urgently ..."
IT firm: "The cost of licences and permits is $865 per year ..."

The client made a simple but crucial mistake - he accepted the first offer. The seller then got greedy and quickly botched up a few additional charges. Of course, these nibbles cannot be significant, otherwise the client may realise what is happening and reopen the negotiation on the main price.

How would you respond to the seller's initial statement? Saying

"Fine, that is within our budget ..." may not be a mistake in itself, if it is followed by a "qualifier" such as "... providing that figure includes *everything* - supply, delivery, installation, training and support, warranty and spare parts. Does it?" If the seller says "No, it doesn't include *everything* ..." then the buyer can reopen or continue negotiating the total figure.

#11: The Flinch or the Wince

> "Practice your shock-horror reaction in the mirror each day,
> when you clean your teeth."
>
> John Winkler, *Bargaining for Results*

SOWING THE SEEDS OF DOUBT

Consultant: "Our rate for a design engineer is $200 per hour."

Client: "How much? Are you kidding me? $200 per hour? That's outrageous! That is $1,600 per day!"

As with all tactics, there are two possibilities here. The client is either truly unpleasantly surprised by the consultant's hourly rates, or he is playing a game. He knows the market rates well, but is still feigning surprise to instil doubt in the consultant's mind. Once the seller starts thinking "He may be right, $200 per hour is high, perhaps I can offer him a discount ..." he is on a weak ground. He is questioning his firm's pricing and may lose faith in the quality and value of his own services.

Doubt is the toughest of enemies.

#12: Salami - Negotiating Multiple Issues

Simple negotiations are about one dominant issue - most often price. When you are buying a known product, you know what you are getting: Same manufacturer, same wholesaler, same service outlet, same warranty.

With more complex negotiations, one of the first dilemmas is how to negotiate multiple issues. Do we discuss them simultaneously, all at once, as a package, or do we use the "salami" approach and discuss them sequentially? By negotiating issues one-by-one or slice-by-slice, we effectively break one large negotiation down into a series of mini negotiations.

Salami happens naturally on large and complex deals. Negotiating a whole deal at once, as a package, is not for the fainthearted. The sequential approach is easier and thus preferred by less experienced negotiators.

On the other hand, negotiating issue-by-issue often leads to a deadlock. The whole negotiation may get stuck on one relatively small issue. The "package deal" approach tends to overcome this pitfall by linking issues and by presenting the less palatable aspects of the deal together with the attractive ones. However, the packaged approach is harder and tougher to carry out.

A PROJECT MANAGEMENT CASE

"Right! Now that we've agreed on the design fees, let's talk about procurement charges for this plant upgrade. I suggest we leave the site supervision rates for our next meeting."

It seems one side is trying to negotiate in a piecemeal fashion. One little negotiation about the design fees, then the procurement fees will be negotiated, and so on. We cannot tell if it's the buyer or the seller talking, so we have to ask ourselves in whose interest would it be to negotiate issue-by-issue?

You have probably guessed that a client is talking to a consultant, who is to design something, manage the procurement side of the project (specifying and buying the equipment and materials required), supervise the installation (or construction), and finally commission the plant. So it seems they are negotiating on some turn-key project here.

Using the salami tactics helps the client to avoid linking and squeeze the best terms on every issue. If a consultant starts using arguments like "Fine, we'll lower our commissioning rates but we cannot at the same time give you a discount on the procurement fees", the client would respond, "We have already agreed on these fees, this is now an entirely different issue!"

HOW TO PROTECT YOURSELF FROM TRICKS & TRAPS

The Sitting Duck Syndrome

"When you are skinning your customers you should leave some skin on to grow again so that you can skin them again."
Soviet premier Nikita Khrushchev, advising businessmen in 1961

If you look timid, confused, gullible or too easy going, you will be treated accordingly - as a sitting duck, an easy prey.

A sitting duck invites all sorts of predatory behaviour. "Sure, we know it's urgent, it will be delivered to you by Friday." Friday fortnight. Your "case" will be put at the bottom of the low-priority pile or even completely lost or misplaced. Your calls will not be answered. You will be shunted from one operator to another and you will never get any answers to your complaints or inquiries.

Your job is to prove them wrong. Surprise them with your

knowledge and your firmness. You are a soaring eagle, not a sitting ducky, and it is their bad luck for mistaking you for one.

The best way to project an image of an informed, no-nonsense, discerning scrutiniser is to actually be one. When you are protected by your anti-bullshit shield, your vibes say "Don't take me for a sitting duck, I have answers for all your tricks and tactics."

Another way to protect yourself is to bluff. If you don't have it, fake it. Pretend. People are suckers for appearances, and even crooks, manipulators and rip-off artists are not immune to visual and verbal mimicry. Give them a taste of their own "medicine".

The 3D Rule: Be Deliberate, Demanding & Determined

To be treated with respect and professionalism, be informed (or at least *seem* so), look determined and demand the best.

The Plausibility Rule of Overcharging

QUICK STORY: Is It a Quote or an Estimate?

I bought a nice Swiss-made watch in Dubai. A few years later, back in Australia, the watch needed a new battery. At the watch repair shop, the repairman started mumbling about his mistake.

Repairman: "How much did I quote you over the phone?"

Me: "$15."

Repairman: "This is an expensive watch, the price for battery change on exclusive watches is $30."

STOP & THINK! How would you respond?

Here is the rest of our conversation:

Me: "Expensive watch? I only paid $400 for it in Dubai."

The repairman fumbles through a folder of some sort. Comes back with a satisfied smile on his face: "See, this watch is listed at a retail price of one thousand dollars in Australia."

Me (happy about my shrewd purchase, but unhappy about this argument): "Well, that may be so, but why would the battery change be more expensive? Does it run on special batteries?"

Repairman: "No, on standard size batteries."

Me: "I don't see why battery change should be more expensive just because the watch is listed as "exclusive". The battery's the same and it takes the same amount of time to do it..."

Repairman, obviously disarmed by my argument, trying desperately the last weapon in his arsenal: "Well, that's our policy."

Me: Preparing to leave, making unhappy faces, shaking my head.

Repairman: "Well, since I quoted you, I'll do it this time."

The amounts involved in the quick story above seem insignificant, and they are. The principles behind it, however, are far from trivial. I chose this minor negotiation for its educational value.

Firstly, just as they use any justification for overcharging, you have the right to justify why you shouldn't pay more.

Secondly, disputes happen because buyers, and even some sellers, don't understand the difference between a quote and an estimate. A quote is fixed, while an estimate is just that, an estimate. The final price of service can be higher (almost always) or lower (almost unheard of, but theoretically possible) than the estimate.

A quote is a fixed price for defined and specified goods or services; an estimate is an approximate price and is subject to change.

So, when you inquire about the price of something, and especially when it comes to service, ask for a "fixed quote". The term is partially redundant, you shouldn't really have to add "fixed", but it can only help, it cannot hurt.

Using others as an excuse is also common. "Our costs have gone up so we had to pass it on to you". Even if it's true, why can't they absorb such a price increase? Most industries have such wide profit margins that they could easily afford to.

Incredibly, even their own incompetence can be used as a pretext: "It took us much longer to complete the job then we thought when we quoted you." Or, to penalise you for using their competitors' parts and services in the past instead of theirs, "It was modified by someone who didn't know what he was doing, so we had to fix that first."

When people run out of excuses, they use the old Rules & Policies trick or its cousin, the common or standard practice trick. "Everybody does it this way, " or "This is a standard industry practice!' they say, as if you care what other crooks and vultures do, and as if that will somehow make everything right again. Don't fall for it. Rules are arbitrary and policies can be challenged and changed.

The Plausibility Rule

Anything plausible may be used as an excuse for overcharging.

How to Negotiate With Tradesmen, Consultants and Other Service Providers

Has this ever happened to you? You have a business project or a personal project at home. Say, you need to remodel your bathroom, overhaul your car's engine or install an air conditioner in your study. Anything that requires services of some kind, a builder, plumber, and the like.

Obviously, you'd prefer a fixed price quote, so there are no surprises later on. So, you get the tradesman to quote you for the job. After some grumbling and a juggling ritual with a pen and a pad, the measuring tape comes out, together with a sinister-looking calculator already programmed to spit out dollars and cents.

Then you'll hear something like "Well, because of _____ (any difficulty they could think of), this won't be easy. I need _____ (special tools, exotic materials, some brains, common sense), so it will take a few more days to do. It will cost much more than what I indicated over the phone ..."

You feel like you don't have a choice, so you accept their inflated price and explanations as to why your project is hard to do well, if at all. You've called six people for a quote and only two showed up. Both said the same thing and quoted an equally disgustingly high price. So close were the figures that you start to suspect collusive tendering or mutual mind reading on the part of the tradesmen.

Tradesman's Trap

Pricing possible yet unlikely difficulties in the quote. This transfers all the risk to the buyer. If those contingencies don't eventuate, the buyer does not get that part of his money back and the tradesman keeps it as an additional profit.

All would be well and you would calmly accept your fate, but things somehow never work out that way (to your advantage). When he rolls up to actually do the job, most of those envisaged difficulties (contingencies you were handsomely charged for) will not happen at all. The job will proceed smoothly and will be finished in no time . Of course, you will still pay the quoted price.

A word of caution: If you thought that only low-brow trades people use this tactics, think again. So called professionals (consultants, accountants, doctors, lawyers and a myriad of other vocations) like this tactic so much, they have actually accepted it as a normal way of doing business.

How to Negotiate Your Way Out of the "Tradesman's Trap"

"Nine times out of ten, the sceptics are right."

H.L. Mencken, journalist, essayist, satirist

So, how do you minimise the likelihood of somebody using the Tradesman's Trap on you? Remember, you can never eliminate the possibility, but you can reduce the risk of being taken for a ride.

After you patiently listen through all those difficulties, disclaimers and demands for more money, you use some basic psychology together with a dash of elementary logic. Start by asking "Have you done such a job before?" Invariably he will say yes, even if he hasn't.

The next question is "Did you face all of those difficulties on every project?" Of course he didn't. He is making it sound as all of those problems will happen on your project. They won't. Perhaps one or two, or none. He is just trying to justify his rip-off price.

Then you continue: "How long will the whole thing take?" After he makes a figure up, you conclude with "Based on your expertise I am confident in your ability to finish this job much faster than that." Now, this is a demand wrapped up in a compliment. He will like that. And the real negotiation of his fees starts in earnest.

After using some of the other approaches outlined in this book, if he still sticks to his (unreasonable) demands, you can either get a few more quotes hoping that you may get lucky and find a honest and competent tradesman or you can try the last resort negotiating tactic: "Come on, _____ (his name), you must have done a similar job for much less money before."

You are using two weapons. His name, the sweetest sounding word in his vocabulary (after the word cash), and the power of precedent. Even if he has done the same job much cheaper before, it doesn't automatically follow that he should or would or could do it for you. But, you may get lucky.

Generic Precedent Plot or "Come on, Jack, ..."

"Come on (*person's name*), you must have done a similar job for much less money before." Or, "Come on, Jack, are you telling me you've never sold this (*what you are buying*) cheaper before?"

The best way to protect your wallet and your sanity is to get a two-part quote. Part one is the basic price, assuming smooth progress.

In part two, you ask him to list the common difficulties and contingencies that could necessitate additional work, and to price each separately. Then you agree to pay for all the setbacks that happened and not to pay for those that did not happen. The risk of escalating charges is still with you, the buyer, but you will not be charged for the work that was never performed.

Does this approach always work? No. Most service providers don't want to go through this exercise. Most would obviously prefer to hit you with additions and variations at the end of the job, as a surprise, knowing that you are then in a vulnerable position.

How to Avoid Being Ripped-off by Grease Monkeys

This illuminating story is about a bunch of mechanics who tried to cheat me out of $500. At the time (about fifteen years ago) that was my wife's weekly take-home-pay. Anyway, the sum in question is of secondary importance here. We are talking about a crucial principle, and using this case study to illustrate how you too can protect yourself in similar situations.

I dropped my wife's car off at the repair workshop and went to work. Two hours later the service manager called, informing me that all four brake pads were worn-out and needed replacing. The cost? $200. And, there were "bad news". Bad news for you actually means good news for them. Servicing your car is a zero-sum game.

"Your discs are badly scoured and they need machining," he said, "it will cost $400." Heck, I was thinking, the whole car is worth $3,000 if lucky! Would you do $600 of repairs on a $3,000 car? That's when they resort to the old scare mongering trick, warning you that "The lives of your family depend on these tires and brakes!"

Something didn't add up. The first warning sign was the fact that all four discs needed machining. It is possible that one or two discs got scoured, but all four at the same time? Grease monkeys pushed it too far this time!

If you really want to twist the truth, do it in small measures. Bluff with restraint. Being too greedy or lying too much always backfires.

Then I remembered that a year before the two front discs were machined by the same shop. How was it possible that the pads lasted only twelve months and that the disks needed machining again?

I mentioned that to the manager. He asked me to stay on the phone while he went to "double-check" with the mechanic. Upon his return, he mumbled something about the front pads not being completely worn out so they could pass. They'd be happy to machine the two back ones for $300. I caught him in an outright lie or at least a gross exaggeration. Plus, if the machining of four discs cost $400, how can the machining of two discs cost $300?

I asked him to put the wheels back on, get the car down from the hoist and do no work on it whatsoever. When I picked the car up, there were two petite Asian ladies there paying their bills. They had worried looks on their faces. You would have, too.

I took the car back home, jacked it up and removed all four wheels. The discs were spotless, like new. Replaced all four pads myself at a cost of $90 and saved $510.

They Are All After You or Your Money!

"All professions are conspiracies against the laity."

George Bernard Shaw, Irish socialist, political activist

If you think I have a bone to pick with car dealers, repair shops and real estate agents, you are right. Perhaps it's unfair to single them out as *the only* predators. All professions have their own repertoires of tricks and tactics. All have polished their performance to a perfection.

They've had to, their livelihood depends on it. Without cross-selling and unnecessary work their incomes would dwindle.

Situations of this kind happen to people on a daily basis. Grease monkeys are everywhere. They don't just wear coveralls; some are dressed in suits, others have stethoscopes around their necks. They may wear wigs and black robes or use gold fountain pens. Beware! You never know when a grease monkey may jump on your back, so you'd better be alerted and prepared.

The Rules of Money

Rule #1: One way or another, it's always about money.
Rule #2: When it seems that it isn't about money, Rule #1 applies.

Let's take dentists as an example. Even when there is nothing wrong with your teeth and they have nothing to drill or fill, you will certainly need cleaning ($80 for a ten minute job) or, if they are really greedy, "deep-root cleaning" ($130 for fifteen minutes).

When there is nothing left to clean, they suggest redoing your old fillings. "But nothing hurts", you protest, "and they look fine ..." The answer you get is nothing short of amazing. "Ah, but they are sort of substandard ..." they would reply, forgetting it was them who did these filings in the first place.

It gets even better (for them). Every time they replace a filling, a hole in your tooth gets larger and larger. And then, one day, you'll be told that your tooth is now structurally too weak ("It can break any time now!") and that it needs a crown. Price? In Australia, between one and two thousand bucks!

The Law of Unnecessary Messing Around

The more they mess around with it, the worse it will get, and the more they will charge you to mess around with it some more.

WINNING TIPS: WHAT I WISH I KNEW TWENTY YEARS AGO

- Consider using no tricks, bluffs or tactics. Be genuine and honest and demand the same from people you deal with.
- One way or another, it's always about money. Yours.
- To be treated with respect and professionalism, be informed (or at least *seem* informed), look determined and demand the best.
- The more they mess around, the worse your situation will get and the more they will charge you to mess around with it some more.
- Trust is good. Constant vigilance is even better.

Pushover No More!

NEGOTIATING WITH DIFFICULT PEOPLE

"Na muci se poznaju junaci!" says a Serbian proverb. Loosely translated, it means, "Heroes rise in difficult times."

Although negotiating with constructive and understanding people isn't trivial, it's nothing to write home about. Dealing with nasty guys is the ultimate test. After reading this chapter, I am convinced you'll pass it with flying colours.

Coming up:

- Discover the reasons behind people's difficult behaviour
- How to assert yourself and protect your interests
- How to win your battles against the Big Guys

14

NEGOTIATE YOUR WAY OUT OF DIFFICULT SITUATIONS

What kinds of negotiations are more difficult for you, negotiating in business, or negotiating in your personal life?

Interestingly, most people are better at negotiation in business situations. When we negotiate on behalf of someone else, we are usually emotionally detached from the deal. We do care about the outcome, but not as much as we would care if we negotiated with our own money. We don't so easily fall in love with a product or service, as often happens in our personal life.

When in love, our reasoning abilities are obscured by irrationality, so keeping a healthy dose of detachment helps us to look at issues more logically and dispassionately.

What is more difficult for you, dealing with your friends, or negotiating with your "enemies"? This question isn't as silly as it sounds and the answer is not as obvious as you may think.

There are two schools of thought here. The adversarial camp espouses the premise of, "Friends are fine - foes are the problem". They claim there is no prize for negotiating and deal-making with people we like and respect. It is negotiating with people we dislike or despise that counts.

The relativist school points to a somewhat paradoxical situation. You know what to expect from vultures and toxic people. With them, you don't feel guilty for being tough or for fighting for what you want.

With friends, however, you have to balance your desire to win (to maximise your gains) with a major concern not to damage the relationship and to uphold the friendship. Such awkward push-pull situations are hard. Compromises always are.

I consider the following negotiating situations the most difficult:

- Negotiating for yourself (with or for your own money).
- Negotiating with your friends and family.
- Negotiating with those who negotiate in bad faith.
- Negotiating with those in power.
- Negotiating with difficult people (aggressives, cynics, avoiders).

The Toughest Negotiation of All

> "Live together like brothers and do business like strangers"
>
> Arabian proverb

You are responsible for negotiating an important agreement with a new supplier. A successful outcome would most certainly propel your career, while a failure to achieve your objectives will most certainly hinder your promotional prospects.

You enter the meeting room where the vendor is waiting for you and cannot believe your eyes. He is your friend, the one you lost touch with a few years back, but a friend nevertheless.

You are both surprised by this encounter, both harbouring mixed feelings about the situation. On one hand, you are glad you have found each other after a few years, and you are relieved that the vendor is not some unpleasant or inconsiderate jerk. On the other hand, you feel obligated towards him, reluctant to pursue your interests firmly, as you would otherwise do.

Putting your relationship first, above business, often results in giving away too much for the sake of the friendship. What other options have you got? Put your friendship aside and negotiate as usual? Try to use your knowledge of his values, strengths and weaknesses to control the negotiation and to maximise your gains? Or explain the issue to your manager and ask that someone else take your place?

Your choice here also has something to do with scarcity. Do you have more friends or more money? You may say to yourself: "I really need this friendship more than a few additional benefits I could get by playing hardball." At other times, you may think differently: "I'm already full on friends. I really need to get out of this deal looking great. My _____ (promotion, business expansion, retirement) depends on it. So, my priorities are clear!"

> 🖉 EXERCISE: How I negotiated in a difficult situation
> _____
> Think about difficult situations you've been through. Choose one that affected you the most, emotionally, professionally or financially. Describe the circumstances and identify the issues that made it difficult for you. How did you negotiate through or around that situation? If you could wind the clock back, would you do the same or would you take a different approach?

How to Identify Those Who Negotiate in Bad Faith

> "In the end, we will remember not the words of our enemies,
> but the silence of our friends."
>
> Martin Luther King Jr., African American civil rights movement leader

Just because somebody negotiates with you does not automatically mean they want to reach an agreement. Concluding a deal is not necessarily the only aim of a negotiation. Some people consider such conduct as negotiating in bad faith. Your investment of time, money and effort is usually wasted in such negotiations.

Why would someone negotiate without any intention of concluding the deal? A very common scenario in politics and diplomacy is posturing for public relations purposes. The negotiators want to score political points by appearing co-operative and reasonable during negotiations that are nothing more than a smoke screen.

Or, the real aim may be to simply delay things, if expecting a development that will change the balance of power to one's favour, or to wear the other side down through protracted talks.

Another, less sinister but equally unethical reason in business is the "three quotes shop around". Many corporate buyers must get at least three quotes for any significant purchase. They often already have a preferred supplier. However, to comply with the company's procedures or probity laws) they have to get two more quotes, just to make everything appear nice, equitable and legal.

Get All Promises and Quotes in Writing

"A verbal contract isn't worth the paper it's written on."

Samuel Goldwyn, film producer (attributed)

The best protection against people who over-promise and under-deliver is to get all their verbal commitments in writing. Simply ask, "Could you get it to me in writing, please?" One of two things will happen. He will either say, "Sure, is e-mail OK or do you want me to mail you the quote?" meaning he stands by it, or, he will play the "Why do you need it in writing, don't you trust me?" game.

Fortunately, this play is easy to neutralise. Just say something like, "Oh, it's not a matter of trust. I do have full confidence in you. This is just so that later I can remember what we talked about."

NEGOTIATING HYPOTHETICAL: Nature or nurture?

The guy you are negotiating with is aggressive towards you. Without knowing him well and without considering contextual factors of this case, what is a reasonable assumption to make?

a) He is confident, sure of himself and his power, feels he's got the upper hand in this negotiation. A definite sign of strength.

b) He is insecure, feeling threatened by you and unable to cope with disagreement and resistance on your part.

c) Who cares. He's just a jerk who needs to be taught a lesson.

STOP & THINK!

a) Unlikely. At a first glance, it would seem this way. However, confident, self-assured people who feel comfortable with themselves, with you and with the deal have no need to resort to aggressiveness, threats and intimidating tactics. Remember, things are seldom what they seem.

b) A prudent assumption. This guy obviously believes that attack is the best defence. I bet you he is just an insecure little boy, too small for his boots, who cannot carry all that responsibility on his narrow shoulders. He is cracking up because he knows he's losing the plot .

c) Maybe, but you are still no closer to the honey. There are two possibilities. He's a nice person who is acting like a jerk, or he is a true jerk. Either way, you better find the way of dealing with him or get your deal done somewhere else.

WHO ARE DIFFICULT PEOPLE AND WHY ARE THEY DIFFICULT?

"There are two races of men in this world, but only these two - the "race" of decent man and the "race" of indecent man. Both are found everywhere; they penetrate into all groups of society."

Victor E. Frankl, Holocaust survivor,
author of *Man's Search for Meaning*

People are difficult for various reasons. It could be bad genes. Some were born aggressive and there is nothing you can do to make them less so. If it isn't nature, it must be nurture. Bad upbringing. Their parents brought them up as demanding, selfish or aggressive children, and now they continue in the same fashion as adults.

Bad luck can also make people difficult. No matter how good-natured, patient or altruistic they may be, a string of bad luck events, one after another, can make even saints loose their cool.

Then, there are testosterone junkies. Bad hormones working over-time. Researches have noticed that men mellow with age, while women become more aggressive as they get older. The explanation is based on the decreasing levels of "male" hormone testosterone in older men and its increasing levels in ageing women. Next time you see a bunch of grannies with moustaches and raspy voices quarrelling at a local market, you know what to expect - trouble.

You Are Not the Cause of Their Difficult Behaviour

"Yes, people that have convictions are difficult. Fortunately, they're rare."

William Dean Howells, author and literary critic

No matter what the real cause of people's difficult behaviour may be, it usually has nothing to do with you. Sure, something you've said or done may have provoked them into the "let me bash you into submission" behaviour, but the problem is not in you, it is in them.

The tendency to blame ourselves originates in early childhood. Little children, when mistreated and abused by their parents never blame the parents. They project blame onto themselves. Mammy and daddy are perfect, and if they are angry with me, it means that I am a bad kid.

If you recognise your current sentiment in these lines, snap out of it. You are never the cause of someone's aggressive or in any other way inappropriate behaviour. The onus is on them to control their emotions and to respond in a mature, constructive way, instead of blowing their tops off.

"The Terrible Twos" Forever

"Insanity - It's difficult to comprehend how insane some people can be. Especially when you're insane."

Larry Kersten, sociologist

Some researchers claim that our basic personality was determined by the time we were three years old. Of those three years, the most critical period was between the ages of two and three, when we moved from the obstinate, selfish and aggressive stance that characterises the "terrible twos" into a more mature stage where we learned co-operation and compliance.

Aggressive negotiators operate along a basic duality of the fight-or-flight response. They either run away from conflict, usually when they judge you to be in a stronger position, or they fight, attacking you at every opportunity.

Stuck in a tantrum-throwing behavioural pattern and too old to change, they are like immature two year olds in adult bodies. Their little toddler brains made a simple causal connection very early in the process: "Whenever I scream or cry or start jumping up and down, mum and dad always give me what I want." Then they extrapolate such a conclusion to other people and hey presto - another jerk is stuck in his loser ways.

✓ CHECKLIST: Why Difficult People Behave the Way They Do

- GENETICS - it is their nature. Their behaviour *is* them.
- HABIT - they got used to behaving in such a way.
- REWARDS - their behaviour brings them rewards; it works for them. It helps them get what they want.
- IGNORANCE - they don't see themselves. They don't realise their behaviour is causing problems for others.
- EXPECTATIONS - they are expected to behave in such a way. It may be due to their culture, upbringing, or due to a nature of their profession or the demands of their job. A purchasing manager for a large oil & gas company commented once, "Igor, all this 'being nice' stuff is fine and dandy in principle, but if I was nice towards my suppliers I wouldn't be doing my job properly; I wouldn't be getting the best possible deals for my company. My job is to be a S.O.B.!" How would you respond?

- MALICIOUSNESS - they are doing it on purpose, to annoy you or harm you. They want to damage your reputation or professionalism, negatively affect your job performance or make you worried or stressed out.

- TACTICS - they are deliberately behaving in a certain way to get an advantage over you. When it comes to money, many otherwise "nice" people (whatever nice means) become obstinate, aggressive, deceitful, opportunistic or inconsiderate.

- INSECURITY - some people become difficult when under pressure. By trying to mask their lack of confidence and insecurity they may over-compensate and come across as inflexible, demanding or aggressive.

Theory X and Theory Y Negotiators

You may have heard of Theory X and Theory Y managers, a concept put forward in the fifties by Douglas McGregor. Although, strictly speaking, it is not a theory but a simple dichotomy, I find it useful not just when applied to management of people in general, but to negotiation as well.

Theory X negotiators believe that people cannot be trusted, that they will lie and cheat, if only given a chance. They advocate constant vigilance, claiming that being accommodating and understanding will only be interpreted as a weakness and used against you.

You may say they are "fixed pie" negotiators: the more pieces of the pie the other person gets, the less is left for you. Theory Xers usually find negotiation an unpleasant, stressful and emotionally charged activity between combatants with fixed positions and mutually exclusive aims.

In contrast, Theory Y negotiators believe in the essential goodness of people. They claim that if respected, listened to and encouraged to search for common ground, the other party will be co-operative.

Once you think about people you negotiate, work or live with, you will most likely conclude that most people don't fully fit either of the stereotypes. We find ourselves in both frames of mind at various times and in different situations. The importance of the situational context cannot be overemphasised. The same generally pleasant and co-operative people can, in some situations, become unpleasant and adversarial.

**There are very few truly difficult people,
there is only difficult behaviour.**

Discern Between Good and Bad People

"Only the bad witches are ugly."

Glinda, the Good Witch of the North, in movie "The Wizard of Oz"

Who are evil people and why are we talking about them in a book on negotiation? The unpleasant fact of life is that over the years you will have to negotiate with them to get what you want. Evil people are in business, in government, in your street, perhaps even in your family. I am sure you have a pretty good idea who they are, you just don't want to admit the fact they are evil.

Or, your mother taught you that calling people evil or nasty is not nice, so you feel guilty even thinking that way. Don't. Evil people don't feel guilty about anything, so why should you feel guilty about recognising them for what they are?

Identifying evil people quickly and accurately is far from easy. If they are bad, we expect them to look bad. Did you notice how in the sixties and seventies evil movie characters were played by ugly, mean looking actors? And, likewise, all good guys were played by the handsome hunks or hearth-throbs? Screenplay writers eventually realised that life is not so transparent or polarised. In real life, many truly evil people look very presentable, even handsome. So, if you cannot go by someone's looks, how can you tell nasty from nice? If visual clues aren't sufficient, we have to use verbal and behavioural indicators.

Even here confusion is possible. With evil people, what you see is not what you get; actually, it's quite the opposite. We often get fooled. Just because someone is charming and friendly face-to-face, does not mean he is benevolent or supportive behind your back.

We often mistake knowledge for intellect - people who are knowledgeable are automatically deemed intelligent. A good talker is often mistaken for a doer. You see this syndrome at job interviews. Just because someone can talk a lot about a subject and knows what to do (in principle), does not mean he will actually do it well or do it all. Sadly, candidates who get hired are not those who can do things well, but those who can talk well.

Wishful thinking

Seeing people as you'd like them to be, instead of who they really are.

Quick and superficial evaluation does not work with the nasties. Deeper probing and testing is in order! Firstly, listen carefully what they say and how they say it. Then, watch for the behavioural giveaways. Sooner or later their true nature will surface. People cannot pretend for prolonged periods of time. And ultimately, trust your feelings. If you feel that "something isn't quite right with that person", then it probably isn't.

✓ CHECKLIST: Evil People Give-Aways

- *You feel uneasy around them.* Have you ever met someone for the first time and instantly disliked them or felt uneasy in their presence? Not all of the people who "rub you the wrong way" are evil, but it is a warning sign nevertheless! If you don't "click" together, the deal won't either!

- *They only think about, talk about and look after themselves.* Sure, they may also look after their family (as an extension of themselves), and even after their stooges, but they will never look after you or your interests. Extreme selfishness is a common trait amongst the nasties.

- *They have no sense of humour.* People who can laugh at themselves are seldom evil. Evil people take everything seriously and personally. Of course, just because someone has no sense of humour, does not make them evil, otherwise all those boring and lifeless people in our midst would be evil. They are just mentally and emotionally dead, yet still physically alive.

- *They lack kindness.* The ultimate test. Disregard how he behaves towards his boss or anyone he needs something from. Of course he will be nice when it suits his purpose. Observe how he treats waiters, taxi drivers, secretaries or contractors.

✗ SELF-PROTECTION TOOL: How to Deal With Nasty People

Life is to short to deal with nasty people. If you judge someone to be dishonest, unethical, selfish, arrogant, unreliable, or just plain evil, look elsewhere. Consider your other options. Do business with nasty people only if you absolutely have to, although I cannot imagine too many such circumstances.

Also, consider the price you may end up paying. Their nastiness may rub on you, so you are in real danger of becoming nasty yourself. People will judge you by the company you keep. You will be guilty by association. If you deal with such people, you will always lose, one way or the other.

While avoidance may be the ideal solution, in some cases we don't have such a luxury - we have to deal with or work with the nasties. What should we do?

Everything we've been talking about in this book that relates to dealing with people applies equally to dealing with evil people, only even more so. There are also some additional protection measures you can take:

- Get everything in writing.

- Watch your back.
- Use multiple levels of protection and concentric lines of defence.
- Get powerful allies, the ones even evil guys are afraid of.
- Don't try to change evil people. That is not your job (unless you are a parole officer, clinical psychiatrist or a sado-masochist).

Shaft or Share?

"This isn't the age of manners, it's the age of kicking people in the crotch."

Ken Russell, film director

What happens when a genuine win-win negotiator meets a nasty, win-lose character? An interesting TV quiz show comes to mind. Its title was "Shafted". I found it mildly entertaining but very educational. It confirmed the universal application of The Bastardry Law.

The final stage of the show is what we are interested in here. The showdown happens between the two remaining competitors who battle for the total pool of money. They have to lock in their choice of strategy (only seen by the TV viewers). The choices are "Shaft" (the other player) or "Share" (with the other player).

What comes next is a crucial part of the whole strategy. The two finalists have an opportunity to convince each other that their intentions are honest, that they are reasonable people and not greedy opportunists. They are then given a chance to change their selection after hearing each other's appeal.

Once they lock their choice in, if both chose "Share", they share the money. If one chooses "Shaft" and the other chooses "Share", the shafter gets all the money and the sharer goes home with nothing, a win-lose deal. If both chose to shaft each other, then they both go home with nothing (lose-lose) and the TV studio executives laugh all the way to the bank.

According to my count, eight times out of ten, at least one of the contestants chose to shaft the other. Is greed your creed? What would you do in such a situation and why?

The Bastardry Law (nasty against nice)

If you are a nice guy or girl and you negotiate with a complete bastard, you are likely to lose.

When a scrupulous, ethical negotiator who follows the rules (you) deals with an unscrupulous, unethical or difficult person who follows no rules, the whole ordeal reminds me of Indiana Jones. With his arms and legs tied, Indy's trying to fend of a vicious Nazi butcher. The difference between you and Indiana Jones is that in real life you lose. *Ze war ist over fur you!*

HOW TO WIN IN NEGOTIATIONS WITH THE BIG GUYS

"The weak have one weapon:
the errors of those who think they are strong."

Georges Bidault, French politician, prime minister

Participants in my negotiating seminars often ask me what to do in negotiations where there is a large imbalance of power, in David-versus-Goliath situations. We will assume here that you are in the shoes of David here, that you are the underdog.

David defeated the Goliath by a single, well aimed sling-shot, but, that is mythology. In real life it is very unlikely just one punch would get you what you want. You will have to combine strategies, enlist help from multiple allies and attack on various fronts.

Whatever you do, don't get intimidated by those who appear stronger, smarter or richer. Appearances can be deceiving. Again, the old adage applies: If you think you can, you can. If you think you cannot, you cannot.

Find Allies (Quickly!)

ALLIANCE, n. In international politics, the union of two thieves who have their hands so deeply inserted in each other's pockets that they cannot separately plunder a third.

Ambrose Bierce, *The Devil's Dictionary*

Taking big guys on is a lonely and depressing task. Luckily, the bigger the Goliath, the more enemies they have. Your first task is to identify who those enemies are and then to form an alliance with them. A common enemy is a very powerful unifying force.

**Everybody has an axe to grind and wants to prove something.
Let them prove it by helping your cause.**

I still remember how my fifth grade maths teacher explained the logic behind the multiplication of positive and negative numbers. [14](+) denotes a positive, while (-) represents a negative number:

TIP	THE ALLIANCE LOGIC
(+) x (+) = (+)	A friend of my friend is my friend.
(+) x (-) = (-)	A friend of my enemy is my enemy.
(-) x (+) = (-)	An enemy of my friend is my enemy.
(-) x (-) = (+)	An enemy of my enemy is my friend.

[14] I still don't understand how the result of multiplying two negative numbers can be a positive number, but that is beside the point.

211

Complain to Government Agencies and Pester Politicians

"If the tiger pauses, the elephant will impale him on his mighty tusks.
But the tiger will not pause,
and the elephant will die of exhaustion and loss of blood."

Ho Chí Minh, Vietnamese revolutionary, statesman

Although most governments don't really care about the well-being of a small guy like you or me, occasionally they need to be seen as they do. Use that opportunity.

Demand as much assistance as possible in return for the money they plunder from you as taxes, duties, tolls, levies and other forms of legalised robbery. After all, they occupy their posts and get handsomely paid because of you, not the other way around, as they would like you to believe.

Since their motto is "To Protect and to Serve", make them earn their keep by protecting your interests and serving your cause for a change.

Of course, things work both ways. If your fight is with a corporation, find who their enemies are in the government, and enlist their support. If you have a bone to pick with a government department, find businesses with vested interests and get some corporate "sponsors" to finance your dispute.

Use Media to Make Your Case Public

"I have never made but one prayer to God, a very short one:
'O Lord, make my enemies ridiculous.' And God granted it."

Voltaire, French writer, historian, philosopher

Media like stories of underdogs struggling for a "just" cause. It is not easy to run commercials all the time (the competition for advertising dollar is fierce) so they are hungry for sensationalistic news. Use their desperation to your advantage.

For instance, if your TV, computer or anything else technical stops working and you don't get much luck from the repair centre or customer support, go in front of a TV station's building and threaten to embarrass the manufacturer.

If airing your grievances on TV does not work, go one step further. Ceremonially dump the offending product in the middle of the street. You may be charged for littering and perhaps for "disturbing public peace", but that would be a small price to pay for your satisfaction. Millions of people will see you on TV or YouTube and sympathise with you. Your fifteen minutes of fame will have finally arrived.

Conventional thinking: If you can't beat them, join them.
***Loser No More!* revenge principle: If you can't join them, beat them.**

Take Them to Court (Get a Pro Bono[15] Lawyer)

Lawyers like publicity, because it attracts new clients, which in turn brings them heaps of money. If your case is unusual, highly publicised in the media, controversial in any sense or simply interesting enough, you should be able to get them to work for you for free.

Whatever fees they forego in your case, they will recoup hundred-fold from other desperadoes who will ask them to take on their cases as a result of the publicity gained on yours.

GET WHAT YOU WANT BY ASSERTING YOURSELF

"At sixteen I was stupid, confused and indecisive. At twenty-five I was wise, self-confident, prepossessing and assertive. At forty-five I am stupid, confused, insecure and indecisive. Who would have supposed that maturity is only a short break in adolescence?"

Jules Feiffer, cartoonist

People tend to judge you by your self-esteem and generally value you accordingly to how much you value yourself. If you are a confident, positive and self-assured individual (and even if you only *seem to be* that way!) , they will treat you with respect. Likewise, if you come across as a timid, insecure and submissive pushover, they will immediately treat you as such.

I'm a passive-agressive personality. Assertiveness has never been one of my qualities. If unhappy with someone or something I would rather fume and blame myself than confront the person who caused my unhappiness.

Speaking from personal experience, it is possible to assert yourself, but only up to a point. Going against your genes, upbringing and social conditioning is an uphill battle.

How do you know if assertiveness is your problem? Oh, I'm sure you know it by now, but if you really want a quick check-up, here is a list of the most common pushover symptoms. If two or more apply to you, you need urgent help.

✓ CHECKLIST: Seven Signs of Low Assertiveness

1. You are reluctant to ask for something you want from others.

2. You feel powerless and cannot say "No!"

3. You're afraid of turning down requests from your co-workers, your boss, family members, even your children or subordinates.

4. You put the others' needs ahead of your own.

---

[15]A shortened version of the Latin phrase "pro bono publico", meaning "for the public good", or in this case "for free"

5. You feel you have no choice but to do what others want you to.

6. You are afraid that if you don't co-operate or submit, you will be seen as insensitive, demanding, aggressive or unreasonable.

7. You are underestimating yourself while overestimating others.

Conditioning Influences That Determine Your Assertiveness

"The best defense against usurpatory government is an assertive citizenry."

William F. Buckley, Jr., writer

We are constantly bombarded with messages, pieces of advice and lessons from outside. Parents, friends, teachers, media, politicians, the society at large, all have something to say or preach.

At the same time, as we grow up and experience life, we make our own conclusions, which are often diametrically opposite. No wander we get confused.

I see life as a constant battle between selfishness ("Look after #1") and altruism ("Love thy neighbour!"). Fans of "The Simpsons" will immediately recognise two archetypes, altruistic Ned Flanders and his selfish, self-centred neighbour Homer Simpson.

How you negotiate will reflect your choice between the two extremes, underpinned by the philosophy you ultimately subscribe to.

ALTRUISM	SELFISHNESS
■ Don't be selfish.	■ Put your own interests first.
■ Be modest and humble.	■ Promote yourself constantly.
■ Let others win, too.	■ Win at all costs.
■ Don't be too demanding.	■ Demand impossible.
■ Let others help you.	■ Help yourself first.
■ Help others whenever you can.	■ Mind your own business.
■ Turn the other cheek.	■ Fight back.
■ Say YES!	■ Say NO!

The Chutzpah Principle

"If I am not for myself, Who will be for me?
If I am only for myself, What am I? If not now, When?"

Hillel in *Babylonian Talmud*

Chutzpah is a Yiddish word of multiple nuances that has no precise English equivalent. In his 1968 book *The Joys of Yiddish*, Leo Rosten, a prominent writer who popularised Yiddish words and introduced them into American cultural and linguistic milieu, defined chutzpah as an idiom meaning "gall, brazen nerve, effrontery."

Nonce of these words alone fully describes the multiplicity of connotations of this term, such as shameless audacity, impudence, presumption plus arrogance or brazenness. Obviously, this not always complimentary term, can also have negative connotations.

Chutzpah negotiating rests on the principle that it is usually easier to ask for forgiveness after the action then to get a permission beforehand.

The Chutzpah Law of Retroaction
If in a hurry, do it first and ask for permission later.

REMINDER	YOUR RIGHTS AS A NEGOTIATOR
	You have the right ... ■ ... to ask for what you want. ■ ... not to justify your demands or decisions. ■ ... to admit your mistakes. ■ ... to change your mind. ■ ... to uphold your values and principles. ■ ... to take as much time as you need. ■ ... to say NO, just as you have the right to say YES. ■ ... to walk away from the deal or the relationship.

Say NO First, You Can Always Say YES Later

"What is a rebel? A man who says no."

Albert Camus, French Algerian author and philosopher

Have you ever said yes to a request although you didn't want or didn't have the time to do it? How many times have you chastised yourself for not being more assertive, for not standing your ground?

The solution is simple: If in doubt, say NO. If need be, you can always change it to YES later. If you say YES and then change it to NO later, you lose your credibility and put yourself in a position of weakness where you have to justify your change of mind to the other side.

If you are unable to say NO, thinking you are being selfish, just repeat the following mantra as many times as necessary to resist the temptation to say YES too easily: "I am not being selfish. I am being fair. I am protecting myself from unreasonable demands. I don't need this person's approval and will stick to my NO. "

The "Getting to Yes" Fallacy
Getting to YES is not that hard. For most negotiators it is getting to NO that is hard. They say YES too often and too quickly.

✗ The Sandwich Tool: YES, NO, YES

If saying an outright "no" is hard for you, sandwich it between two ye-ses. The format of the sandwich tool is : "Yes, we would like to (do something) but no, we cannot (do something else). However, if you (do something else) then yes, we can (agree or work together)."

For example, imagine a consultant talking to a prospective client who wants things done his (wrong) way: "We would like to help you on this consulting project, but we cannot work under the proposed structure. However, if you agree to follow our standard, proven methodology, then we can guarantee the results and meet your requirements on this project. Would that be acceptable?"

The Sandwich Tool

General YES - Specific NO - Conditional YES

The first YES is generic and sets the scene in a positive way: "Yes, we would like to do business with you". Or, in personal relationships, "Yes, I love you and care about you."

The middle NO is specific. It's about an issue that is not negotia-ble. It means "We cannot agree to that," or "What you did was not acceptable."

The final YES is conditional. It clearly spells-out your demands and sets a precondition for continuation of the relationship or project: "However, with a four-week delivery we can supply the required quan-tity of the widgets you want. Yes?"

WINNING TIPS: WHAT I WISH I KNEW TWENTY YEARS AGO

- Everybody has an axe to grind and wants to prove something. Let them prove it by helping your cause.
- If in a hurry, do it first and ask for a permission later. It is easier to get forgiveness than permission.
- Very few people are truly difficult, there is only difficult behaviour.
- Conventional thinking: If you can't beat them, join them. *Loser No More!* revenge principle: If you can't join them, beat them.
- Getting to YES is not that hard. We say YES too often and too quickly. Getting to NO is hard. If in doubt, say NO!

Hesitant No More!

APPLYING YOUR SKILLS IN PRACTICE

If reading and knowledge were sufficient, librarians and university lecturers would be driving Lamborghinis and I would be rich and retired in the Bahamas or any other place with no taxes, sunny climate and a plentiful supply of cocktails.

Timely action and decisive implementation are the crucial differentiators between the also-runs and the true pros.

Coming up:
- Bridge the knowing-doing gap
- Put your knowledge into action
- The paradoxical side of negotiation

HOW TO BRIDGE THE KNOWING-DOING GAP

"Dal dire al fare c'e di mezzo il mare."
("Between saying and doing lies the ocean.")

Italian proverb

Reading is Not Enough - You Have to Take Action

The simplest thing to change is understanding. Acquiring new knowledge is the easiest step towards success. Applying it in real life is far more difficult.

Since negotiation is a natural part of life, you will never become a successful negotiator if you don't know much about life. Conversations, conflicts, purchases, problems, and projects - whether large or small, personal or business-related - all will add to your understanding of negotiation.

In his *Epistulae ad Atticum* (*Letters to Atticus*), Cicero, Roman philosopher and statesman, aptly said "Advice is judged by results, not by intentions." Indeed, the ultimate value of this book is in the application of its lessons in everyday life. By merely reading it, you won't achieve anything. That would be like trying to become a better public speaker without giving speeches, or learning to ride a bicycle without actually hopping onto one. So, go out and get them: Life is too short not to negotiate!

Thoughts - Actions - Results Sequence

"You always project on the outside how you feel on the inside."

Denis Waitley, self-help author and motivational speaker

To improve the quality of your results, you have to improve the quality of your actions first. By the same token, to improve the quality of the decisions you make and the actions you take, you have to improve the quality of your thinking. I call this progression the "Thoughts - Actions - Results Sequence".

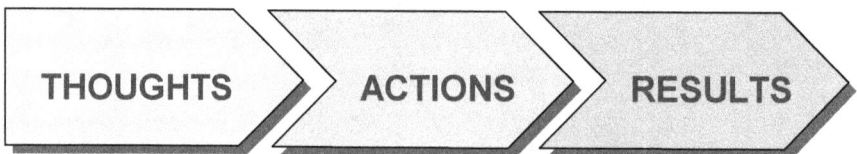

THOUGHTS > ACTIONS > RESULTS

This progression doesn't apply only to negotiation. It's of universal value. In public-speaking (a close relative to negotiating), convincing presentations come from clear thinking. If your thinking is muddy, your presentation will be confusing and boring.

So, fix your "inwards" first (your self-image, inner thoughts and attitudes) and the "outwards" (your actions and the results of those actions) will automatically fall in line.

The Crawl, Walk, Run Rule

"One pound of learning requires ten pounds of common sense to apply it."

Persian proverb

Life offers numerous opportunities for sharpening your deal-making skills. The best way is to start with simple, low-risk situations and gradually move towards more complex deals. Expand your comfort zone by starting small and moving into bigger and tougher negotiations. By negotiating in low-stakes, low-stress situations first, you will be able to negotiate better in high-stakes, high-stress situations later.

The Crawl, Walk, Run Rule

Start practising in simple, low-stakes deals and gradually move towards more complex, high-risk deals.

If you make a mistake or two on a small or relatively insignificant deal, it won't cost you much. Consider it an educational expense, an investment in your future. If possible, practice with somebody else's money. Get somebody else (such as your employers or clients) to pay for your real-life education!

Don't be Afraid of Success

"Audentis fortuna iuvat." ("Fortune favours the brave.")

Virgil, *Aeneid*

We've talked about procrastination and fear of success at the start of this book. Just in case you've missed it, read The Procrastination Conundrum again.

Don't be one of many who wake up from their stupor, grey-haired and near the end of a boring, unproductive career or a string of broken relationships, with a sudden realisation that you have been living far below your true potential.

I don't want you to accept less than you deserve, or to sell yourself, your employer, your family, your business or your country short. I want you to have no regrets. I hope you will look back at your past negotiations and other endeavours with pride and look forward to new ones with confidence.

The Last and the Most Important Exercise

Trying to change too much, too quickly is a recipe for certain failure. Many corporate initiatives and management projects fail primarily for that reason. Wisdom in life consists of deciding what should be changed and what is better left alone.

By biting more than you can chew, you will feel overwhelmed by the enormity of the task and will start procrastinating. To avoid these traps, I find it helpful to divide action steps into two categories.

Firstly, make a list of actions you will take straight away, these that are relatively easy and quick to implement in practice. You can call them "low-hanging fruit."

Things that are more difficult to do or steps that require persistence and long-term planing, should be listed under "Longer term actions".

✎ EXERCISE: Implementing ideas from this book
---

a) Immediate actions - things I will do right now:

1. _____

2. _____

3. _____

4. _____

b) Longer term actions - things I will do soon:

1. _____

2. _____

3. _____

4. _____

Bounce Back, Baby!

> "Nije sramota pasti, sramota je ne dići se."
> ("It's not shameful to fall, it's shameful not to get up.")
>
> Serbian proverb

Negotiating is one of the loneliest, most difficult and most frustrating businesses in the world. Many times you'll question your abilities, feel discouraged and disillusioned. You'll have to fight all those negative thoughts and maintain a positive attitude.

If you don't believe in yourself, nobody will. Apart from belief and a positive mental attitude, you'll also need stamina, perseverance and hard work (and a bit of luck, of course).

To deal with discouragement, setbacks and occasional losses, good negotiators need a strong psychological immune system. Such psychological resilience helps them recover faster and bounce back quicker. No matter how many times you get knocked down, all you need is to get up after each setback and you will eventually have made it. The

difference between success and failure often comes down to psychological resilience.

Be Not Only a Graceful Winner, But Also a Graceful Loser

"We must believe in luck.
For how else can we explain the success of those we don't like?"

Jean Cocteau, poet, playwright, filmmaker

Graceful winning and graceful losing usually go together. Negotiators
who don't win at the expense of others, who don't boast about "ham-
mering them into the ground", go quietly about their business and
don't make a big deal out of either winning or losing.

Those who want to squeeze the last dime out of the "opponent" are
usually sore losers. When they win, they ascribe such success to their
skills and hard work. When they lose, they either blame the outside
factors (the circumstances, bad luck, the government, the markets or
the competition) or claim that the other side acted unethically or ille-
gally. They complain, scheme revenge and allow destructive emotions
to take over their reason.

Sore and revengeful losers don't make good negotiators. While la-
menting their fate or commenting about the other side being unfair,
they usually have no qualms about being unfair and unreasonable
themselves - if only an opportunity presents itself. Double standards
are a prominent feature of their egos.

The Paddling Duck Syndrome

Remember my claim that we humans hype our gains and hide our
loses, in order to be perceived as more successful than we really are?
"The Paddling Duck Syndrome" is its close relative. When I go with
my daughters for a walk to a nearby lake, they are fascinated by the
ducks' apparent lack of effort. They seem to glide effortlessly. Due to
the shimmering surface of the water we cannot see the frantic paddling below.

Likewise, we can only see the magic in the performance of tennis
players, ice skaters and various other sports stars. They did not become successful through luck and wishful thinking, but through gruel-
ling practice and ongoing sacrifice, which we never see.

Some people want to appear cool and leave an impression that
they are extraordinarily talented, that success comes to them without
much effort on their part. Don't fall for this impression management
ploy or expect the same to happen to you. You can be cool and composed on the surface, but you have to keep paddling like crazy to continue moving towards success.

THE PARADOXICAL SIDE OF NEGOTIATION

The Laws of Inverse Effort

> "The harder you try, the dumber you look."
>
> Larry Kersten, American sociologist and author

The dating game messed up my entire adolescence. It was frustrating, illogical and often even surreal. The main culprit was my complete lack of understanding of the female psyche and my own mental programming. I remember many girls who were interested in me, sending all sorts of IOI signals (Indicators of Interest). Yet, it was to no avail. I didn't recognise the signals and on rare occasions when I did, I ignored them. I wanted the girls I could not have and wasn't interested in those I could.

This syndrome works the other way, too: The more a boy wants the girl, the less the girl wants the boy. The cooler and less interested the boy appears to be, the more the girl goes crazy about him. The same principle applies not just to dating but to other worthwhile human activities, too.

The First Law of Inverse Effort

The harder you push for something, the less likely you are to get it.

There are two more Laws of Inverse Effort, and they have something to do with destiny or karma if you believe in such things.

There are two situations in life that cause misery. One happens when we stubbornly keep pushing for something, despite the fact that we would be better off cutting our losses and moving on.

The Second Law of Inverse Effort

Some things are *not* meant to be, and no amount of time and effort expended will make them happen.

The other, equally frustrating situation develops when we give up too soon, not knowing that we would have succeeded had we just persisted for a little while longer. The goal was within our reach, the victory was assured, but we could not see what was around the corner. Our human inability to predict the future is the basic cause of both afflictions.

The Third Law of Inverse Effort

Some things *are* meant to be, and no matter what you do to prevent them from happening, they will happen.

The implications of these laws are obvious. We have already talked about this issue in negotiations, when to stay and conclude a deal and when to walk away. We should know when to keep pushing and when to give up. Easier said than done.

The same conundrum applies to other aspects of life. Should we stay in a dysfunctional marriage for the sake of the children and keep up the appearances, or should we go through a psychologically and financially devastating divorce? I can think of many such lose-lose life situations, where most or all of the choices are unappealing, but don't want to depress you any more than necessary. It would be unwise to end a personal improvement book on a sour note.

The Hindsight Predicament

Life is a one-way street that can only be negotiated by going forward, yet we can only understand it by reflecting backward.

Nobody Wins in All Cases and Nothing Works All the Time

"Fanaticism consists in redoubling your effort
when you have forgotten your aim."

George Santayana, writer and philosopher

Many hopefuls assume that practical negotiating principles, strategies and tactics work in all situations and for all negotiators. This is a dangerous assumption.

Life is a messy condition and negotiation is such a complex process that outcomes depend on many factors. However, this does not render those principles, approaches and tools useless or diminish their appeal. Screwdrivers and hammers are two very different groups of tools, intended for two very different purposes. So are the negotiating tools. They all have their merits, uses and limitations. There is a time and a place for each.

Interestingly, style often beats substance. It doesn't matter that much what you do, but how and when. You may have the best recipe, but if your execution is sloppy, you will end up with a lousy dish.

Furthermore, what worked once may not work again. That doesn't mean the recipe is wrong, the situational factors could have conspired against you. Even the best cooks don't succeed all the time, just as the best negotiators don't.

The Repetition Paradox

What worked yesterday may not work today.

There Are No Shortcuts to Success

"... that life is an inherently mysterious business
and that there are no easy answers or simple formulas."

M. Scott Peck, *A World Waiting To Be Born*

Every now and then, a participant in my negotiation course would say something like, "Igor, I am a practical person and I need a list of five quick things I can use, simple steps that work all the time." We want certainty, predictability and repeatability. When we do something right, we want to know that what worked once will work again. We hope for quick shortcuts and simplistic solutions.

The "Neat & Tidy" Delirium

The "Neat & Tidy" school of management is a fairy tale; it does not work in a messy, uncertain, unpredictable world, the real world.

The bad news is that such shortcuts seldom work. A life-skill such as negotiation distilled down to seven or nine items? A serious reality check is in order!

Indeed, things should be simplified, but only up to a certain point and no further, otherwise we start losing the essence of the issue, and not just the peripheral factors. Where that point lies is a contentious matter that often ends up in disagreement.

Personally, I subscribe to the situational school of thinking. To decide how far to go, each situation has to be dealt with on its own merits.

The "Neat & Tidy" school of thinking is passé; "Fuzzy & Paradoxical" is in. Just because most popular self-help books oversimplify and promise you the Moon, does not mean they are right! Would you rather be right or successful?

WINNING TIPS: WHAT I WISH I KNEW TWENTY YEARS AGO

- Reading is not enough - you have to take action.
- Understanding is the easy part; implementation is much harder.
- Start practising in simple, low-stakes situations and gradually move towards more complex, higher-risk deals.
- Simple does not mean easy.
- What worked yesterday may not work today.
- The harder you push for something, the less likely you are to get it.
- Life is a one-way street that can only be negotiated by going forward, yet we can only understand it by reflecting backward.

The Final Thoughts

The Last (and the Most Important) Lesson

I owe a lot to my mother, just as you probably do to yours. She made a complacent little boy into a conscientious achiever. She also taught me the most important values in life - hard work, honesty, decency, and above all, the value of life, not just human life but *all* life.

♥ QUICK STORY: There are no pockets on a shroud

It happened in the mid-sixties in my native Yugoslavia, when my mother was a young nurse and I was about five. A woman from a wealthy family was diagnosed with cancer and remanded in the hospital. Doctors gave her only weeks to live. She had a little daughter, about my age, who regularly visited her dying mother.

Although most of her family's businesses and factories got nationalised after the Second World War, they were still considered extremely wealthy. At home, they dined from the finest porcelain dishes and used silver cutlery, she once mentioned.

One day, during lunch, my mother apologised to the lady patient about the sorry state of the aluminium cutlery and the chipped enamelled plates that were then used to serve hospital meals.

The lady looked at my mother as one would look at a well-meaning, but still naive child. "My dear Sister Ela," she said, "there is nothing to be ashamed of. I've never cared about these things, and they mean absolutely nothing to me now. I would give away everything I have, this very instant, if only I could stay with my daughter and watch her laugh, play and grow. There is only one thing on my mind now, the thought that I will never see my little girl again."

The Law of Spiritual Perspective

There are no pockets on a shroud. No matter how much you end up having, you can take nothing with you when you leave this world.

The Boomerang Principle: Make Others Feel Special

"You cannot succeed by yourself. It's hard to find a rich hermit."

Jim Rohn

When people realise that you are a decent and honest human being who is genuinely interested in them, their behaviour towards you will markedly improve. They will go out of their way to help you get what you want, because they know that you will also help them get what they want.

I call it The Boomerang Principle. What you throw at others comes back eventually. The return is always in kind.

The Boomerang Principle
When you make others feel special, you become special yourself.

Of course, don't expect immediate rewards. Your payback may come at odd times and in most unexpected ways. Ultimately, this is the gist of everything: Be kinder and nicer to people.

Once you get the things you want, don't hoard them or keep them under a lock. Enjoy them and share them with others. The strangest thing in life is, the more you share things, the more you will enjoy them. That is the ultimate aim of the game. Share your sorrows and share your joys. Don't go through life alone.

Instead of Farewell

"Half of what I say is meaningless,
but I say it so that the other half may reach you."

Khalil Gibran, *Sand and Foam*

I worked hard on this book, but I've also had lots of fun writing it; I hope you've had some fun reading it. I apologise for not being able to make this book shorter, sweeter and smoother.

Endings are sad, if you've enjoyed our time together. Or, they bring relief that the whole damned thing is over. I hope you feel sad right now, not relieved.

Should you need any help with your current or upcoming negotiations, I'd be glad to be of service. Don't hesitate to get in touch with me. Let me know about your experiences, problems or interesting negotiating cases. I'd really like to hear from you.

My e-mail is: igor@careerprofessionals.com.au

You may remember the First Law of Punditry. I wouldn't have called it the First Law for nothing, would I? So, there must be a second one, and sure enough, here it is:

The Second Law of Punditry
The time will come when the student outgrows the teacher.

Once you learn all you can from each teacher, move on. Find another teacher to guide you through the next stage of your journey. I hope you have learned as much as you could from me and I wish you many helpful and wise teachers along your way. Remember, it is not the destination that ultimately matters, but the journey itself. May your journey be exciting and interesting. See you on the road!

INDEX

101 Rules & Ruminations

1. Negotiation is a journey. Travel light and enjoy yourself along the way.

2. Losers wait and hesitate, until it's too late. Winners get on the ball.

3. Some things take a certain time, and no amount of money, effort, planning or praying can make them happen faster.

4. When the student is ready, the teacher will appear.

5. We all hype our winnings and hide our losses.

6. Hoping for better results while using the same old ineffective techniques is insane.

7. The less authority you have, the more important your negotiation skills.

8. If you don't take control of your future, somebody else will.

9. The more you lose, the less likely it is you will win again.

10. The more you win, the easier it becomes to win more.

11. To improve your outcomes, you have to first improve yourself.

12. Nobody envies a loser. When others start being jealous of you, you know you are on the right track.

13. Negotiation is the ability to minimise pain and maximise gain.

14. Simple does not mean easy. A good cookbook does not guarantee a perfect meal.

15. Life is no fairy tale; it requires hard work and even harder negotiation.

16. You ether make your own choices or allow others to choose for you.

17. The challenges we brave and the choices we make determine the consequences we face.

18. Experience is an expensive way to learn and somebody has to pay for it. Make sure it is not you. Learn at somebody else's expense.

19. Life is not a neatly designed and carefully rehearsed management seminar. It's messy, confusing and often irrational. Luck

often wins over logic, style over substance.

20. Negotiations are predictable and, therefore, controllable.

21. Imperfect (real) people cannot produce perfect (ideal) agreements.

22. Every destination is a starting point for another journey.

23. Whoever has to implement the deal or live with its results or consequences is the best person to negotiate it.

24. You cannot solve people problems by technical means.

25. Don't try to fix the system or the other person. Fix the problem.

26. We don't see things as they are, we see them as we are.

27. When the cause of a problem isn't found, we invent it.

28. An obvious solution is seldom the optimal one.

29. The party that feels the need to justify themselves to the other side is perceptually in a weaker position.

30. To get something, you have to ask for it. If you expect others to bring you the things you want on a silver tray, you are in for a long wait.

31. Power + Preparation + Practice = Perfect Performance

32. The taller the building, the deeper the foundations. The more complex the deal, the longer the preparation required.

33. Expect the best but be prepared for the worst.

34. The longer and the more complex the objective you are trying to achieve, the more likely the negotiation will fail.

35. Judge your success by the price you had to pay to get the prize.

36. Be careful what you wish or pray for - you may get it.

37. How you start isn't that important. What really counts is how (well) you finish.

38. Too much preparation analysis leads to negotiation paralysis.

39. You can't tell how well you are prepared until you start negotiating.

40. Whoever has or controls the money makes the rules.

41. We can fool some people some of the time, but we can fool ourselves all of the time.

42. First, get to know your limits. Then, work on expanding them.

43. The exercise of power is costly, messy and risky.

44. Never praise something you want to buy, especially not in front of the seller or their agent.

45. Never deal with others from an inferior posture; assume a posture of power. Stay calm, confident and composed.

46. The more you keep giving away, the more others will expect from you.

47. A strong opening gets you halfway towards getting what you want.

48. Your aim is to be respected and treated fairly, not to be liked.

49. People are predictable, therefore, they are controllable.

50. Many situations, things or people aren't what they seem to be. Often they are completely opposite.

51. You are not there to be cute, you are there to get what you want.

52. The more experienced you get, the more inflexible you will be.

53. Professionalism is not a qualification or occupation, but a state of mind and an approach to work and life.

54. Do the best you can, where you are, with what you've got.

55. Life is not black and white. Learn to recognise shades of grey.

56. Buy swimming pools in winter and gas heaters at spring sales. Or, when everybody zigs, you zag.

57. The amount of money, time and effort each side puts into a deal is the best indicator of their commitment to it.

58. Good deal means parties are happy with the deal, committed to it and ready for new deals.

59. Keep your eyes on the prize and your mind on the price.

60. Be careful what you ask for in your contracts - you'll have to pay for it. The more details you specify, the higher the price gets!

61. The harder we work to get it, the more we appreciate it.

62. Never accept the first offer.

63. There is no such thing as a fixed price.

64. Negotiate price last. Money does not solve all problems.

65. Help others get what they want and they may help you get what you want.

66. Don't just give things away - ask for something in return.

67. We want different things and in a different order of importance.

68. If you are getting all you are asking for, you are not asking enough.

69. To be happy after a purchase, once you've bought it, stop looking.

70. Money is not the root of all evil, the lack of money is.

71. Delay is the cruellest form of denial.

72. The more time, money and effort invested in a negotiation, the harder to walk away from the deal.

73. Poor negotiators follow the rules; mediocre negotiators decide when to follow and when to break them; master negotiators make the rules.

74. Being one step ahead of your counterpart is usually enough for you to control the negotiation.

75. It isn't always necessary to do everything right. Just make less dumb mistakes than your opponent.

76. Secure agreement on easy issues first. Start your negotiation with common interests and easily agreed upon items.

77. Make your desire for success bigger than your fears.

78. Problems created by others become your problems when they start impacting your performance or hurting your interests.

79. It is better to be paranoid than sorry.

80. You can't prevent others from shitting on you, but you should under no circumstances allow them to rub your nose in it.

81. Contracts are next to useless. You don't need them with people you trust, and they won't protect you from those who want to shaft you.

82. Things rarely just go wrong suddenly; usually there are warning signs along the way. Keep your eyes and ears open.

83. If you really feel you must use tricks or tactics, make sure you never use the same tactic on the same person twice.

84. Once the service is delivered, the perception of its value is lower than the perceived value before the consumption of the said service.

85. Just because there is a way out, that does not necessarily mean you'll be able or willing to take it!

86. Doubt is the toughest of enemies.

87. A healthy dose of cynicism and scepticism is indispensable if you wish to become a truly great negotiator.

88. Trust is good. Constant vigilance is even better.

89. If you look timid, confused, gullible or too easy going, you will be treated accordingly - as a sitting duck, an easy prey.

90. To be treated with respect and professionalism, be informed (or at least seem so), look determined and demand the best.

91. Anything plausible may be used as an excuse for overcharging.

92. Money Rule #1: It's always about money.

93. Money Rule #2: When it seems that it isn't about money, Money Rule #1 applies.

94. If in a hurry, do it first and ask for permission later.

95. Some things are not meant to be, and no amount of time and effort expended will make them happen.

96. Some things are meant to be, and no matter what you do to prevent them from happening, they will happen.

97. Life is a one-way street that can only be negotiated by going forward, yet we can only understand it by reflecting backward.

98. What worked yesterday may not work today.

99. There are no pockets on a shroud. No matter how much you end up having, you can take nothing with you when you leave this world.

100. When you make others feel special, you become special yourself.

101. The time will come when the student outgrows the teacher.

www.ingramcontent.com/pod-product-compliance
Lightning Source LLC
Chambersburg PA
CBHW061159220326

41599CB00025B/4532